# THE KREMLIN SCHOOL OF NEGOTIATION

**Igor Ryzov** is a business coach for companies across Russia, and has been a business technology teacher since 2006. He runs open and corporate 'Hard Negotiations' training sessions. *The Kremlin School of Negotiation* won the 2016 PwC award for best business book in the Russian language.

**Alex Fleming** is a translator working from Swedish and Russian into English. Her previous translations include works by Maxim Osipov, Therése Söderlind and Cilla Naumann, and in 2015 she was awarded the British Centre for Literary Translation's Emerging Translator Mentorship for Russian. She is based in London.

# THE KREMLIN SCHOOL OF NEGOTIATION

## IGOR RYZOV

Translated by Alex Fleming

CANONGATE

This trade paperback edition published in Great Britain in 2021
by Canongate Books

First published in Great Britain, the USA and Canada in 2019
by Canongate Books Ltd, 14 High Street, Edinburgh EH1 1TE

First published in Russia in 2016 by Eksmo Publishing House LLC

Distributed in the USA by Publishers Group West
and in Canada by Publishers Group Canada

canongate.co.uk

3

*British Library Cataloguing-in-Publication Data*
A catalogue record for this book is available on
request from the British Library

ISBN 978 1 83885 291 7

Typeset in Garamond by Palimpsest Book Production Ltd, Falkirk, Stirlingshire

Printed and bound in Great Britain by Clays Ltd, Elcograf S.p.A.

MIX
Paper from
responsible sources
FSC® C018072
www.fsc.org

# CONTENTS

# AUTHOR'S NOTE

What prevents us from achieving our goals? The answer, of course, will depend on the situation. Whenever a person has a goal they want to accomplish, they will first (if they are mildly practical, at least) consider what obstacles they will have to overcome. And often they'll find that the list of potential obstacles could quite easily go on forever.

So what prevents negotiators – even very experienced ones – from achieving their goals? Inflexibility, unwillingness to compromise, personal ambitions . . . yes, that list could also go on for a while.

In my workshops, I am often asked similar questions. When I answer, I always give thought to the specific circumstances at hand. However, over the years I have come to realise that it would make sense to provide some more general answers, too. This is how the idea for this book was born, although it should be said, it isn't only about providing answers. With this book, I wanted to create a teaching aid to guide you through one of the most complex disciplines of any business course – a negotiation manual, if you like. In it, I have included exercises that will not only help you to discover a variety of effective negotiation methods, but, more importantly, to put them into practice straight away. This book will become your very own negotiation tool, a personal arsenal of 'combat' techniques.

When I say 'you', I mainly have in mind those who have already discovered negotiation as both a science and a true art. This book will be of use to anyone who wants to prepare for negotiations in advance, considering all of the possible steps and alternative scenarios that might arise. These are no empty words: in my own studies – which include time spent at the Camp Negotiation Institute in the USA – I have always tried to put the most valuable lessons into practice. Every thought set down on these pages has passed through my own personal prism of perception, experience and awareness. Barring the odd historical or diplomatic reference, all of the examples in this book come from my own experience. The recommendations and advice have been honed over time, and their advantages thoroughly analysed. So who has been doing this analysis, and when?

Well, reader, at the risk of sounding arrogant, the answer is: me. A man with over seventeen years' experience in sales and purchasing. A man who has spent almost half of his sixteen-hour working day leading tough – often at first glance hopeless – business negotiations.

Let me establish one point up front: despite the book's title, these negotiation techniques in no way encourage rudeness or excessive pressure. Quite the opposite, as it happens.

Modern life often pits us against a wide range of characters

– from 'yobs' to 'louts', 'ball-breakers' to 'princes' – with whom, like it or not, we still have to do business. These people's negotiating styles can, if not completely discourage and confuse, make it hard for us to get the results we need.

In this book, I will also present to you the special techniques for tough negotiations employed, among others, by the Russian secret services. Here, you will learn some basic strategies that will allow you to put yourself in the driving seat and maintain command in complex negotiations. In addition, you will also get the chance to perfect and put into practice skills that will help you to steer tough negotiations. These skills must be honed, so this book comes complete with extensive exercises. Negotiation is, first and foremost, about practice. Good luck!

## LOOK OUT FOR THESE SYMBOLS:

| | |
|---|---|
| ⚠ | important information / key points |
| ☞ | examples and situations |
| 🥊 | definitions and rules |
| 💡 | conclusions |
| 💬 | anecdotes |
| 🗡 | stratagems |
| 🌐 | examples from history and diplomacy |
| ★ | questions for the reader |
| 📓 | exercises |

# INTRODUCTION

I am sure we all have a clear memory of the things we enjoyed doing when we were little kids; as we grew up; when we got our first student cards . . . Well, when I was a student I, like many of my friends and classmates, took up karate. It was an exciting sport with a certain prestige, and besides, damnit, I was a *man*! You can probably picture how our training sessions looked: a giant sports hall, a coach teaching kids specific moves, skills and techniques. Of course, there was one golden rule: no fighting in the streets. We'd spar, of course, but within the sports hall contact was always limited – it was something dangerous, forbidden. Even so, we could (and generally did) consider ourselves successful fighters: after all, we took part in meets and workshops, went to sports camps, learned and perfected new moves, showed off our skills at various competitions – which we won, of course, earning ourselves belt after belt. So we were justified in thinking we were serious fighters. We had complete confidence in our skills and in ourselves. However, one very banal event put us all back in our place.

Late one night, me and the guys were on our way home from practice. Three kids that looked like bad news came up to us and asked us for 'a smoke'. Now, in that sort of situation, a request for 'a smoke' never feels completely harmless; it was fairly reasonable for us to expect it to be followed up with some trick straight out of the playbook. But hey, we did karate, we weren't about to let them scare us! So what did we do? You guessed it. Without the slightest doubt in our own professionalism, we immediately decided to fight. Of course we did: we were sportsmen, we had mastered a true martial art – we definitely had the upper hand. On paper, that is. But.

Yes, there was a 'but'. And it turned out to be pretty decisive. You can probably guess that our calculations came up short. We got whipped. Pummelled, even. I'll be honest, it was a big knock, both physically and emotionally. Those street thugs turned out to be way faster and stronger than us. And although they had nothing on us when it came to our training in specialist combat techniques, we didn't even get a look-in.

Turns out, a street thug is stronger than any sportsman trained in a sports hall. Why? Well, while a sportsman may have specific skills and training, they'll be lacking experience of hand-to-hand contact. The real fighter to be reckoned with is the one who not only has a perfect mastery of technique, but who also knows the tricks used on the street.

Reader, take note: never underestimate street tricks. Theory may tell us they shouldn't work, but, more often than not, in practice they do – and how! We were just kids, still so inexperienced. We underestimated the strength of the street.

Where am I going with these reminiscences, you may ask? Surely I'm not suggesting that, instead of their fists, these poor karate kids should have solved the problem with some skilled negotiations? That *is* what this book's about, right?

Yes, this book is about negotiation. But it's mainly about *how* you negotiate. When entering into negotiations, you are essentially engaging in combat. Of course you need to know what theory suggests is the right course of action. But you also need to know how to hold your own against the 'street fighters' who won't play by the same rules.

The book you hold in your hands brings together a number of scholarly approaches employed in negotiations today. But it also contains a wealth of life experience, amassed over years of leading negotiations – in business as well as in life, with public authorities and the business community alike.

# 1.

# MASTERING THE
# KREMLIN SCHOOL
# OF NEGOTIATION

*Better ten years of negotiation than one day of war.*

— ANDREI ANDREYEVICH GROMYKO,
former Soviet Ambassador to the United Kingdom

What is negotiation — a science, or an art? Many will argue that of course it's a science: after all, there are clear laws, refined systems and methods that, once mastered, give you everything you need to become a good negotiator. Which is undoubtedly true. Others, however, will argue that of course it's an art: after all, not everyone needs these laws — some people are just born with it. These people don't simply *know* how to negotiate, they *feel* it, and they can negotiate at any time, with anyone and about anything, with great success. Their words and gestures are like Picasso's brush strokes. This is also true. But this gift isn't given to everyone, no matter how many people aspire (and diligently study) to reach Picasso's heights. Which is why I believe that negotiation is both an art that is inseparable from the individual, and a science consisting of clear-cut laws, concepts and goals.

## IDENTIFYING YOUR NEGOTIATION OPPONENT'S GOALS AND MOTIVES

Essentially, negotiation can be viewed as a sort of sport: after all, sport is the place where art and science intersect. But, just as becoming a professional sportsperson requires constant work and regular training, no single book or course will make you a great negotiator. Only you can do that. So, dear reader, view this book as something of a description of the training process. Everything else is down to you. The more you practise, the more noticeably your skills will improve, and the more achievable your goals will become. What form this practice takes is up to you. Whether you practise through drills or at club meetings, with sparring partners or in the workplace, there is only one rule: the more you practise, the better the results.

Consider the question:
is it possible to win or lose negotiations?

Many schools of negotiation maintain that yes, negotiations can – and must – be won. There is even the oft-prescribed approach of the 'win–win' negotiation, which we'll talk about later. Others maintain that the key to negotiating is never losing; that victory is paramount.

My point of view (and of this I am convinced) is this:

Negotiations **cannot** be won or lost. What you **can** do, however, is determine exactly where you are in the negotiation process, and what the next steps need to be.

It is very dangerous to view the negotiation process from a win/loss perspective, for several reasons. Firstly, when our minds are fixed on the win or loss at hand, we focus on tactics at the cost of strategy. Negotiations become duels, and negotiators duellists. Secondly, in the grand scheme of things, something deemed a 'win' isn't necessarily good, nor a 'loss' necessarily bad: it's impossible to predict how agreements will affect future processes. No one knows what the future holds; all we can do is guess. And while today we may be celebrating an apparent negotiation 'win', tomorrow we may be lamenting such a bad deal. I can give you any number of examples of this.

An acquaintance of mine did some – to his mind very successful – negotiating with a travel firm, and secured a nice discount on a group tour. He thought he had **won** that negotiation. However, two days later the travel firm went bust, leaving him out of pocket and down a trip. So does that then mean he **lost**?

I spent years working in the drinks distribution market, and have seen many similar situations first-hand. For example, after drawn-out negotiations with one major seller, my team was delighted to finally sign our contract. 'We've won, we've done it, we've got the contract!' we thought. But not long afterwards the other company went under, without paying us in full for products we had already supplied. What could we do? This is why it is extremely important to always know what your next step after negotiations is going to be.

⚠️

Negotiations aren't the final round in a bout to determine winner and loser; they are a **process** – at times a very long one. This is why from the start you need to rid your mind of any thoughts of negotiations as just another round in a duel. Negotiations should only ever be viewed as a process.

Rudolph Mokshantsev, author and PhD, suggests that negotiations are a complex process comprising:

- the pursuit of an agreement between people with differing interests;
- the discussion of parties' differing positions in order to find an acceptable solution;
- debate between two or more parties in order to overcome incompatible goals;
- the trading of concessions, in which one party's concession is a direct and calculated response to a preceding concession from the other party;

- ongoing communication between parties with differing and intersecting interests, through which the parties either reach an agreement or fail to do so, depending on the expected implications of such an agreement.

Negotiations presuppose a dialogue between equal partners that are relatively independent of one another, although in reality this may not be the case.

## Negotiations as a dialogue between parties that may lead to an agreement

If we are to speak of negotiations as a science, then the science of negotiation is grounded in mathematics and psychology. The weight accorded to each of these two sciences in the negotiation process will depend on the sphere in which these negotiations are being held. In diplomatic negotiations, for example, mathematics – that queen of sciences – holds particular sway, although psychology shouldn't be discounted completely. In business negotiations, on the other hand, the balance of mathematics and psychology tends to be roughly fifty-fifty, whereas in domestic negotiations psychology is generally the guiding factor.

Some negotiation models based on theory alone urge us to approach negotiation from a place of logic, to put the psychological aspect to one side. An example of this is the suggestion that negotiators find the 'mean' solution as a compromise.

While straightforward enough in theory, this task can be a dead end in practice. Let's say a seller names a price of 10,000 roubles for a product, expecting to sell it for somewhere between 8,000 and 9,000 roubles. A buyer makes them a counter-offer of 8,000 roubles, although they are actually prepared to pay somewhere in the region of 8,500–9,500 roubles. From a theoretical perspective this is all very straightforward: we simply add the two and divide them to get a mean of 9,000 roubles. And, as I'm sure you'll agree, this all looks perfectly lovely – in theory. But in the real world, things are far more complicated.

Ivan and Fyodor are negotiating the sale/purchase of a car. Ivan is selling his car for one million roubles, but Fyodor only has 800,000. So Fyodor phones Ivan and says, 'Vanya, buddy, I'll give you 800 grand.' Ivan, having weighed up his own interests against the logic of compromise, immediately agrees.

On the face of things, this is a fair, successful negotiation. We could even go so far as to call it ideal: both sides get what they want. Both Ivan and Fyodor should be very pleased. They should both feel like winners. But this is just at first glance.

Now, try to put yourself in Fyodor's, the buyer's, shoes. Sure, you got what you wanted for the money you had, and you didn't even have to rack your brains to find some extra cash (as you would have done had Ivan dug his heels in a bit more). But didn't you stop to think how strange it was that Ivan suddenly cut his price by 20 per cent? This question will soon become a torment. 'Why would he agree to my price so quickly? There must be something wrong with the car . . .' And with that, your new car – the one that mere hours ago gave you such joy – is causing you pain, filling you with doubt and anxiety.

Now put yourself in Ivan's, the seller's, shoes. You will also be tearing yourself apart. 'Why did I agree to his price so quickly?' you'll ask yourself. 'Obviously I wasn't expecting the full million, but I could have wrangled another 100,000 roubles from him, 50k at least.'

So where does that get us? It appears that even ideal negotiations are far from perfect in practice. Neither side of this
deal came away fully satisfied.

Studies have shown that the probability of reaching a square
deal like this one is 0.16, or 16 per cent. But because this
probability is actually twice as high as that of striking a deal
through a model that involves a more gradual narrowing of
differences (which is 8 per cent), many negotiators plump for
this option. However, for the most part, the results of these
'square deals' are later called into question. Psychology gets in
the way. Whereas a model involving a gradual narrowing of
differences puts psychology front and centre right from the start,
a reliable companion and aide during the negotiation process.

People aren't computers. We all have emotions.
It is crucial to view your opponent as
a subject rather than an object.

At times, we reject even interesting proposals made by our
opponents without quite being able to explain why. Of course,
we will eventually find ourselves some sort of explanation. 'But
how were we supposed to take that coming from an opponent?
It's common sense that they would do such-and-such instead!'
Well, yes, logically speaking. But then emotions come into play.
This is why specialists highlight three vectors as being particularly important to the negotiation process. It is these three
vectors in particular that we will study over the course of this
book. These are:

- the ability to defend one's interests;
- the ability to manage one's emotions; and
- the ability to manage the emotions of others.

Negotiations are, above all, a process. With this process in mind, we must identify both the type of negotiations we are taking part in and our opponent's motives.

Many sales specialists believe that if a buyer invites them to negotiations it means the buyer is automatically *interested* in doing business with them, and that this will therefore be the purpose of the negotiations. This is a rookie mistake.

For several months, Andrei, the manager of a company selling construction materials, has been negotiating with the procurement manager of a construction company. Andrei knows for a fact (nor is the buyer hiding this) that the construction company is currently buying in its materials from a competitor. During these negotiations, the procurement manager has repeatedly stressed that they enjoy working with this competitor. They are happy with the quality and price that the competitor offers, as well as their fast service. The buyer isn't refusing to negotiate with Andrei, but they never manage to get down to the nitty-gritty. Andrei keeps on offering them discounts, shares and better terms, all in the hope of poaching their business. After four months of futile efforts, Andrei learns by chance that the buyer has been using his quotes to get better terms from the competitor.

In this example, it is clear that the buyer's motives have nothing to do with a future partnership, but Andrei doesn't see what is really driving the discussions and so falls straight into the trap.

This happens quite a lot. A man decides he wants the best possible deal on a car, and so conducts his own pseudo request for tenders. He goes to every car dealership in town, using one single phrase to get the best possible price: 'Your rival offered me a better deal.' He is, in effect, putting his competitors head to head. The dealership managers, believing he's negotiating because he intends to buy from them, get caught in his net.

Fred Charles Iklé, an American sociologist, political scientist and author of books including *Every War Must End* and *How Nations Negotiate*, outlines the following types of and motives for negotiations:

- **Negotiations with a view to extending existing agreements.** Such negotiations are often held in the trade sphere to extend the validity of a contract, or to add certain clarifications or changes to a new contract to reflect the current state of affairs. Such negotiations are also not uncommon when extending labour contracts.
- **Negotiations with a view to normalising relations.** These presume a transition from a conflict situation to a different relationship between the parties (neutrality or co-operation).
- **Negotiations with a view to finalising redistribution agreements.** These negotiations are when one party takes an aggressive position and demands changes to agreements that are to their advantage, at a cost to other parties. Such negotiations take place when haggling over a price or other material resources – an increase or decrease in rent, for example.

- **Negotiations with a view to reaching a new agreement.** These are intended to establish a new relationship and new obligations between parties. Negotiations with a new partner, for example.
- **Negotiations with a view to gathering information.** Indirect results may not be reflected in agreements, and in some cases the negotiations may not even lead to an agreement at all. Examples of this type of negotiation include talks to establish contact, identify partners' points of view or influence public opinion.

Iklé wrote his books in the twentieth century. In light of present-day practice, we can extend this list to include:

- **Negotiations with a view to misleading an opponent.** These are, quite simply, an imitation of the negotiation process. Opponents often enter the negotiation process and deliberately draw it out, safe in the knowledge that time is on their side. In this type of negotiation, every one of your proposals will be met with a 'maybe', a 'we'll need to consult on this' or similar.
- **Provocation.** Negotiations with a view to showing the other party's inability to negotiate.

It is very important to identify your opponent's primary motive in the early stages of the negotiation process, and to use this knowledge when deciding on your next steps.

I once acted as a mediator in negotiations to settle a dispute between two companies and a bank. The dispute concerned a joint debt repayment for an enterprise that had gone bankrupt.

Every meeting came to nothing, but our opponent kept on initiating negotiations, declaring their willingness to settle the matter in a 'constructive' manner. Yet when it came to the negotiating table, the same party kept putting forward absurd demands. Whenever the talks broke down, we couldn't understand what was preventing us from reaching an agreement. Then it dawned on us: our opponent simply didn't want to share their part of the debt. Their goal was to avoid it. Meaning their main task was to prove our inability to negotiate. Once we'd figured out their real motive, we were able to fundamentally change the course of the negotiation process.

The negotiator's primary task is to identify what type of negotiations their opponent is leading and, with a better understanding of the process at hand, to select an appropriate negotiation strategy.

## WHO IS STRONGER IN NEGOTIATIONS – THE LION OR THE FOX?

Some five hundred years ago, Niccolò Machiavelli – that great bard of public administration – wrote:

Since a ruler has to be able to act the beast, he should take on the traits of the fox and the lion; the lion can't defend itself

against snares and the fox can't defend itself from wolves. So
you have to play the fox to see the snares and the lion to scare
off the wolves. A ruler who just plays the lion and forgets the
fox doesn't know what he's doing.[1]

Now, I realise that the negotiator is no ruler, but negotiation
carries with it the same requirement to *get smart*, shall we say.

I have already mentioned how, in negotiation, two points
are particularly important. One is the ability to defend one's
interests. As far as Machiavelli goes, this is pretty much
comparable to the ability to be a lion. But the ability to be
a lion is not enough on its own, as you might not notice the
snare.

The thing is, when we defend our own interests, we can
inadvertently lay down our own snares – the very ones
Machiavelli warns against. What snares are these, you ask?
Emotions. Emotions that prevent us from defending our interests, progressing and realising our goals. To use our emotions
the right way, we need to play the fox. Together, these abilities
are key to negotiation. Like a ruler, a negotiator should take
on the traits of the lion as well as the fox.

In other words, the ability to play the fox as well as the lion
lies at the heart of effective negotiation.

Before exploring the methods and tactics for defending one's
interests (à la the lion) and managing one's emotions (à la the
fox), I would first like to look at one of the toughest and most
brutal schools of negotiation. Yes, you read that right. Brutal.

Legend has it that this school was born in Russia in the
1920s, and it still has its followers and advocates to this day.
It is known by many as the Kremlin school of negotiation.

So what is it? Before answering this question, we should note that this was a school born of the Soviet Union, a country under constant external pressure. A country whose diplomats, no matter where they were stationed, had to show real toughness and decisiveness simply to withstand such pressure.

Andrei Andreyevich Gromyko, one of the most prominent diplomats and political figures of the age, was a master of the Kremlin school of negotiation. A remarkable man, and a diplomat of his time, he outlived virtually every General Secretary of the Communist Party of the Soviet Union. His diplomatic career started young, when he was just thirty, and, under Joseph Stalin's rule, at an extremely precarious time. Gromyko's first major posting was as the USSR's ambassador to the USA.

What is this man known for? Well, in the West, he earned himself the nickname *Mr Nyet*, meaning 'Mr No'. You can probably guess why. Yet the man himself maintained that he heard the word 'no' much more often than he said it. And if he did say it, it was almost always with one sole aim: to prevent himself from being manipulated. Or rather, not himself, but the country he was representing. The ability to negotiate – including in its tougher and more brutal forms – was an integral skill for every diplomat of the time.

So what teachings does the Kremlin school of negotiation build on? This school is based on five postulates, or gambits. Let's take a closer look at each one.

## The five postulates of the Kremlin school of negotiation

*Postulate 1: keep quiet and listen attentively to what your opponent says*
Keep quiet and listen. What's so tough – so brutal – about this, you ask? At first glance, nothing. Nothing at all. But let's take

a closer look. What happens when your opponent stays quiet and listens to you? You talk. When people listen to us – especially if they are attentive, taking note of what we say – we expose ourselves. To keep quiet and listen is to play human flaws to your advantage.

People are talkative. We toss 'breadcrumbs', unwittingly giving away unnecessary information, answering questions no one asked. Anyone who works in procurement will have mastered this ploy and will already know just how effective it is.

The dialogue below gives you an idea of how this gambit typically goes.

**Sales representative (SR):** I would like to present our product to you. Here is our business proposal.

**Buyer (B):** Yes . . .

**SR:** Well, initially we would propose our starting conditions, but after three months we can give you a longer payment window.

**B:** Go on.

**SR:** We can also offer you a discount – and a promotion.

**B:** Right.

**SR:** And free shipping.

Often all it takes is for us to listen for our opponents to start dishing everything up to us on a silver platter. But when we drop these information 'breadcrumbs', offering up insights we haven't even been asked for, we make our opponent's task much easier and complicate things for ourselves.

When we listen, we win our opponent's favour. We make it clear that we are interested in what they have to say. And when a person sees their opponent show a genuine interest in what they have to say, it is only natural for them to start to reveal more, because they want to be as useful as they can. After all, it's so rare for anyone to actually listen to us nowadays!

However, don't let yourself get too relaxed. This is a very serious trap.

I agree with Eliyahu Goldratt, originator of the Theory of Constraints: in negotiations, it is important to be 'paranoid', so to speak[2] – always looking and planning for possible dangers. Every single word we say must be carefully weighed up. When we drop our metaphorical breadcrumbs, we give away extremely valuable information, presenting our opponent with a hook that they will most certainly use to try to reel us in.

An example from the Second World War: after the Soviet Union's entry into the war, the prospect of the opening of the second front became a key question. For the Soviet Union in particular, knowing when the USA and UK planned to do this was paramount. This issue came to a head in the run-up to the Tehran Conference, a strategy meeting of leaders of the USA, USSR and UK that took place between 28 November and 1 December 1943. All of the official Soviet agencies – including the secret service – were working around the clock to try to find out their allies' plans.

Not long before the conference in Tehran, Kirill Novikov, then acting Soviet ambassador to the UK in London, was instructed to urgently inform the UK Foreign Office that he was to be included in the Soviet government's delegation for the summit in Tehran. He was told to request permission to travel to Tehran with the UK delegation. Of course, he explained that there was no other way of him getting from London to Tehran. The British agreed.

Novikov flew on the same flight as Churchill, head of the British delegation. In Cairo, where the flight made a stopover, a dinner was served for Churchill. As the guests dispersed, Churchill offered the Soviet diplomat a drink 'for the road'. They had a friendly, unconstrained conversation, and Novikov gave the British Prime Minister his full attention, hanging on his every word. Out of the blue, Churchill asked, 'Mr Novikov, I suppose you want to know when we will open the second front?' before immediately continuing: 'Not before 2 May 1944.'

Novikov was stunned. All of Soviet reconnaissance had been straining to get this information, and he had just got it from Churchill himself.

Upon arrival in Tehran, Novikov wrote a quick memo and Stalin was immediately informed. So when discussion of the second front came up at the conference, he already knew the Western Allies' position, meaning he had an extra move up his sleeve. On 1 December 1943, the participants of the Tehran Conference signed a historic document announcing that Operation Overlord would be launched in May 1944.

*Postulate 2: ask questions*

The negotiator listens. Then they ask questions. In doing so, they can steer the conversation as their own interests dictate. Negotiators who find themselves listened to and asked questions will often take the bait and talk more; offer more.

This is a key moment in any negotiation. It is at this moment that the opponents are assigned their first roles. We will go into roles in more detail later, but for the time being I would just like to highlight a few key points.

At this early stage of negotiation, it is through tactics like these that the first negotiation roles are assigned: namely, those of 'host' and 'guest'. The 'host' is the one who asks the questions; the 'guest' is the one who answers them. The 'host' enquires; the 'guest' offers. And with this, that most well-known pair of roles begins to take root: you offer me something, and I'll choose if I want it. I am the 'host'.

When you entertain a guest in your home, you get to ask the questions. But remember: in negotiations, the *host* isn't the party doing the hosting in a geographical sense, but the person asking the questions. The *host* is the one who controls the agenda, even if their opponent believes the opposite is true. The opponent thinks that because they are doing all the talking, they must be running the show. They equate talking with leading. Not so. The person controlling the conversation is the one asking the questions; the one listening.

Negotiations in an official's office:

**Visitor (V):** We would like to ask you to free up some land for us to construct a supermarket.

**Official (O):** What do you plan to sell?

**V:** Consumer goods. These are important items for residents, and we have experience in this retail segment.

**O:** Tell me more.

**V:** Well, we have had branches operating in many Russian regions since 2000, and we have a wealth of experience and positive reviews.

**O:** And in this region?

**V:** None as yet.

**O:** Then come back to me when you do.

From the very first second, the official takes on the role of 'host', asking their 'guest' a variety of questions before coming to a decision – the one that is most advantageous to them.

In my experience, this is often a point of confusion for many retailers. 'Where did I go wrong?' they will ask. 'I gave them all the information they wanted and politely answered their questions, but in the end they went with someone else.' To which I answer: when we answer questions, we become the 'guest'; we give our opponent the role of 'host' and, in doing so, the right of refusal. And, having won that right, the buyer is certain to make the most of it.

You must fight for the role of 'host'. This is crucial. If you feel you're being asked more questions than strictly necessary, know that with every question asked you are being drawn further from your goal. So you must break this chain and seize back the initiative through counter-questions.

Let's see how some well-placed counter-questions could have led to a very different outcome in the dialogue above.

**V:** We would like to ask you to free up some land for us to construct a supermarket

**O:** What do you plan to sell?

**V:** Consumer goods. These are important items for residents, and we have experience in this retail segment.

**O:** Tell me more.

**V:** Well, we have had branches operating in many Russian regions since 2000, and we have a wealth of experience and positive reviews. But tell me, do you think your residents would appreciate having a wide range of affordable goods within easy reach?

**O:** That's an interesting question . . . I think so, perhaps.

**V:** I would be very grateful if you could take a look at our plans and give us your expert opinion. Would you prefer them by email, or on paper?

**O:** I prefer paper documents.

Through their counter-questions, the visitor wrests back the role of 'host' and in so doing puts themselves in a better position to progress in negotiations.

After answering a question,
always ask your opponent a counter-question.

On a packed metro carriage:

'Excuse me, are you getting off at the next stop?'

'Yes.'

'And are the people ahead of you getting off at the next stop?'

'Yes, don't worry.'

'Have you asked them?'

'Yes, I have.'

'And what did they say?'

'They said they're getting off.'

'And you actually believed them?'

*Postulate 3: impose a scale of values or 'depreciate'*
Next, whoever is playing 'host' will start to introduce their own

value system. This marks the next stage of negotiations. As soon as this scale of values has been introduced, the state of play changes completely. This is because the party in the role of 'host' can now raise up or pull down the 'guest' at will, based on their own values.

Three hundred prominent scientists have assembled in a large hall. A bag is brought into the hall containing fifteen items. The scientists have no idea what these items are. The contents of the bag are emptied onto a table, and the scientists are given the task of arranging the objects by order of significance. There is an added twist: these objects have all been retrieved from a shipwreck. The scientists are given thirty minutes to complete the task. After this time has elapsed, a man from a law enforcement agency (this is clear from his physique, appearance and way of holding himself) comes into the hall and asks the scientists if they have completed their task. Needless to say, they have not: three hundred scientists could not come to a consensus in such a short space of time. To which the man says, 'And you call yourself smart? You couldn't deal with such an easy task as that!'

Can you see how the scientists' sense of importance might suddenly take a dive?

But back to negotiation. Anyone who has worked in sales will probably have experienced the following situation more than once.

A buyer well-versed in negotiation methods takes a look at

your proposal, tosses it to one side and asks: 'So, what, you think you're unique? You think I can't get this anywhere else?' As intended, these comments will start to make you feel that bit smaller.

In another example, a boss says to his subordinate: 'What, you think you're a star or something? That you're the only one who can do this?'

Turning points like these almost always lead to one thing only: the person being addressed instantly slides a step or two (read: falls headlong) down their own scale of values.

A history exam at a university. The exam takes the form of an interview.

One student has paid the examiner a bribe of 1,000 roubles, the second 500 roubles, and the third nothing at all. The first student comes in for his exam. The examiner asks:

'In what year did the Great Patriotic War start?'

'1941.'

'Good. A.'

The second student enters and is asked:

'In what year did the Great Patriotic War start?'

'1941.'

'And when did it end?'

'In 1945.'

'Good. A.'

The third student enters and is asked:

'In what year did the Great Patriotic War start?'

'1941.'

'And when did it end?'

'In 1945.'

'And how many people died?'

'20 million.'

'Now name them all!'

**A colleague is 'depreciated'**

Maria is a driven young woman working in an in-house marketing and publicity team. She graduated from a top university and has five years' experience at some major firms behind her. But whenever she speaks to her manager, a forty-five-year-old man who likes to throw his weight around, he always says things like: 'Masha, dear, you probably don't have the experience for such a complex assignment yet,' or: 'Your degree's hardly going to cut it on an assignment like this.' Maria, meanwhile, is running around like a headless chicken trying to prove herself to her manager.

*Postulate 4: 'roll out the red carpet'*

Now you're probably wondering why Maria simply does her manager's bidding? Surely she knows a situation like this is unsustainable – how much should a person have to prove? That's because after 'depreciating' Maria, her manager always rolls out the 'red carpet' for her. Now, I don't mean a red carpet in the sense of a ceremonious greeting; view it as more of an appealing path to follow. Something along the lines of: 'Fine, Masha, if you insist, I'm prepared to give you a shot at this while I consider it. Just make sure . . .'

When a 'depreciation' puts someone in a subordinate role, it is only natural for them to feel somewhat uncomfortable in that position – which means they will do anything they can to get out of it. This is when a tough professional negotiator – like Maria's manager – will make use of the play we call 'rolling out the red carpet'.

As it happens, this play actually has its roots in an old Chinese stratagem.

**Show your enemy there is a road to life**

Government troops have surrounded a band of thieves in the mountains. The thieves are many in number, and they are well armed and well stocked with provisions. Despite suffering great losses, the government troops haven't been able to capture any of them. They turn to an old commander for advice.

The commander asks them about possible means of escape, and is assured that not even a mouse could get past the government troops. To this he replies: 'Then of course they'll fight until the bitter end. Since you have cut off their road to life, all that remains for them is to fight to the death. Show your enemy there is a road to life! Surreptitiously leave a passage unmanned in an inconspicuous spot. The thieves are many in number, and they are all different. Some of them will regret their choices; others may have been recruited by force. And some of them will simply be cowards. Once they see a way out, they will run through it one after the other. And then even your average postal worker will have no trouble rounding them up!'

That is what they did. Sure enough, the thieves were caught, brought to the capital and put to death.

A person who feels backed up against a wall has two options: they can either make a desperate attempt at resistance, or simply do nothing and let themselves be crushed. Similarly, a negotiator who feels backed up against a wall can choose one of three courses of action: they can either attack, escape or play dead.

Truth be told, none of these options lead to great results for either party. To make matters worse, what they do lead to is a sense of pressure or manipulation. This is where the play described above comes in handy. If you can show the person backed up against a wall a possible way out; if you can bring it out as an opportunity for 'victory' while saving face, then the outcome will change quite markedly. This is why it is always worth preparing two techniques prior to negotiations: one that will give you the upper hand, and another that will let your opponent lose while still saving face. Should the latter come to pass, when your opponent is backed up against a wall you need to know how to roll out the red carpet for them to walk down, wilfully choosing their own defeat. Only then will they be satisfied with the outcome of the negotiations.

For months a young man has unsuccessfully been trying to get a passport for international travel. All of his applications to date have been refused for a variety of reasons, each time with a request for some new document or other. Exasperated, he has found some leverage over the person handling his case – through their boss. The boss has assured him he will have a word with the handler.

Returning to the passport office with all the swagger of a champion, the man kicks open the door and says, 'Didn't I tell you? Now give me my passport!'

'Yes sir, here it is.'

This story has a very sad ending. At the border, the chip in the passport turns out to be defective. Now what are the chances of that happening? Oh well, better luck next time.

All because the young man didn't give his opponent the chance to save face and lose with dignity.

Treat your opponent not as the role they perform, but as the human they are. Everybody has emotions, and these are often what govern our actions.

Instead, this man should have rolled out the red carpet for his opponent. For example:

'Maria Stepanovna [the handler, after her manager has already had a word with her], last time you told me to re-write my statement. Could you check everything is in order this time?'

'All right, I'll take a look. Oh, will you look at that, it's fine.'

A simple gesture like this in no way detracts from your status – quite the opposite. After all, it brings you closer to the outcome you want.

The red carpet rule is the essence of the **fourth postulate** of the Kremlin school of negotiation: making the opponent an offer they can't refuse.

This play might sound something like this: 'Well, fine, seeing as you're here, if you can offer me a discount I'll take a look at your proposal.' In the majority of cases, your opponent will happily accept.

So, to begin with we listened to our opponent carefully. Then we asked questions, steering the conversation towards our objectives. As we did this, the opponent gave us lots of unnecessary information, things we hadn't even thought to ask. And then we smoothly and discreetly introduced our own scale of values and gave the opponent a sharp dip in importance. And now our opponent finds themselves in a role and position they would very much like to get out of.

Now is the moment to roll out our red carpet, giving them the way out they're so desperate for. Of course, our opponent will seize this opportunity with both hands: the position they have unexpectedly found themselves in is so unpleasant. Not to mention the fact that the terms of this 'surprise escape' do go some way towards achieving what they wanted. But only to some extent, and only at first glance.

If statistics are to be believed, then this method gets results in roughly 80–90 per cent of cases. But is 90 per cent always enough? At times only 100 per cent rock-solid results will do.

Which is why one more lever is brought into play, one that allows the user to crank their negotiation success rate up to 98 per cent.

*Postulate 5: put the opponent in the zone of uncertainty*
As a buyer I know from a major federal chain once put it: 'No one has ever squeezed better terms out of a supplier than those the supplier squeezes out of themselves.'

So what does it mean to put someone in the zone of uncertainty?

You say something like *'I'm not sure how my management will react to your refusal,'* or *'I don't know if it'll be possible to bring you into our distribution network.'*

It's hard to put in words what happens in a seller's mind when they hear this. You see, the seller has already been picturing all of the upsides of this deal, and the knock-on effect it will have for their business. Faced with uncertainty, who wouldn't start to ask, beg, even plead – whatever it takes to coax out another chance? Who wouldn't promise their opponent all imaginable (and unimaginable) bonuses, agree to any number of concessions?

Why does this happen? Fear gets a hold on us. Fear is a most powerful weapon.

Fear can also be described as a state of *over-motivation*, of 'need'. The term 'need' is described well in Jim Camp's book *Start with NO*.[3] This is when a person feels compelled, for whatever reason, to conclude a deal, get the sale, get the documents signed.

And this isn't the preserve of business relationships. A sense of 'need' is not uncommon in interpersonal relationships – for example, when one partner feels they 'need' the other.

All of this is a state of *over-motivation*. When a person can't take a step back and soberly evaluate the current situation, their brain starts to see all manner of negative consequences. As a result, they latch onto any bones they are thrown. And who's throwing these bones? The tough negotiator. You can find any number of examples of this in films depicting the events of the 'hard nineties' in Russia and other former Soviet states.

The nineties saw many groups of racketeers approach local businesses to suggest the use of their 'services'. The majority of businesses would agree on the spot, fearing possible reprisals if they refused. But some strong-willed individuals refused to do business with such groups. That's where things get interesting for us.

At this point, let's say one of the gang members says to one such businessman: 'No problem. You don't want our help, that's your business. Just tell us straight: if it's a no, then it's a no. Just say the word.' And then they walk away.

Now, at this point all the businessman can think about are the grimmest possible consequences of his refusal. He's in a state of fear, of *over-motivation*. Before long, the businessman comes crawling back to the criminals, the roles now firmly reversed: he is the one persuading *them* to let *him* take advantage of their valuable offer. He automatically falls into a dependent role.

This tactic has a 98 per cent success rate. But there are situations in which even this tactic won't work – namely if the person feels no such sense of fear or 'need'.

The zone of uncertainty is, nevertheless, a very powerful play, and using it can easily secure some movement in your direction from your opponent.

Let's imagine a manager is yet again asking his subordinate to stay late after work to finish a project. The subordinate is neither prepared nor willing to work in his free time. Now, at this point many managers would start to threaten the subordinate, barking out a list of orders and acting in a way they consider to be 'tough'. In fact, this is exactly the sort of behaviour that will provoke further resistance and disloyalty in their colleague.

This is when it's time to remember the 'zone of uncertainty' play. All you need are a couple of phrases: 'Fine, Ivan, if you don't want to stay, don't. I'm sure we'll manage without you.' With this, the manager puts those toughest of negotiators – fear and uncertainty – to work in their subordinate's mind. And believe you me, those two certainly are persuasive.

So now we have seen all five postulates of the Kremlin method. But this method also makes use of what is known as the 'pendulum of emotions'.

No living person's emotions can be completely neutral. Our pendulum of emotions is always in a state of flux: even when we are calm, our pendulum will oscillate slightly. And the task of the negotiator using the Kremlin method is to swing the pendulum to its maximum amplitude, so as to more effectively influence our actions and dealings.

Let's see what happens to our pendulum of emotions during each of these five postulates.

Postulates 1 and 2: the negotiator listens to us and asks us questions. This puts us in a pleasant, even happy frame of mind. The pendulum swings out towards the positive edge of its range.

Postulate 3: we are 'depreciated'. The pendulum swings in the opposite direction.

After the fourth postulate, once the 'red carpet' has been rolled out, our pendulum moves back into the positive. That is where we want it to stay.

If this isn't enough to seal the deal, then one more step is added – postulate 5.

Under what circumstances is it ethical
to use such negotiation methods?

Before we answer this question, let's evaluate the effectiveness of this method.

**How to measure the effectiveness of any negotiating system**

A system is evaluated on three points:

1. The negotiation system should, where possible, lead to a reasonable agreement.

2. It should get results effectively.

3. It should improve (or at the very least not worsen) relations between the parties.

On the first and second points there is no doubt that this school of negotiation gets results, and it clearly leads to an agreement.

Which begs the question:
to what extent does the Kremlin method improve relationships?

The answer to this question will also answer our question of ethics. Let's take a look.

Every coin has its flip side, and I have to examine both.

In theory, the answer should be a resounding no: it worsens them.

The opponent leaves the negotiations feeling happy with the outcome. At that point in time, they genuinely believe that they have found a win–win scenario: both sides have won and they have also met the goals they set out for themselves. After all, they got the contract (letter, sponsorship, etc.). Gains have been made. At some point, however, this person will start to get a feeling I liken to a hangover – when your head starts to clear after a big night, and you realise that something isn't right, that you've done something wrong. Only in this case it's that something isn't right, but that *someone else* has done something wrong to you. This 'hangover' feeling can soon begin to grate.

This is one reason why the Kremlin method isn't always conducive to long-term relationships, which is a major factor to consider in our modern world. Now, if you don't need long-term relationships – if this is just a one-time negotiation that you want settled here and now – then this method is undoubtedly very effective. But if you have your sights set on long-term communications – even just one more exchange with this party – or if their recommendation is important to you, then this negotiation method is not for you.

That being said, in practice things aren't always so black and white.

In 2006, when Russia introduced an import ban on Moldovan wines, our company experienced some difficulties. This ban meant that all of the wines in our warehouse would have to be destroyed. And that our regional partners owed us a lot of money for these very wines.

Of course, many of our partners started to speculate on the situation, trying to shift as much of the risk and loss onto us as possible.

Initially we made the decision to write off these debts, in the hope of preserving these relationships and encouraging future business. But then a combination of circumstances made us change tack and toughen our policy. We insisted that our partners accept their share of the risk, and pay what they owed us for the wine that we had had to destroy. With some companies, the matter even went to court.

It is worth noting that, despite us having handled everything in a 'civilised' manner, some of the companies from the first list turned their backs on us and stopped working with us. But the very companies that ended up 'taking a hit' continued doing business with us, some even more so than before.

Businesses prefer to work with strong, reliable opponents who stand up for themselves. In practice, people respect strong, decisive opponents.

Never sacrifice your own interests to maintain a relationship. That is no marriage of equals. Strategically, you stand to lose both the relationship and your negotiation benefit. Your opponents are most likely simply banking on your desire to 'do the right thing'.

So where does this get us with the ethics of the Kremlin method?

As with any weapon, this method can be used for good as well as ill. It all depends on your goal. If you use the method in a competitive setting, with no fraudulent intent, then it can be regarded as one of any number of resources. But it's another matter entirely if the method falls into the arsenal of a not-so-honest negotiator.

For this reason, it can be beneficial to look at how to stand up to negotiators who have near-enough mastered the Kremlin method, while also honing your own methods.

A reminder: developing three basic skills will take you far in the art of negotiation. These three skills will help you to become a true negotiator and leader and to get results. Let's recap what these are. The first is the ability to defend your interests, i.e. to play the strong **lion**, see your goal and pursue it. The other two are the ability to manage your emotions and the emotions of your opponent, i.e. to be a circumspect and slightly cunning **fox**.

## BEING THE LION IN PURSUIT OF YOUR INTERESTS

Above all else, defending your interests is knowing how to fight for them. We can draw an analogy between this and physical combat, even war. In fact, negotiation algorithms have much in common with those of military operations, which is why virtually every negotiation method has some grounding in Sun Tzu's *The Art of War*, written some 2,500 years ago.

War is a form of combat that plays out through the positioning of bodies and objects in space. It only differs from other forms of combat – wrestling, or a fistfight, say – in the specific equipment used, and in the all too real possibility of inflicting irreversible physical damage on the opposing side. Fistfights lack both the weapons and the irrevocably destructive objectives of war.

However, where negotiations follow the same formulae as physical combat (or war), there is one crucial difference: the final outcome. Where physical combat is about the positioning of bodies in space (the seizure of territory, objects, etc.), negotiation actually boils down to a fight for social roles (boss/subordinate, vendor/buyer, teacher/student, decision-maker/implementer, etc.). As negotiators, it is crucial that we understand who holds what role.

We have already seen one such pair of roles, that of 'host' and 'guest'. These are the most important roles that can be assigned in negotiation. The movement towards these roles begins as soon as the first questions are asked and the first answers given. As noted, it is after these roles are established that a value system is introduced, and one party is put into an undesirable role that they then want to shift. This role can indeed be shifted, but only by a) knowing how to fight for a social role, or b) engaging in combat (dismissing an objectionable dealer, say, getting into a scuffle or even grabbing an object or money). There are no other options.

So what is a role? Roles are an extremely powerful thing. If a negotiator knows how to recognise the roles at play, then they can predict others' behaviour and use that knowledge to adjust their own – usually with great success. The thing is, if we put a person into one role or another, then sooner or later they will start to move exactly as that role dictates.

This principle was the subject of an audacious experiment in the USA.

### The Stanford Prison Experiment (1971)

Wanting to better understand the nature of conflict within the correctional institutions of the United States Navy, the Office of Naval Research agreed to fund an experiment led by behavioural psychologist Philip Zimbardo. Zimbardo fitted out a basement at Stanford University to create a mock prison, and recruited male volunteers who agreed to be assigned a role of 'prisoner' or 'guard' at random. All volunteers were students at the university, and they received $15 per day (which, with inflation, equates to almost $100 in 2018).

The participants all underwent tests of their physical health and psychological stability prior to the experiment. After this, they were randomly divided into two groups of twelve: 'guards' and 'prisoners'.

The 'guards' were given uniforms bought from an army surplus store, which were based on the uniforms of actual prison guards. They were also given wooden batons and mirrored sunglasses, which meant their eyes were impossible to see.

The experiment started with the 'prisoners' being sent home. They were then mock-arrested by state police, who assisted with the experiment. The 'prisoners' had their fingerprints and mugshots taken, and they were read their rights. After this, they were stripped, searched, and given a number.

In contrast to those of the guards, 'prisoners' were given uncomfortable uniforms to be worn without underwear, and rubber slippers. They were addressed only by the number sewed onto their uniform. In addition, they had to wear a small chain around their ankles, intended to serve as a constant reminder of their imprisonment.

The 'guards' worked in shifts, although during the experiment many of them were happy to work overtime. Zimbardo himself took on the role of Prison Superintendent.

The experiment was supposed to last four weeks. The 'guards' were given a single task: to do the rounds of the prison. Barring the use of physical force towards the 'prisoners', they could perform these rounds in any manner they chose.

As early as day two, some 'prisoners' had started a revolt, barricading the entrance to their cell with their beds and mocking their overseers. To put an end to the disturbance, 'guards' attacked the 'prisoners' with fire extinguishers. Before long, the 'guards' were forcing their wards to sleep naked on a bare concrete floor, and use of the showers was made a privilege. The sanitary conditions in the prison deteriorated to a shocking degree: 'prisoners' were forbidden from using toilets outside of their own cells, instead having to make do with a bucket. Occasionally, as a punishment, 'guards' even prohibited the buckets from being emptied.

One-third of the 'guards' revealed sadistic tendencies: they bullied the 'prisoners', forcing some of them to clean waste tanks with their bare hands. Two of the 'prisoners' were so emotionally traumatised that they had to be removed from the experiment. One of the replacement participants was so shocked by the scenes that met him upon arrival that he swiftly started a hunger strike. As punishment, he was locked in a dark closet in lieu of solitary confinement. The other 'prisoners' were given a choice: they could either go without blankets or leave the troublemaker in 'solitary' all night. Only one person was willing to sacrifice his own comfort for the sake of the other 'prisoner'.

Roughly fifty observers followed the work of the 'prison', but it was only Zimbardo's girlfriend, who came to interview some of the participants, who voiced alarm at what was happening. Stanford's 'prison' was closed six days after opening its doors. Many guards expressed regret that the experiment had ended sooner than anticipated.

It is hard to overstate the importance of roles. If, in negotiations, we are viewed as one in a long line of others, or if we fall into the role of 'dependent', we will immediately start looking for a way out – for example, by suggesting tantalising terms or making concessions. All because we want out of that role. This is exactly why we need to learn how to negotiate.

Returning to our warfare analogy, we can differentiate between two stages of negotiations: manoeuvring and combat.

In *On War*, Carl von Clausewitz, a prominent nineteenth-century military theorist, wrote, 'Fighting is a trial of strength of the moral and physical forces by means of the latter.'[4]

This means that in battle, 'strength of the moral forces' – i.e. our strength of spirit – is key. Everything else is secondary: what matters is having the willpower to see you through. When it comes to defending our interests – or playing the lion – our confidence in our own strength will naturally be of great importance. We must have enough strength of spirit to fight for our interests.

So when does combat begin? It begins when both sides have an equal understanding of what they are fighting for, and what is at stake. Let's take a look at the following situation.

Two years ago, a supermarket chain installed a very cheap security system in their stores. It is constantly breaking down, causing them many headaches. They should probably change it, but how much will that cost? Is it really worth the effort?

A company supplying security systems is aware of these issues, and they are trying to convince the manager's assistant to change the bad system for their better quality, more expensive one.

The supplier's sales manager comes to the supermarket's HQ and launches into negotiations by saying: 'Maria Stepanova, I know your system is always breaking down. I'd like to propose you replace it with my system, which is both reliable and great quality.'

What sort of response do you think they will get? The answer is fairly predictable: 'No, we're fine, thanks, you can show yourself out.'

At the risk of jumping a few steps ahead, I can say that this is exactly why this firm came to me for help.

Essentially, when you reveal your negotiation benefit – what you want to achieve – to the opponent, this marks the start of combat. This is because it is only once the benefit has been pinpointed that bargaining and other 'uses of force' can begin.

Combat is the stage of negotiations at which parties fight for a benefit. Both sides clearly understand what having the benefit would mean to them and to the other side. The benefit could be material – a salary, a price, commercial terms, etc. – or it could be completely unrelated to material values: a trip to the cinema, perhaps, or a visit to your mother-in-law at the weekend.

Why couldn't the security system supplier achieve their goal and sell the equipment?

In my view, the answer to this question is obvious. The sales manager chose the wrong negotiation method. They went into negotiations along that old Napoleonic principle of 'We'll engage in battle, and then we'll see.'[5] This is, in fairness, a particularly Russian approach. For some time even I felt it was the right approach to take, but with the benefit of experience, I now insist on replacing Napoleon's principle with one of Sun Tzu's: 'The victorious strategist only seeks battle after the victory has been won, whereas he who is destined to defeat first fights and afterwards looks for victory.'[6] By which I mean that before entering negotiations it is essential to *forecast* the results.

Here, you need to consider whether you have the three key components of the negotiation process: strength, means and resources.

If your opponent is armed to the teeth but you don't have so much as a penknife, then negotiating won't bring you anything good. This is what happened in the example above. It is crucial to learn how to arm yourself for the negotiation process, rather than hoping for a free ride.

This means that, before entering negotiations, you need to make a thorough forecast for success. It is only ever possible to enter negotiations with all guns blazing – i.e. revealing your position and benefit – if you are certain what the outcome of combat will be, if your forecast is positive and if you have all three components of the negotiation process in hand. In any other situation, you need to do some manoeuvring.

Now, manoeuvring shouldn't be mistaken for a refusal to negotiate. Manoeuvres are simply the process of making preparations, clarifying information, finding reinforcements and more.

Two oligarchs meet. One asks the other: 'How are things? What's new?'

'Oh, we're in clover. Two months ago I bought a villa in Cyprus for my daughter, then a month ago I bought a fancy three-storey house in central Moscow for my son, then a Merc 600 for myself, my wife and kids . . . So overall, things are good.'

After a three-second pause, he adds: 'Hey, do me a favour, lend me 500 bucks for a few weeks?'

The other replies: 'You can kiss my . . . ankle.'

'Ankle?'

'Oh, sorry, don't you like being misdirected? Wouldn't know how that feels.'

When the security system supplier came to me, the first thing I asked them to do was to make a forecast. And we immediately found the rub. Every single person I asked, from the director down to the sales manager, was making optimistic forecasts. As is often the case in practice, their optimism was well founded: the equipment they were selling was of a high quality, whereas the equipment their potential client had was bad. But this was their fatal error: they were viewing the situation from *their* perspective, rendering their forecasts completely inadequate.

Basically, their forecasts were like a street cleaner looking up at the royal palace and making plans to marry the princess. He can plan all he wants, but – here's the catch! – besides his own wishes, he's got nothing on his side. He is short of the second and third components: resources and means.

A lot rests on the accuracy of these forecasts. They affect how we hold ourselves, how we act and what we plan to do in negotiations. When evaluating possible negotiation outcomes, we must look at the situation not from our own perspective but from that of our opponent. What matters is not how we approach our opponent, but how *they* view *us*.

To make an adequate forecast, you must look at the situation – and at yourself – from your opponent's perspective.

This is how I recommend making a forecast:

Draw up a simple matrix, which I'm going to call the *'forecast matrix'*. This matrix should have two vectors: *'importance'* and *'irreplaceability'*. These two vectors will serve as a measurable indicator of how our opponent views us.

Prior to negotiations, consider – on a scale of zero to ten – how much your opponent needs you and your goods or services (or how much they need you as a worker/employer, etc.). This will be your rating on the 'importance' vector.

You then need to evaluate – once again, on a scale of zero to ten – how hard it would be for your opponent to find a replacement. This will be your rating on the 'irreplaceability' vector.

Depending on your ratings, you will fall into one of four categories. This category is how your opponent views you, and you should plan your next steps on this basis.

First, let's familiarise ourselves with each of these four categories.

*Supermarket*
Your opponent isn't interested in you, and you are easily replaced. This is the category that the security systems supplier had fallen into. As a result, it was immediately clear that the forecast was not in their favour. When a person sees their opponent as one of many items on a supermarket shelf – an item they weren't even looking for in the first place – they will have little interest in the products or services on offer. And, naturally, if you are to engage in combat with that person, i.e. immediately reveal the benefit you seek, there is a high chance that you will very soon be leaving with nothing. What is the point even haggling with you when you are both easily interchangeable (just look at all of those products on the shelf!) and unimportant?

For a forecast like this, I would categorically advise against opening with a fight for your benefit. Here, manoeuvring is key. Focus on strengthening your position. That's what we did.

First of all, I found an acquaintance who could set up a meeting with the supermarket chain for us. Of course, I could have gone in on my own, but going in on someone else's recommendation is much more effective.

During the negotiations themselves, I proposed nothing. Instead, posing as a consultant from a company seeking to expand its supply market, I asked the assistant for advice on the manufacturer of the security system they were using. Of course, she started to open up – and reader, let me tell you, it's been a long time since I've heard so many uncomplimentary words. With every complaint she voiced, my position became stronger.

When I felt that my importance to her was at its peak, I went on the offensive.

'Maria Stepanova, why don't you change your equipment for a superior system? I mean, I would be happy to do you a quote – if that's of interest, of course.'

If you've fallen into the 'supermarket' category, then to all intents and purposes you are simply one of many identical products on the shelf; your opponent might not notice you, or they might not even stop to look at the shelf at all.

If an employee wants to ask for a raise, then before going to the manager, it's worth them thinking about what category they fall into in their employer's eyes. If they fall into the 'supermarket' category, then what will negotiations actually achieve? Now, I'm not saying that you should ever refuse to negotiate – certainly not. I'm simply saying that what you need is a manoeuvre, one that will either 'inflate' your significance (on the 'importance' vector), or highlight just how unique you are (on the 'irreplaceability' vector). Only after that should you begin to fight for the benefit.

*Opportunity*

You are pretty unique, but as it stands your opponent has little interest in you. What should you do? Enter combat, or manoeuvre?

Let's look at an example.

A company producing metal hangars has developed and marketed a hangar with a particular shape that makes it cheaper to construct and maintain than traditional hangars. Having taken its home market by storm, this company now has its sights set on neighbouring markets. Its managers all set out to woo potential buyers, but things don't quite go to plan. Yes, the hangar is innovative, the potential buyers all agree, but who uses them? None of their potential clients agree to 'do themselves a favour' and get on board.

Once again, this was all down to an inaccurate forecast. Because they had marketed an innovative solution, these innovators assumed they would automatically fall into the 'opportunity' category, which is to say they gave themselves a high rating on the 'irreplaceability' vector and decided that that would be enough for success. However, they didn't take into account the fact that, no matter how unique they were, in their prospective partners' eyes they simply weren't important.

Hence it follows that this category also demands an initial manoeuvre. First you need to create value for your potential clients, then you can outline your benefit.

Here I should note:

Value is something your opponent is willing to pay you for.

I would advise a company like this to build a demo hangar, which would serve as a first important step: it ensures the market has at least heard of them.

*Lever*

By its very name, this category implies there may be pressure on you. If there is interest in what you have to offer but you face a lot of competition, then I recommend boldly stepping into negotiations and revealing your benefit.

'What, straight into combat, without any manoeuvring?' you might ask. This I can understand: to all appearances, this category hardly differs from 'opportunity'. Only the vector has changed: here, rather than 'irreplaceability', the high rating is for 'importance'. However, the two do differ in quite marked ways.

While prior preparation for negotiations is still essential, in this category there is some room for bargaining off the bat. Naturally, your opponent will try to put pressure on you by emphasising that there are other options available to them, they have companies queueing up to work with them and the like. But if you prepare your negotiations and arm yourself well (we'll look at techniques, plays and negotiation preparations in more detail later), then success awaits. In this category, you have all three components of success in your hands.

Once again, I would like to note that combat is not a 'tough' position: it is simply the stage of negotiations that begins when both parties understand the benefit the other side seeks. The negotiations themselves can be as tough or as gentle as you want: that is down to you and your opponent.

If you're a valued employee who meets targets and whom the company has an interest in retaining, you can boldly ask for a raise. Your employer will negotiate with you, whether they have a potential replacement for you or not. This is in contrast to the previous two categories, where there was no scope for bargaining.

*Partner*
There is interest in you, and you are hard to replace.

Now, in this category it might appear that success is in the bag, but you can't relax just yet. Yes, go into combat; yes, go out there with all guns blazing to declare your benefit. But be careful: your opponent won't be dozing. For purchasing agents, for example, suppliers who fall into this category are a big danger. Managers of 'stars' face this headache all the time. This is because once we reach the top right-hand corner of the matrix, we often start behaving not as a partner but as a counter-lever. We lean in to our position, throw our weight around more.

You can be certain that the other party – be they a purchasing agent or an employer – will always be on the lookout for a replacement. So you need to be aware that even if you've won the battle, you can still lose the war. Don't forget the relationship aspect of negotiations; here it's more important than ever.

And so we can see that, even in this category, it is practically impossible to get by without some form of manoeuvring. Yes, go into combat; yes, reveal your benefit, but in later negotiations you will need to manoeuvre to encourage trust in you. And for this, you need to foster the three most important components of trusting relationships. They are:

1. Attentiveness to the opponent and their values.
2. An ability to listen.
3. Professionalism.

At the start of the 2000s, we were supplied by a well-known factory in Moldova. In the early days our partner made every effort to accommodate our wishes, and we grew together. Supply volumes continued to increase, and by the mid-2000s these were quite considerable (around seven million bottles per year). At this point our partner, realising how dependent we were on them, started imposing their own rules. They introduced unfounded price increases of quite a significant margin, as well as minimum sample sizes. As a result, we started to lose trust in them, and, naturally enough, we made the strategic decision to transfer 30 per cent of our supply to another producer. Our new producer was, of course, delighted with the situation. And our old partner very quickly started fussing over us and making their excuses. But it was already too late.

If you fall into the 'supermarket' or 'opportunity' category, forget combat for a while and focus on manoeuvres. Combat (bargaining) is possible only when your opponent feels you are important.

Before beginning negotiations, make sure you possess the three most important negotiation components: strength, means and resources.

Make a forecast using the forecast matrix, and only then decide whether to make a manoeuvre (arm yourself and improve your position) or to head straight into combat. When it comes to building your strength and arming yourself, I would recommend studying the Chinese stratagems. Several of them feature in this book. You will remember, under the fourth postulate of the Kremlin school of negotiation (rolling out the red carpet) was the stratagem 'Show your enemy there is a road to life'. For the negotiations on security systems, I drew on the following stratagem:

**Fool the emperor and cross the sea**

Once the emperor had marched his 300,000 troops as far as the sea, he began to lose heart. All that lay before them was water, endless water. Their enemies' kingdom, Goguryeo, was 1,000 *li* away. How would they get there? Why hadn't he listened to his advisers when they had warned him against this campaign? Embarrassed, he turned to his commanders for advice. They requested some time to think. The commanders feared that the emperor might cancel the campaign, so they appealed to the artful general Xue Rengui for advice.

The general said: 'What if the emperor could cross the sea like dry land?'

The commanders nodded – that would be good.

Then he told them that no one should look at the sea until the next day.

Xue Rengui prepared everything.

The next day, the emperor's officers told him that a rich farmer who lived by the water's edge wanted to offer the troops provisions for the crossing. He had invited the emperor to his home to discuss the matter. The emperor, feeling his mood picking up, set out towards the sea with his retinue. He himself couldn't see the sea, however: 10,000 skilfully placed fabric panels (usually used for tents) obscured his entire field of vision. The rich farmer respectfully invited the emperor into his home. The walls were decked out with expensive curtains, and rugs covered the floor. The emperor and his companions sat down and started to drink wine.

After a short while, the emperor thought he could hear the whistling of the wind all around him, and the pounding of waves rang in his ears like thunder. The goblets and lamps in the room all started to sway and shake. Surprised, the emperor ordered one of his servants to pull back the curtain. His gaze fell upon the endless dark sea.

'Where are we?' he asked uneasily.

'The entire army is crossing the sea to Goguryeo,' one of his advisers explained.

Faced with this *fait accompli*, the emperor's determination grew. Now it was with courage that he travelled east.

## RECOGNISING YOUR OPPONENT'S BEHAVIOUR:
## FOUR BEHAVIOUR TYPES, FROM THE 'TEENAGER'
## TO THE 'TANK'

And so, we have now outlined the two stages of negotiation: combat and manoeuvring. Let's take a closer look at the combat stage – the fight for your goal.

In combat, the most important thing to rely on is your strength of spirit. Quite simply, whoever's is greater will win. Let's remind ourselves of von Clausewitz's much-cited definition of fighting: 'Fighting is a trial of strength of the moral and physical forces by means of the latter.'[7]

In negotiation, 'fighting' is the stage at which we fight for gains. This stage only comes into play when certain conditions are present:

⚠

1. There is a clash of interests.

2. Both sides clearly understand what benefit they seek as well as that of the opposing party.

3. Both sides want to gain said benefit.

This is precisely where strength of will can play a decisive role. Why? Because this is where the moral forces of the two sides go head to head. Whoever's is greater will win. You must be ready for this. In other words, you must constantly train and hone your willpower. As Napoleon once said, 'The moral is to the physical as three is to one.'

Let's take a look at the **four behaviour models** of people in combat – how people behave when fighting for their benefit and defending their interests.

Before getting into this, it should be noted that these behaviour models must be viewed along two vectors. The first vector is '*motivation*' (to achieve a result). This is equal parts self-confidence and belief in one's cause. The second is '*courteousness*'.

Confidence is an important factor in combat. The outcome often boils down to which of the negotiators is more motivated. As for *courteousness*, it is worth taking a closer look at what this means in this context. Nowadays, many associate the word '*courtesy*' with 'compliance'. This is wrong. *Courteousness* means treating people properly, behaving appropriately, using socially acceptable language and other similar concepts – none of which is synonymous with compliance.

So these are our two vectors – confidence (results-oriented motivation) and *courteousness*. It is through these two criteria that we will explore the four possible behaviour models adopted when defending one's interests.

If necessary, can we disregard the '*courteousness*' vector in negotiations?

Remember your response – at the end of this section we will come back to this critical question.

Before examining each of the behaviour models, I would like to emphasise that these are completely unrelated to any typology of personality. This is simply a model of the behaviour an individual adopts *when fighting for their goal*. In essence, each and every one of us has it within us to behave according to any one of these models, based on the circumstances at hand.

*The teenager*
This behaviour model is normally presented by people who lack confidence (i.e. have little motivation) and are discourteous to boot. Aggressive attacks on weaker parties are generally typical of this model. 'Teenagers' are quick to make things personal, and often speak very informally, using this as a means of projecting confidence in themselves and the rest of the world. However, this aggressive behaviour is in fact a mask for their own insecurity. Sound like a teenager to you?

Once I saw a woman get onto a trolleybus with her child, who looked about nine or ten. The woman bought a ticket for herself, but the child ducked under the barrier. Nothing too unusual there. But then things took a much more unusual turn.

A ticket inspector walked up to the woman and demanded that she show a valid ticket for both her and her child. The woman openly admitted to only having one. With that, the inspector's facial expression instantly changed, and, with no regard for anyone else on the trolleybus, he started rudely and disrespectfully demanding that she pay a fine. The woman handed him the money without argument.

'So what, you're trying to bribe me now?' he shouted, before grabbing hold of her things and trying to pull her off the trolleybus.

At this point I stepped in. I walked up to the inspector and said, 'Excuse me, why are you behaving like this?' Of course, he then tried to channel all his anger onto me. But as soon as he saw that I was emotionally stronger than him, he stepped aside and listened to what I had to say. I explained to him that what he was doing was actually against the law, and then ran through the possible consequences of his actions.

And what do you think his reaction was? He turned tail and ran! Literally – he even forgot all about his offender, and he didn't take her fine.

For me, this is one of the simplest and clearest examples of the behaviour of someone who lacks both confidence and *courteousness*.

If you encounter a 'teenager', it is important to show them that you are emotionally stronger than they are. When they sense your strength, they will be forced to change their negotiation strategy and stop their provocations. One way of demonstrating your strength is to look your opponent straight in the eye and pause for a few seconds. Your response needs to be firm and confident, so that your opponent understands that the power is on your side. Under no circumstances whatsoever should you mimic their behaviour. Meeting boorishness with boorishness will simply turn you into a 'teenager' too: your motivation will drop, and the only thing to be gained from that discussion will be you letting off steam.

Buddha and his followers were once passing through a village in which his enemies lived. The villagers came rushing out of their homes, surrounded Buddha and his followers and started hurling abuse at them. Buddha's followers started to get annoyed. Were it not for Buddha's calming presence, they would have been ready to give as good as they got.

Then Buddha turned around and said something that stunned both his followers and the villagers.

'You disappoint me. These people are simply going about their business. They are incensed: they believe I'm an enemy to their religion, to their values. So it is natural for them to be shouting insults. But why are you getting angry? Why are you letting these people manipulate you? You are letting them control you. Are you not free?'

The villagers hadn't expected such a reaction. Baffled, they fell silent. Now Buddha turned to them.

'Have you said all that you wanted to say? If not, then you will have another chance to get it all off your chests when we return.'

The villagers were completely confounded. One of them said, 'But we were shouting insults at you! Why aren't you angry?'

'You're free people, and you have every right to do what you did. But I will not react to it. I am also a free person. Nothing can force me to react, and no one can affect or manipulate me. I am the master of my own manifestations, and my actions are born of my inner state. But I would like to ask you a question. The people in the village next to yours welcomed me; they brought me flowers, fruits and sweets. I thanked them, but told them that we had already eaten. I told them to take the fruits back to their homes with my blessing: we couldn't take them with us as we do not carry food. Now let me ask you: what should they do with what I didn't accept from them – what I returned?'

One man from the crowd said, 'They probably took the gifts home and shared them with their children and families.'

Buddha smiled.

'So what will you do with your insults and abuse? I do not accept them. If I refuse to take those fruits and sweets, the giver has to take them back. So what can you do? I reject your insults, so you too can carry your burden back to your homes and do with it whatever you please.'

If you cross paths with a 'teenager', make sure you keep your aim at the front of your mind. People in this state will often reveal their inner Porthos, and simply fight for the sake of fighting. They have no motivation to achieve anything in these negotiations, no benefit in their sights. So you should remember the words of Winston Churchill: 'You will never reach your destination if you stop and throw stones at every dog that barks.'

I once ran a workshop in Tula. I arrived in the city early, and went to park my car by my hotel, where the workshop was also going to take place. The parking lot was empty, so I parked my car in the first spot I liked.

No sooner had I got out of the car than an attendant came up to me and gruffly told me to move my car, as that particular spot was for the bank. Now, where my first instinct would typically be to answer back and start a bickering match with him, it's important to remember your priorities. At the time, all I wanted to do was to park my car, check into the hotel and get ready for the workshop.

'Fine, I'll move it. Where should I park?'

'The hotel spaces are numbers 101–108.'

'Thank you.'

And that's where my story with the parking attendant ends. However, I was to revisit this encounter very soon afterwards, when this very topic came up in the workshop. One young man jumped out of his seat and angrily said, 'Yes, I had to deal with that jerk this morning! I gave him a piece of my mind.'

I was interested to dig a bit deeper into this situation.

'And where did you end up parking your car?'

'Two blocks away.'

'So let's see: your car's parked further away, and you've spent half the day in a bad mood. And that rude parking attendant, how do you think he feels?'

Silence.

'Were you able to mend his ways?'

'No.'

Don't try to re-educate people or moralise with them. You'll either lose sight of your benefit, or turn into a 'teenager' yourself.

There is, however, another way of dealing with a 'teenager': find a third party who is better able to negotiate and who has a vested interest in the result.

A young man worked as a buyer for one of our distribution networks. Having modelled a tough manner from his older colleagues, but not fully grasping the nuance of when and how to use this 'toughness', he earned himself the reputation of an incompetent jerk. Which, I have to say, he was. No matter what a supplier proposed, he would bluntly and rudely refuse them, taking great pleasure in the power he wielded. He would drive young women to hysterics, and men almost to fisticuffs. But what's most interesting is that no one tried to go straight to his line manager. We, however, did just that. As a result of these negotiations, we got the contract, and a week later that particular 'teenager' was throwing his weight around the job centre instead.

It's always worth seeking out someone who has a greater interest than the 'teenager' in seeing an issue resolved.

There's no point getting into a showdown with a jerk on a plane: much better to call in a specially trained, interested party. And the best way of not having to negotiate with an indifferent jerk is to go straight to their manager.

If you encounter 'teenage' behaviour, under no circumstances should you fight fire with fire. Always keep your goal in mind, and let the circumstances guide you:

1. Make a one-time show of strength.

2. Ignore their behaviour and stand your ground.

3. Check if you would be better off speaking to someone else.

4. The 'red carpet' and 'zone of uncertainty' can also be used to good effect here.

### *The mouse*

These are people who value *courteousness*, but who lack confidence (low results-oriented motivation). This behaviour model is the least successful when it comes to fighting for the goal. Why? Because people who fall back on this model tend to concede everything to everyone. But that's not all – not only do they make unnecessary concessions, they make excuses for doing so: 'I'm a nice person – it's just so easy to hurt me!'

When does a negotiator turn into a 'mouse'? When they lack confidence in their cause; when they are unsure of their own position. If this person values *courteousness* they will become a 'mouse'; if not, 'teenagerhood' awaits.

I am often asked questions like: 'How can I sell something I don't completely believe in?' or 'How can I change a supplier's terms if I find the new ones unfair?' I get thousands of questions like these. The answer is simple: sell it to yourself first. Find the strength of your position. Regardless of what the situation is, it is crucial to convince yourself first, and only then go into negotiations.

A manager gives his subordinate an assignment: 'Go and tell the client that if they don't pay us today, we won't do business with them any more.' His subordinate nods in response. The negotiations go as follows:

'I'm asking you, please pay us. We need the money by tomorrow.'

'No, that's not going to happen.'

'Well, my manager said that if we don't have the money . . . You know, it'll be hard for me to get him to authorise future deliveries.'

'So what, you don't need clients? We get lots of offers like yours. And you keep on making all these demands.'

'I'm asking, not demanding. I would really like to keep our relationship, but—'

'Then go tell that to your crazy boss.'

Not only did the negotiator not defend his own interests, he also conceded his benefit, lost face in front of his opponent *and* threw his manager under the bus. So who is to blame here, and what can be done? Both are to blame: both the manager who didn't see his subordinate's lack of confidence, and the employee who couldn't justify his position and so started delicate negotiations in the position of a 'mouse'. As for what can be done: proper negotiation preparation, which in this case is finding solid ground to stand on.

⚠️

Under no circumstances should you enter negotiations if you don't truly believe in your cause. When a negotiator doesn't believe in the strength of their own position, they are doomed to failure.

If this sort of behaviour feels like your default, then now's the time to be honest with yourself. It's important to acknowledge that this model simply leads to you making excuses for your own failings and not seeing your own areas for growth.

This isn't the only shortcoming of the 'mouse' behaviour model. The second is compliance. A negotiator like the one in the example will almost always be forced away from their initial plans and make concessions. Of course, an almost new, well-kept car is always going to be easier to sell than a rusty piece of scrap metal. But, as you'll see later, even the latter has USPs to be found.

Once I witnessed negotiations being held in the office of the chief engineer (CE) of a construction holding. A contractor had sent a representative (CR) in for negotiations.

CE: So, what do you want?

CR: Well, I'm sorry, but we have . . .

CE: What's all this mumbling? Are you as bad at building as you are at talking?

CR: Oh, no . . . We would like to review these deadlines. I would very much like to find a mutually beneficial outcome here.

CE: What are you trying to tell me? Nothing changes. But now I'm starting to think maybe it isn't worth continuing this project with you.

CR: Wait! Well, if you can't agree to these terms, we'll do all we can to meet the old ones.

CE: Yes, you do that. Oh, and I'd like you to do something else for me, too.

CR: Yes, of course, we value your business.

The following anecdote nicely encapsulates where trying to please everyone can often get you.

A father, his son and a donkey are travelling along a dusty city road in the sweltering midday heat. The father is riding the donkey, and the son is leading it by the bridle.

'Poor boy,' says a passer-by, 'his little legs can barely keep up! How can you just laze around on that donkey when your son is clearly exhausted?'

The father takes this man's words to heart. As soon as they turn the corner, he gets off the donkey and makes his son ride it.

Very soon, another person passes them and loudly announces: 'Has he no shame? The little one riding the donkey like a sultan, while his poor old father's left trailing behind!'

These words pain the boy, so he asks his father to sit on the donkey behind him.

'Good people, have you ever seen such a thing?' a woman in a hijab starts to cry. 'Tormenting an animal so! The poor donkey's back is practically breaking from the weight, while these idlers simply lounge around. Poor, unhappy creature!'

Without a word, father and son get down from the donkey, shamefaced.

They have hardly made it a couple of steps when an acquaintance of theirs comes up to them and starts ridiculing them:

Why are you just walking that donkey around town? It's not carrying anything, and neither of you is riding it!'

The father shoves a big handful of straw into the donkey's mouth and puts his arm around his son's shoulder.

'No matter what we do,' he says, 'there'll always be someone who disagrees. From now on I think it's best we decide how to travel for ourselves.'

We can see that it's impossible to please everyone all the time. So not only is it important to know how to keep your eyes on your goal, it's also important to know how to assert yourself. *Courteousness* alone just isn't going to cut it. Confidence in the position you hold is key. Take heed of the old rule of thumb of any good lawyer:

If you're right, act, and if you're wrong, you simply haven't put enough time into crafting your argument.

If you can't find a reason to believe in your position, then you need to admit what you've got wrong. That will be your strength.

Now, for a bit of light relief, here's an advert I took the trouble of re-writing in full (maintaining the style and spelling of the original):

**For sale:**

Volga GAZ-3110, 2005.

Mileage 75,000–79,999km, 2.4l, petrol, sedan, colour: black

I'm selling my Volga! To be honest, it's a dubious buy, but then the price is purely symbolic. For just 30,000 roubles, this cruiser could be yours! A 2005 model, its condition is, shall we say, contradictory. It's got 72,000km on the clock, but by that you should read 172,000. Or, to be completely honest, 272,000. For the life of me, I'll never understand how it could have covered such a distance . . .

But the important thing is that the machine's still on the move! Getting around town's no problem (except that, without AC, in summer the car feels like it's on fire). It tears off from traffic lights faster than many foreign cars (especially when they don't realise they're drag racing). Tip-top on the roads too. The only limit to the speed you can get her to is your own self-preservation instinct. Personally, on those rare occasions when I've got her up to 180km/h, I've found myself staring wide-eyed, not moving, hardly even breathing.

There's a broken part by the left-hand door. This really helps you to find the car in big parking lots, and it gives the beast a distinctiveness you won't find anywhere else. The body features a couple of parts that you could consider to be in good condition.

The saloon's internal trimmings are made of some incomprehensible linoleum-based whim. You'll just have to live with that. On the back of the driving seat there's this really sharp thing that kills when it randomly digs into the base of your spine. I've never figured out what it is, why it's there or how it could even have come into being.

There's an air-conditioning button, but that's the only part of the air conditioning that's made it this far. There's also an on-board computer, and I suspect this artificial intelligence (and not you) is what really dictates when the engine starts and when it dies.

The heater – the flame of Sauron itself – works in winter, so no need for Mum to be sad. But unfortunately the hot air points downwards, and when the heating's off in summer, if you drive at more than 110km/h in sandals then it'll really burn the toes on your right foot. So in summer it's best to wear a trainer on that foot.

I haven't smoked in the car for the last month and a half. Before then I did. A lot. But no more than the car's previous owner and his many friends, who would all pile in and smoke together, in winter, with the windows closed. The uncharacteristically grey colour of the ceiling means there's no hiding that.

One big plus: the muffler's gone, so the beast roars like a demon! It sends even super manly bikers running and keeps them at a distance, offering you a more comfortable drive.

> But one of the biggest plusses of this car is that highway patrol categorically do not want to stop you. Even if you pass straight in front of them with your seatbelt unfastened and your lights off, all they'll do is watch you go with a pitying look. What that's all about I've never been able to guess. Plus, expensive (and less so) cars are really afraid of cutting into your lane.
>
> At times this gives you the feeling of being in a presidential cortège – until that sharp metal thing in your backside brings you back down to earth.

And so, dear reader, how do you think the seller got on with finding a buyer? The price, of course, was purely symbolic, but we're not talking petty cash. Thirty thousand roubles for the pleasure of driving some scrap metal to the dump?

For your information: the car was sold the very day this advert was posted.

> Read the following scenario and consider Mikhail and Ivan's reasoning. Who was right?
>
> A family acquires a plot of land. They build a small house, which they plan to use as a holiday home in summer. However, in the spring they discover that water accumulates on the plot and drains poorly. Ivan, joint-owner, finds a contractor online who agrees to fix the problem.

Mikhail, the contractor, diligently measures and calculates everything before giving Ivan a quote. Ivan is happy with the quote, which is 200,000 roubles for the work and materials. Ivan pays an advance of 140,000 roubles, and Mikhail gets to work.

Once a week, Mikhail calls Ivan to discuss his progress. In some of these calls, Mikhail mentions that new details have come to light, but says that the issue can still be resolved.

The work is completed, and the day of reckoning arrives. Mikhail informs Ivan that he owes him another 160,000 roubles. Ivan is confused: they have a verbal agreement and a contract stating that the remaining balance due is only 60,000 roubles. Mikhail argues that there were issues with the land, that the job was more complicated than expected and that additional materials were required. When Ivan asks Mikhail why he didn't ask for his approval, Mikhail simply shrugs and replies that it goes without saying.

Email me your answers at igor@ryzov.ru, and I will make sure to get back to you.

And so, we have now seen how not to fall into the position of 'mouse'. But, given the type's weaknesses, would you be happy to come up against a 'mouse' in negotiations? Let's see. Here, the golden rule is this: tempting though it may be, don't try to take everything from them. Having promised you the world, chances are that the 'mouse' will hide away and no longer negotiate with you. Which means you're still left without your goal.

Let's come back to the example we looked at above, of the negotiations between the chief engineer and the contractor's representative. Delighting in his own inflexibility, the chief engineer considers himself the victor, when he is actually leading himself and his organisation to losses. He enjoyed his power, but gained no benefits.

You see, although the contractor made promises, do you think they'll actually follow through? I can assure you, you can find thousands of reasons and pretexts as to why a deadline might be moved. What's more, the negotiator who couldn't defend his interests is more likely to relay the results of the negotiations to his manager in the following way: 'He wasn't going to listen to us; he started threatening to break off all business.'

People are inclined to justify their own behaviour; he's hardly going to tell himself the truth – that he couldn't convey their position to the customer. And the manager (who, being only human, is no stranger to emotions) might, in the heat of the moment, decide that if the customer won't meet them halfway, then they'll just play it by ear and see what happens.

If a negotiator is behaving like a 'mouse', there's no point putting pressure on them and taking everything. Show them there is a road to life (as already described) and roll out the red carpet. They will happily walk down it.

How might the chief engineer have conducted discussions, based on the strategy 'Show your enemy there is a road to life'?

1. If you (or your representative) don't trust the strength of your position, then under no circumstances should you start negotiations. It is important to find something you can base your arguments on; where the strength of your position lies.

2. If you can't find a good argument for your position, then you need to admit what you've got wrong. That will become your strength.

3. If you come up against a 'mouse', don't try to take all you can from them. Use the 'road to life' play; give them a way of leaving the negotiations with their dignity intact. The red carpet play would also work here.

*The tank*

This is a very common behaviour model, and it's pretty self-explanatory: the 'tank' is a confident person, but not a *courteous* one. Our society often approves of this behaviour, and as a result tank-ish behaviour is precisely what many strive for. So what sort of behaviour are we talking about? Well, a 'tank' is typically guided by their interests and their interests alone. Others' interests mean absolutely nothing.

But there's no hiding it, 'tanks' do achieve great success in life, and negotiation, of course, is no exception. So it should come as no surprise that this behaviour model is often used in negotiation. More than that, it's often very successful. It doesn't even stand comparison to the 'mouse': the latter comes out far too unfavourably, and the success of 'tank'-style negotiators is exaggerated even more in contrast.

However, there is one serious downside to this model: it is angled towards instant results, not on aligning strategic relationships.

The executives of a supplier (S) and client (C) have come to an agreement regarding the rollout of a new accounting system. The deadlines and budgets for the project have been set out, but the functionality required (the scope of the work) has yet to be finalised.

A deadline is approaching, and S asks C to review the schedule, to which C replies: 'We're sick of this! First you start the work, and only then do you start your grumbling.'

**S:** But listen, we just want to update our agreement.

**C:** You're just swindlers and frauds.

**S:** Wait, what are you suggesting?

**C:** Well, that's how you're behaving – that's your style of work!

**S:** But we're just trying to—

**C:** YOU! YOU'RE TRYING? Don't make me laugh, you gold-diggers!

The client in this example is behaving like an archetypal 'tank'. It's all about them. Nothing else matters.

**What can you do when you meet a 'tank'?**

An experienced negotiator will say: even a 'tank' gets their comeuppance every now and then. There are three strategies for dealing with a negotiator who has adopted this apparently fail-safe behaviour model.

1. The 'two dogs' strategy. You have to prove that you're stronger.

2. Don't encourage your opponent's behaviour. Meet toughness with softness and in doing so disorient them.

3. Use a burst of 'breakthrough force' at the right moment. If you're being pulled into a whirlpool, don't flounder and tire yourself out: gather strength, and then give a strong burst of kicking.

When choosing your strategy, it is essential to first evaluate which of you is the stronger party. Here it is very important to make a sober evaluation of your strengths and potential and an adequate forecast of the outcome of the fight. If you are stronger, then it is entirely possible that if you enter combat using the 'two dogs' strategy, you will come out on top.

An audience member once told me the following story.

He had recently acquired a plot of land near Moscow with an area of $1{,}712\text{m}^2$. Before making the deal, the sales manager at the vendor company, Marina, sent him a site plan for the plot, on which it was stated that the total land area was 1,701m$^2$. When questioned about the inconsistency in the figures, Marina assured him that the figure on the plan was a mistake, that they would correct it and that everything would be fine.

My audience member checked every single one of the sales documents to ensure the correct figure was given throughout. Having done that, he felt comfortable signing the contract, and the documents were sent for registration. Marina assured him that he would have the correct plan within a week.

A week later, after following up on the as-yet-unsent documents, he got a 'What's the hurry?' in reply. He grinned and bore this none-too-courteous response. Ten days later, the plan arrived in the post. When he opened it, there it was again: 1,701m$^2$.

Back to the negotiating table. His phone call to Marina went like this:

'Marina, I've been sent the old plan again.'

'And? It's a simple mistake.'

'Marina, do you understand how this looks?'

'Hey, why are you getting so stressed out? Like I said, it was a simple mistake.'

'Marina, when will I get the correct plan?'

'Our specialist is off sick at the moment, but once he's better we'll send it to you.'

'OK, please put me through to your manager.'

'He isn't going to speak to you.'

'Look, this is the second time you've sent me a site plan that contradicts the information detailed in our sales agreement, and based on which the price I paid was agreed. Are you familiar with the laws on this sort of practice?'

'But—'

'I'm sure you're well-versed in Russian law and how this would be classified. I insist on this issue being resolved, and hope that this is simply another misunderstanding. I also insist on receiving an official response from your company.'

'But our specialist is unwell—'

'That's not my problem. It's up to you to fix this. Am I making myself clear?'

Fifteen minutes later, the correct plan was with him, along with the company's apologies.

This story is a good example of the 'two dogs' strategy: one of the parties (the vendor) growled, and the other party (the buyer) growled back. In this instance, not only did the buyer have the moral upper hand, he could also arm himself with his knowledge of the law. The ability to negotiate is crucial, but a knowledge of the law and your rights is no less so.

However, if you have analysed the situation and your options and come to the conclusion that this strategy is high-risk, then it's best to abandon it. If you use it in such a situation, not only do you stand to lose your benefit, you will also gain the reputation of being the losing side if you do.

If in an encounter with a 'tank' you feel like the weaker side, then in no way should you encourage their behaviour by responding to rudeness with rudeness. It is better to respond to attacks with softness, which will disorient them, and to seek out their weak spots (arguments, positions, etc.). This isn't so hard to do. The key is to remember that 'tanks' deliberately use their bluntness and pressure to pull you into an *emotional* mode of negotiation.

There's a reason why 'emotional' is italicised here. Specialists in negotiation processes distinguish between two modes of negotiation: the emotional and the rational. Essentially all negotiations begin in a rational mode. However, far from all of them progress in the same manner, much less conclude in it. Transitioning into an emotional mode is the aim of the provocateur, which is usually what 'tanks' happen to be. The provocateur deliberately draws their opponent onto an emotional level, making them feel undesirable emotions that will lead to irrational decisions. And as Jack Nicholson says in the film *Anger Management* (2003), 'The angry man opens his mouth and shuts his eyes.'[8]

More often than not, once a negotiator has been drawn onto the path their 'tank' opponent has chosen for them, they will try to concede something early on to soften their opponent's apparently negative mood, 'bribing' him, earning some favour. This is a big mistake. Once the 'tank' gets an inkling that their opponent is prepared to make concessions, they will take even more drastic action.

In the early 2000s, we started doing business in Russia and things progressed well. However, my deputy (as we were soon to find out) wasn't particularly well qualified for the job, nor did he have the strongest moral compass. In the early stages of the company's development, he justified his position in the group, but he soon became a burden. He didn't want to change or grow; he was happy with things the way they were. But we weren't. We decided to part ways.

He wrote a resignation letter, and we calculated all of the payments he was due by law. But that arrangement didn't suit him. He started demanding huge sums in compensation.

After resigning, he took on the role of deputy director at a car factory, one that so happened to own the land on which our warehouse and car park were situated. On this score, he had more strength of spirit than I did. I slipped into the role of 'mouse', and tried to accommodate his wishes.

That was a mistake. I thought that if I gave in and paid him the pay-off he was claiming, we could maintain a good relationship. Far from it! He started circling our organisation like a hawk, terrorising our drivers and warehouse manager, and trying to stir up fights between our partners and me.

I had to fix my mistake. I decided there was nothing I could say to my former deputy. But I did have a talk with the director of the car factory, his immediate superior:

'Nikolai, we've decided to move.'

'Why? What's happened?'

'We've got the impression you don't want to do business with us any more.'

'What, why? You're faultless with payments, and you rent a large space . . . Why would you decide that?'

'Your deputy is demanding additional payments from us, and he's forbidden us from entering and doing loading works at night. And more besides.'

'Igor, I'm shocked.'

'Nikolai, I'm sorry, but because of this we just can't accept your terms.'

'I think I see what's happening: he used to work for you, didn't he? This must be something personal. But I assure you, Igor, he has no right to do this!'

After that my former deputy gave us a wide berth, and a month later he left the car factory.

Sometimes you have to pay dearly for your mistakes.

Never try to exchange a benefit for the opponent's favour without a fight. You will lose your benefit, and you won't gain their favour.

Later we will come back to how to avoid falling into a provocateur's net, when we discuss the role of emotions in negotiations in more detail. But, running ahead slightly, I would like to note: instead of exchanging emotional fire with a 'tank', ask yourself: what wins out, emotions or reason? The answer, as history has proven, is clear: intellect first.

So now we have looked at two strategies for negotiating with 'tanks'. Both the 'two dogs' and 'softness against toughness' are perfectly reasonable courses of action, in certain circumstances. Both offer clear plusses as well as minuses.

The third strategy – 'breakthrough force' – is the most effective, but it takes some effort.

---

**⚠**

If in negotiations you are completely unarmed and find yourself against an opponent who is armed to the teeth, then negotiations aren't going to bring you anything good. The primary task of the negotiator is to master the art of arming oneself (finding strength) during the negotiating process. And to use that strength (or the opponent) at the right moment, and in their own interests.

---

A company, Omega, supplies produce to Sigma. Their produce is in demand, sells very well and has loyal customers. Omega is constantly trying to improve quality, and runs promotional campaigns. Due to a change of export terms, Omega has decided to approach all of its buyers with a request to reduce the payment period for goods supplied from forty-five to thirty days.

This is how discussions between the sales manager (SM) and purchasing agent (PA) go:

PA: Are you out of your mind? All of your competitors are offering me better terms.

SM: Once again, we hope that you'll be able to accommodate us on this.

PA: What? Do you realise I have crowds of people like you knocking at my door? All of them prepared not only to offer a longer payment period, but better prices, too?

SM: Yes, we have many competitors. However, we would ask you to consider the possibility of raising prices.

PA: No, you're demanding, I . . . I don't even know where to begin! No, no, no!

SM: Can I ask you a question?

PA: Ask away!

SM: Is your issue with this payment period such a deal-breaker that — hypothetically speaking — if we can't come to an agreement now you would be prepared to break our contract?

PA: . . .

SM: Then I propose we take a look at what we're prepared to do if you accept our proposal.

PA: And what are you proposing?

This is now a constructive discussion. Had the vendor started offering discounts and the like from the start, he would have been drawn deeper and deeper under the ice. But he kept his focus and, at the right moment, 'kicked' in the right direction. You'll say this strategy is pretty risky. I agree: there's always some level of risk. However, in situations like the one just described, the risk is absolutely justified. If the payment terms are so crucial, then they can explore other terms that would allow these to be introduced.

Every day, a man feeds nuts to a group of monkeys. One day he says, 'Dear monkeys, I'm running out of nuts. From now on I'm only going to give you 3kg in the mornings, and 4kg in the evenings!'

The monkeys are outraged.

'OK, OK!' the man laughs. 'I'll give you 4kg in the mornings, and 3kg in the evenings!'

The monkeys are overjoyed.

It's also important to remember that 'tanks' don't only provoke through their words. Their actions and gestures are also very powerful weapons for immersing their victims in emotion.

I once happened to be present as a high-level executive was holding negotiations. Unimpressed with the work of one manager, he called him into his office. When he stepped inside, the executive stood up and walked towards him, extending his hand. The manager, as anyone would, took the extended hand for a greeting, so he extended his own hand in response. At that very moment, the executive swivelled away and, instead of welcoming the manager, picked up a glass on his desk. It's hard to put the manager's facial expression at that moment into words.

We will see what the right way of responding to attacks like this is in the next section, where we will look at emotions.

If you come up against a 'tank', it is very important to make a forecast of the outcome of combat. If you are stronger, or at least comparable in strength, then the 'two dogs' strategy is appropriate. In all other situations it is much more advantageous to hold off on encouraging your opponent's manner. Instead, wait and gather the negotiation resources you need for a forceful 'kick'.

*The leader*

The American writer Larry Wilson, a contributor to the book *The One Minute Salesperson*, has a striking motto: 'Leadership is about someone following someone else because they want to, not because they have to.'[9]

Experience shows that in negotiation, the best tactical and strategic results are achieved by those who skilfully combine concern for their opponent with confidence when defending their own interests. People who demonstrate this behaviour model will typically keep their own interests in mind, without infringing upon those of others. They demonstrate both confidence and *courtesy*. They know how to assert their opinion, but also how to show concern for their opponent. They manage to withstand pressure, yet know how to exert it when needed.

A 'leader' listens to and understands their opponent, assesses situations well and steers the negotiation process. They can be either soft or tough, as the situation requires. They act in their own interests, but don't forget those of their opponent. They know how to create forecasts and make decisions that won't infringe upon their opponent's interests.

A 'leader' knows how to influence their opponent's behaviour. Soft to touch but firm in substance, they are like a fist in a kidskin glove.

So why the name 'leader'? Any 'leader' should inspire people to follow them, and they should also look after their followers. It is much the same here: the motto of such negotiators would be something like: 'Assert your interests without infringing upon those of others', as opposed to the 'tank', who will impose their own interests without sparing so much as a thought for anyone else.

'Leaders' tend to reach their goals faster and at less cost, for a few reasons. One: they better see and understand their own interests, and they are able to assess whether they are in a position to fight, and what for. Two: they are able to see the wider situation and approach it through their opponent's eyes, making their worldview more rounded. Three: a 'leader' doesn't prove, he reasons, using only strong arguments to boot.

A 'leader' always approaches their opposite number in negotiations with respect. They are prepared to listen and seek out alternative solutions, but at the same time they are not prepared to lose sight of their own interests just to please the other side.

> **⚠**
>
> If you are sitting opposite a 'leader', then steer clear of emotional games, manipulation and pressure. A 'leader' will make easy work of turning your energy back on you. You will have to come to an agreement in a completely rational mode.

So with that, we now know how to behave in negotiations if your opponent is demonstrating one of these four behaviour models. But which behaviour model do you, dear reader, most fall back on when you negotiate? I can already hear the indignant replies: *Obviously that depends on the situation! You've already said that anyone can present any of the models, and you stressed that these behaviour models are not a typology!*

Reader, hold your horses. What I want to gain from this is simply that, now that you have an idea of the different behaviour models, you can pinpoint your own as well as that of your opponent. The following table can be of use here:

|  | Teenager | Mouse | Tank | Leader |
|---|---|---|---|---|
| **Speech** | Loud, abrupt: 'Oi, wait!' 'Hey!' 'Gimme . . .' | Quiet, hesitant: 'Would you possibly mind if . . .?' 'Might it bother you if . . .?' 'Would you please be able to tell me if . . .?' | Loud, imperious tone (fighting talk): 'You should . . .' 'You will . . .' 'You have to . . .' | Exact, clear, concrete: 'I would like . . .' 'I have . . .' 'I'm prepared to . . .' |
| **Eyes** | Flitting around | Looking down | Piercing gaze | Direct, open gaze |
| **Body** | Slouching, energetic gesticulations | Constrained movements, slouching | Fists and jaw clenched, chin up, energetic gesticulations | Shoulders straight, natural movements |
| **Approach to life** | 'I don't care' 'Do what it takes to avoid doing anything' | 'It's all my fault' Opinions easily swayed, polite and obliging | 'Don't argue with me! You'll regret it!' The only opinion that matters is my own | 'I know my interests' Prepared to listen to others and take their wishes into account |
| **Feelings** | Resentment, fury, anxiety | Anxiety, fear, uncertainty, a sense of hurt and guilt | Rage, vindictiveness, superiority | Confidence, calm, fairness and self-esteem |
| **You feel like a** | Follower | Follower | Leader | Equal |

Now not only can you see your own areas for growth; in negotiations (during bargaining or a fight for your benefit) you can easily determine your opponent's behaviour model and adjust your behaviour accordingly. All that remains is to remember that only a 'leader' is able to shift their behaviour, effectively making use of Sun Tzu's advice:

> When able to attack, we must seem unable; when using our forces, we must seem inactive.[10]

To conclude our exploration of the behaviour models, let's evaluate each one based on our negotiation criteria.

As we know, whatever negotiation technique you select, it should meet the following criteria:

1. Leads to a reasonable agreement.
2. Is effective in getting results.
3. Improves (or at the very least doesn't worsen) relations between the parties.

Now that we have this measuring tool, let's take another look at each of our behaviour models:

*The 'teenager'*
• Rarely reaches agreements.
• Doesn't gain results.
• Sours relationships.

*The 'mouse'*
• Agreements may be reached, but calling them 'reasonable' is a bit of a stretch.

- Results leave much to be desired.
- Concern for relationships and others' interests are, however, their forte.

### The 'tank'

- Reaches agreements by any means necessary. At times their only goal in battle is to reach an agreement on their own terms, maintaining their dominant position. Engages in combat for power.
- Results often suffer because the 'tank' disregards the relationship and forgets that, at times, it will be more advantageous for the other party to simply stop doing business with them than to honour the agreements they have forced through.
- Other people and interests hardly feature in their mind.

### The 'leader'

- Clearly sees their goal, remembers their asset and, where possible, finds a way to co-operate with opponents.
- Dealings progress.
- Relationships develop.

Now, remember how at the start of this section I posed the question: *If necessary, can we disregard the 'courteousness' vector in negotiations?* I asked you to remember your answer, to compare it with what I would say at the end.

Well, here goes:

> Maximum results are achieved by negotiators who adopt the 'leader' model when fighting for the benefit. For this, it is important to have a strong level of results-oriented motivation and to act in a *courteous* way – as the situation dictates.

## REGULATING TENSIONS AROUND THE NEGOTIATION TABLE

Every negotiator has a set of tools at their disposal. Similarly, every negotiator has certain ways of regulating how heated things get at the negotiating table. That is to say, what level of 'toughness' is acceptable. But, to return briefly to the previous section, we should remember that only the negotiator who adopts the 'leader' behaviour model can make use of these regulators in a purposeful way. This, as we saw, is because anyone who adopts the other behaviours lacks either confidence or *courteousness*. Which means that in the heat of the moment they will be unable to assess whether to ramp up the emotional intensity at the negotiating table or tone it down.

So what are we really talking about? In short: tension regulators.

Negotiation specialists single out four such regulators. Let's take a closer look at each of them.

*Regulator 1: people*

During negotiations, we often make value judgements about people or events that concern them. Or even worse: we make judgements about a person's personal qualities. As soon as negotiations become personal, the process becomes more heated.

In a negotiation, it's one thing to say, 'The figures you're showing me don't really add up', and another thing entirely to say, 'How incompetent do you have to be to come up with figures like this?' In the former case, we are in a rational frame of mind: we can discuss the figures our opponent has given us in more detail. In the latter, we launch straight into a heated fight, one we provoke because we let our emotions come into play. We have cast our judgement, and are thereby no longer capable of rational thinking. Our later actions will be governed by our emotions.

Caliph Ali battled his enemy for some thirty years. His enemy was very strong, and the fight continued; a whole lifetime of war. Eventually, an auspicious moment arrived: Ali's enemy fell from his horse, and Ali pounced at him with his spear. It would only take a second for his spear to pierce his enemy's heart, and then everything would have been over. But in that tiny space of time, his enemy did something that changed his fate: he spat in Ali's face. The spear stopped.

Ali wiped his face, stood up and said to his enemy, 'Tomorrow we begin again.'

His enemy was confused. 'What do you mean?' he asked. 'I've waited for this moment for thirty years – waited hoping that I would finally put my spear to your chest and end it all. That luck did not befall me, but it has befallen you. You could finish me off in a heartbeat. What has got into you?'

Ali said: 'This has not been an ordinary war. I have taken a vow, a Sufi vow, to fight without anger. For thirty years I have done so, but now my anger has come. When you spat on me, for a split second I felt anger, and this war became personal. I wanted to kill you: my ego entered into play. Until then, for thirty years there had been no problems: we had been fighting for a cause. You were not my personal enemy; in no way was this personal. I wasn't interested in killing you; I simply wanted to win. But in that moment I forgot my cause: you became *my* enemy, and I wanted to kill you. And that is why I cannot. So tomorrow we begin again.'

But the battle did not begin again. Instead, the enemy became a friend. He said: 'Now teach me. Be my master and let me be your student. I too want to fight without anger.'

We are used to judging events, people and everything around us. For example, I have heard remarks like: 'That bitch kicked me out.' What does that actually mean? All it means is that a woman told them something and, tactfully or not, asked them to leave her office. That's the rational assessment. And it is only in this frame of mind that we are capable of adequately regulating our behaviour.

As soon as we get mired in value judgements, combat immediately heats up. The following example shows how situations have the potential to play out very differently if a person presents the facts, or simply goes on their own impressions.

A young man is meeting his fiancée's parents for the first time, for a meal in their home. When he arrives, his fiancée and her mother haven't finished setting the table, and so they give their guest some newspapers and family photo albums to keep him entertained. The young man is holding a ballpoint pen to do the crossword, which he is nervously twisting in his hands.

Suddenly the pen pops open, and the spring shoots out of it and into a bowl containing some family oddments. Mechanically, the young man reaches into the bowl to pick it up, but as he does so he sees his fiancée's mother walk into the room out of the corner of his eye. He knows that whatever he says, whatever explanations he gives, will be useless. He needs to bring his fiancée into the conversation – she can be a mediator.

That, I'm afraid, isn't the subject of our book. But let's assume he knows these techniques and is prepared to get his fiancée involved. If he tells her his suspicions and gives her his view of events – that her mother probably saw him and could have suspected him of rooting around in their things – he might be jumping the gun. At the end of the day, he doesn't actually know what her mother thought. Nor can he. This, in turn, will mean his fiancée doesn't fully trust what he says. She may start to think he's making excuses, and when she gives her mother his explanation, she won't believe it either.

So it's essential to lay out the facts alone: he was sitting, twisting the pen, it came unscrewed, the spring jumped out and landed in the bowl, and her mother saw.

You have to learn to speak the language of facts, especially in negotiations – even more so if you are dealing with a complicated opponent. As soon as you start to get personal or give your own personal opinions, the fight will intensify. It is crucial to separate the person from the issue being discussed.

This is the first regulator: if you don't want a fight to heat up, don't get personal. Instead, set out the facts and try to make fewer value judgements. Separating the individual from the issue at stake is key. If we lump everything together, our negotiations will move from a rational to an emotional mode, and as a result things will get personal.

*Regulator 2: positions and ambitions*
Let's look at a situation described in Stephen Covey's book *The Seven Habits of Highly Effective People*.

Two battleships assigned to the training squadron had been at sea on manoeuvers in heavy weather for several days. I was serving on the lead battleship and was on watch on the bridge as night fell. The visibility was poor with patchy fog, so the captain remained on the bridge keeping an eye on all activities.

Shortly after dark, the lookout on the wing of the bridge reported, 'Light, bearing on the starboard bow.'

'Is it steady or moving astern?' the captain called out.

Lookout replied, 'Steady, captain,' which meant we were on a dangerous collision course with that ship.

The captain then called to the signalman, 'Signal that ship: "We are on a collision course, advise you change course 20 degrees".'

Back came a signal, 'Advisable for you to change course 20 degrees.'

The captain said, 'Send, "I'm a captain, change course 20 degrees".'

'I'm a seaman second class,' came the reply. 'You had better change course 20 degrees.'

By that time, the captain was furious. He spat out, 'Send, "I'm a battleship. Change course 20 degrees".'

Back came the flashing light, 'I'm a lighthouse.'

We changed course.[11]

What do we see here? An inflexibility of views and convictions. An unwillingness to compromise. When put together, this can be described in one word: ambitions. Ambitions are often what prevent negotiators from examining the heart of the issue and coming to an agreement. Such tough, unflinching positions and ambitions are precisely what cause opponents to draw one another into a nonsensical fight.

In the next chapter, which is devoted to the art of compromise, we will see how this behaviour affects the negotiation budget and subsequent decision-making.

I once took part in negotiations between the buyers (B) for a fairly large company and the regional manager (RM) of a supplier. The supplier was a relatively small company that wanted to work with the buyer by any means necessary. Here is part of their conversation.

B: Don't you realise who you're talking to? We have companies queuing up to work with us!

RM: Look, we simply can't work at a loss.

B: I don't think you heard me. If you want to work with us, then we'll need a discount of 10 per cent.

RM: We can't accept that.

B: My desk is practically buckling under all of the offers I'm getting.

RM: We don't give those sorts of discounts to anyone. Don't you understand? No one would work at a loss.

B: Then our negotiations are over.

Doesn't this remind you of the lighthouse and the battleship? Neither party can explain to the other what they really want. Hiding behind a tough and inflexible position, we often lose sight of our benefit and simply fight for the position we hold, setting ourselves up for failure.

I stopped these negotiations here. I wondered what the two sides were actually fighting for. It turned out that the buyer would have agreed to a 5 per cent discount, and the regional manager to 7 per cent. So perhaps it might have been better for them to forget their inflexible positions and worry about the deal at stake, no?

On the face of it, our positions often mean a lot more to us than our goal does. Especially when in the position of a 'tank'. When in this role, we forget all about our benefit, instead devoting our attention to asserting our own ambitions. And when this happens, the negotiator is simply fighting for power, an appearance of strength and importance.

The appearance of success is, in reality, simply a value judgement given by a collective. And the only thing these sorts of ambitions do is interfere. Whereas real success – ambition in the good sense of the word – is a product of personal effectiveness.

My family and I were once on holiday in Thailand to bring in the New Year. On New Year's Eve, the hotel's dining tables were all laid beautifully. Each table was set for eight people, and each guest received an invitation to the dinner with a table number written on it. There were seven people at our table.

Then a young couple came over to our table and showed us their invitations, which showed our table number. Well, what can you do, we would have to sit as a nine. It was no big deal – there was more than enough space at the table. As there were only eight chairs but nine guests, the young man decided to take a chair from elsewhere. None of the guests had arrived at the table next to us, so he took one of theirs. When the guests at the neighbouring table arrived, they were outraged and demanded he return the chair.

'You've taken our chair! Give it back now!'

'They didn't give me a chair, so I took one that wasn't being used.'

'The cheek! We have kids, give it back!' (By this point they're shouting).

'I'm not giving anything back, I haven't got anything to sit on. This is my chair!'

Other people started getting involved on both sides, and what was a minor squabble quickly started to escalate. By this point no one even cared about the chair – it was simply a matter of principle.

Their exchange started to remind me of that of the lighthouse and the battleship. I called a waiter over and asked him to bring another chair. As soon as the chair arrived, the sides, who were still mouthing off aimlessly without listening to each other, realised there was nothing left to fight for and finally calmed down.

Conflicts often arise in negotiations because people mistake aims for means. When negotiators argue from a place of ambition, they often restrict themselves by the framework of these very ambitions. The more you try to convince your opponent of the inflexibility of your initial position and the firmness of your convictions, the more you will start to believe them yourself.

Once again, let's return to our key point. Whatever negotiation technique you have chosen, it should meet these three criteria:

1. Leads to a reasonable agreement.
2. Is effective in getting results.
3. Improves (or at the very least doesn't worsen) relations between the parties.

Ambitions can often turn the decision-making process into a true battle. This is what happens when one side declares: 'You'll get the contract, but only on my terms.' In other words: 'I'll win, but you'll get the honour of being good.' Such negotiations usually lead only to resentment, hurt and anger. And this resentment can last a lifetime.

Negotiations often spill over into a fight for positions or ambitions because parties enter the negotiation process without properly outlining a range of possible solutions. If we only have one possible solution in mind when entering negotiations, we are setting ourselves up for tough negotiations from the get-go.

*Regulator 3: having a range of options*
A participant in a workshop once came up to me after losing yet another 'duel' and asked: 'What's going on – why is my negotiation opponent not listening to me? I'm making him such a great offer, but he won't agree, and whenever I try to prove how good it is he just won't listen.'

This boils down to the fact that, when preparing for

negotiations, both opponents only developed one single option, deciding that it would also work for the other side. And what, do you think, is the likelihood that the two will coincide? In my experience, not great.

When preparing for negotiations, think through every possible option that could work for you. Several of them. And they all have to be grounded. Options from the 'I want' side of things will, once again, draw you into a battle for ambitions and lead to you both digging your heels in.

When doing this, particular attention should be given to drawing up a polygon of interests. Yes, you read that right. We'll look at how to do this later on.

As I have already mentioned, if the negotiator has a narrow perspective that sees only one possible option and one single interest then negotiations will become heated, often causing Newton's law of 'equal and opposite forces' to spring into action. When this happens, negotiators will dismiss even interesting or potentially profitable ideas for no ostensible reason.

Often people mistake having a range of options for a willingness to make concessions. In reality, however, the opposite is true: when you have options at hand, there is no need to reveal them to your opponent immediately; all you need to do is listen, draw conclusions and stow them away in your range of options. And should you come to put another option forward to the opponent, then you can pause on it, or at least make an attempt at putting it to paper before moving on to the next.

It is very important to learn how to get to the heart of a problem, rather than attempting to solve it through banal, often irrelevant, bargaining for ambitions. If it is at all possible to find your benefit and reach a decision, then that is worth pursuing. And if not, then you should insist on a solution that you can ground in fact. Try to bear the Tibetan adage in mind: 'He who proves isn't right. He who is right has no need to prove.'

*Regulator 4: a fight of the tenses*
It is possible to either intensify or calm the emotions around a negotiating table simply by shifting the focus of the fight forwards or backwards in time. For example, if we are constantly dwelling on the past, then negotiations become pointless: the prospect of reaching an agreement is, in practical terms, unrealistic.

We cannot change the past. Any attempt to shift our perspective backwards in time in order to convince ourselves not to act in a certain way is pointless. We should know our past, accept it and build on it. Fighting to change it is pointless and non-constructive.

> 'A year ago you supplied us with defective goods, I don't want to see you.'

An opponent may use a phrase like this as a means of retaliation. It is very important not to dwell on this, but to bring the conversation back to the present or, even better, the future. People don't enjoy talking about the less agreeable moments of their past; they far prefer discussing their pleasant futures and how you can help them to get there.

> 'I am truly sorry for what happened, but our quality control system is now set up to eliminate such errors, and we are prepared to offer you an extended warranty.'

As soon as you feel that your opponent is drawing you into a fight for the past, try not to be drawn – it is not constructive and, ultimately, it's pointless. The past cannot be changed. Squabbling over it, however, does have the potential to sour the present.

'You didn't deliver on your promises.'

'Well, you didn't transfer the entire sum on time.'

'If you'd at least started the work, I'd have transferred the advance.'

'And how are we supposed to work without money?'

Does an agreement between these parties seem likely to you? In this instance, you should get to grips with what caused the dissatisfaction and then move on.

If a person is constantly battling over past ground, it means they are still experiencing feelings of guilt, anger or blame. Wound up by their memories and a desire to change past events, they air their grievances with anyone who will listen. There is no point in this person negotiating; it will only end in conflict.

However, when in capable hands, a fight for the present is a valuable regulator. It is important to learn how to fight for the present, because it is indispensable if we are to develop an adequate view of what is going on around us. This is, admittedly, a tough stage of combat: a person who is fighting for the present is effectively in a state of war with the world around them. But you will get clear, positive results earlier on: either you get what you want, or, failing that, you gain a better understanding of your opponent's actions and intentions.

Many people avoid this battle because they are afraid of losing. But sometimes in negotiations it's OK to put your benefit to one side and focus instead on building a more accurate worldview. In some instances, this is even more strategically advantageous than an instant win.

'OK, I'll call Nikolai at some point to specify this.'

'Call him now.'

'I've left his number at home.'

'I'll give it to you, I have it.'

'You know, I've left my phone somewhere.'

'No problem, call from mine.'

'Look, stop, I'm not calling anyone.'

By pursuing this point, it becomes clear that there isn't going to be any call. So now we know what's going on; we don't need to get our hopes up. The fight for the benefit (combat) as described above is a clear example of a fight for the present. Yes, it's tough, yes, there's a (not inconsiderable) chance we'll lose our benefit, but we will gain an understanding of our opponent's true motives, from which we can start setting out our future line.

I once took part in very complex negotiations involving multiple parties. The negotiations were to finalise a voluntary settlement with a bank regarding a debt repayment. Two of the parties were debtors. Present at the negotiations were representatives from the bank, the representative of one of the debtors and the second debtor himself.

Bank: Well, we are willing to sign the voluntary settlement.

Party 2: I am too. Are you? [Turning to Party 1's representative.]

Party 1: Yes, we are, please set up a meeting with my boss.

Party 2: Well, why don't we just call him? Providing everything is fine, we can then prepare the report and he can come here to sign the agreement.

Party 1: Uh, he may be out of the country.

Party 2: That's no problem, this issue is more important than roaming charges. Let's call him and go through this together on speakerphone.

Party 1: I doubt he'll talk it through over the phone.

Party 2: But we can still try. Don't you agree? [Turning to the bank's representatives.]

Bank: Yes, we're ready to draw up an agreement, so why not get this resolved now?

Party 1 [Leaping up]: I didn't come here to sign an agreement, but to find out your positions.

The upshot of this dialogue: we now know that one of the parties clearly had no intention of coming to an agreement at all; they were simply buying time. This sort of information is priceless.

I repeat: the future is very important to people. In order to soften negotiations, you can (and sometimes need to) shift your fight into the future. I'm talking about things like not splitting pennies now, but discussing the technology you will use to distribute *future* earnings. Marriage contracts, a founders' agreement setting out how partners' expenses will be managed – these are all great examples of an ability to engage in a fight for the future. The fight may take place in the present, but it has its sights on making it easier to resolve complex issues in the future.

However, if we let ourselves get carried away by the future, we can turn into someone who idealises their goals and lives only by their plans, expectations, hopes and fears.

It is very important to be competent in issues of tense. Focus on the present; don't fear it. Draw on past experiences, but don't let them become the object of your fight. Use the future to enrich your present. In negotiations, it is important to recognise that memory and expectation are acts of the present. The past and the future are the background to the present. The present must be our focus.

Let's run back over all four tension regulators we can use at the negotiating table.

*People*
Getting personal leads to an intensification of the fighting. If our opponent targets us personally, they are trying to pull us into a tough fight where they will feel more comfortable.

*Positions*
When our fight is driven by our ambitions and positions, we forget about our goal and start to assert an 'unshakeable' point of view. As a result, we get carried away while the results we want drift out of reach.

*Having a range of options*
Always go into negotiations with an outline of your range of options (benefits) and a polygon of interests. You must be prepared to ground every option, and you should also demand as much from your opponent.

*A fight of the tenses*
Fighting for the past is pointless and not constructive. When we get bogged down in a fight over past events, we lose sight of our goal. It can be useful to focus on the future if we need to calm the emotions at the negotiating table. Fighting for the present may be tough, but it will bring us a more accurate worldview, even if it doesn't always secure us our benefit. However, you should only engage in this fight if you are prepared to take some losses.

# LEARNING TO TELL A COMPROMISE FROM AN UNNECESSARY CONCESSION

*Ironically, the most solid, unshakable beliefs*
*are the most superficial ones.*
*Deep convictions can always change.*

— LEO TOLSTOY

I n this chapter, we will explore concessions, compromises and how to tell the two apart. But before defining these terms, I would like to introduce the concept of a 'negotiation budget'.

Have you ever given much thought to what this really is? Many would say that the budget is, above all, the money spent on negotiating. In that sense, it can be viewed as a sort of benefit. But it is worth looking at this concept from a slightly different angle.

• • •

## CREATING A NEGOTIATION BUDGET: FOUR KEY COMPONENTS THAT AFFECT RESULTS

While the negotiation budget will of course depend on the value of the contract in question and other related concerns, it is also largely dependent on these four parameters:

- Time: the time we spend on the negotiations themselves.
- Energy: the energy we put into preparing and holding these negotiations.
- Money: the cost not of the contract, but of the ongoing negotiations.
- Emotion: the emotional toll of the negotiations.

The following equation for calculating the negotiation budget is based on Jim Camp's model.

Let's take a look at these four criteria sequentially and evaluate their impact on the overall negotiation budget.

*Time*

We all know the saying 'time is money'. And it's true – it really is. But even in our everyday life, even when we know and remember this simple maxim, we don't always value our time as much as we should.

Think about it: I'd say about 80 per cent of our working life is made up of things that we could put to one side, things that don't bring us any particular benefit in the here and now. Probably only around 20 per cent of tasks produce a specific, tangible result. And where negotiations are concerned, we will often spend 80 per cent of our time around the negotiating table discussing matters that not only bear little relevance to the negotiation process itself, but that have little – if anything – to do with the matter at hand.

Experienced negotiators know how to use time to their advantage. For example, in some situations an opponent might deliberately start to draw out their responses. You won't get a better indicator of something like this happening than the words: 'You know, this isn't formulated very precisely . . . I'll need to think this through and discuss it with my colleagues . . . When can I call you back? How about in a week?'

This negotiator is buying time. Why? Because they are well aware of what this means to your negotiation budget. So, from their perspective, in order to put pressure on your negotiation budget, they need to increase this particular item of expenditure. That is to say, to increase the amount of time spent on the process itself.

What is this component worth? A lot. But of all of the components highlighted at the start of this chapter, it's the least weighty: in Jim Camp's equation, it gets a unit value of 1.

*Energy*

This component ranks third in its importance and unit weight.

It's obvious that we put a lot of energy into negotiations – no one needs proof of that. But what is this energy, and where does it go? Into negotiation preparations, the negotiation process itself, travel and more. I'm sure you'll agree that the question of travel – and who does it – is an important one. Of course, negotiations demand energy regardless, but it's a different matter entirely if you're the one doing the travelling, particularly if you have to travel to another city or region. Picture yourself travelling from Moscow to Vladivostok, a distance of about 6,500km. Can you imagine how draining flights, hotel stays, travel around town while pondering your situation are? These are all aspects of energy. Energy can even be crucial in the negotiation process itself.

Here's an example.

I once flew to Murmansk for negotiations. It was winter, in the depths of polar night. I'm not even going to go into how draining it is for a Muscovite to be up in the Arctic Circle in constant darkness. Even before setting out for Murmansk, my team and I had put a lot of energy into just setting up this meeting, which had not been a quick process. Anyway, so there I was, having flown in to see them, and what do they tell me: 'You know, we aren't in a position to negotiate with you right now.'

In this example, it's clear that our negotiation budget took a blow that day. Note also how my opponent acted on two components at once: time and energy.

Having already looked at time, we have seen that it has a unit weight of 1 in the negotiation budget. Energy, on the other hand, has a unit weight of 2. In negotiations, energy is the more valuable. Because it's one thing to spend *time* sitting comfortably in our office reading books, speaking on the phone, holding timetabled meetings or simply waiting for the appointed date. And quite another to have to travel somewhere for one single purpose.

*Money*

There's no escaping it: the goal of any organisation is profit. And when we spend money on negotiations (especially if we spend more than expected), the budget of any activity will have to go up.

Let's define the concept of money in the negotiation process. A lot falls within this category: the money we spend on communication (phone bills, travel to meet a client), gifts, marketing materials, shipping and forwarding, not to mention remuneration for the work of everyone involved. In short, it is all the expenses incurred for and during the negotiation process.

At times this financial component of the negotiation budget can simply skyrocket – when flying back and forth from Moscow to Vladivostok, say, or organising some sort of congress to prove the advantageousness of a proposal – or even simply when multiple parties are involved in the project who need to come together for talks.

When these costs are very large it's easy to get preoccupied by how much money we're actually spending. Which is why this component is very important to the overall negotiation budget, and it has a unit weight of 3.

Let's briefly explore why this component gets more weight than energy. After all, in the Murmansk example I gave before, energy certainly proved its weight.

Let's say we're travelling from one part of Moscow to another. The expenses for this trip will be minimal; all it requires is energy and time. However, if we instead have to fly from Moscow to Kamchatka, then all three components will come into play: time, energy and money. Our costs will increase significantly, meaning that our negotiation budget will go up, too. Incidentally, this is exactly what happened in my Murmansk example, and it's also why money has the greater unit weight: three times greater than that of time, and 50 per cent greater than that of energy.

*Emotion*

The final component of the negotiation budget is emotion. And, as you have probably guessed, it is also the most valuable. Why?

Because when emotions are stirred during the negotiation process, a person can no longer reason logically; they are unable to add up the costs, evaluate a benefit or join up the dots. How often have you heard remarks like 'But I can't give up now – I've put so much into this!' in negotiations? If you have, it means it's likely that the negotiations in question have already gone over budget, and the emotional component in particular is sweeping it off the scale. So it isn't surprising that the emotional component of the negotiation budget is accorded the highest unit weight: 4.

Let's return to the negotiations I described in Murmansk and try to figure out the budget of these negotiations.

We spent **time**. On travel, of course, but also on preparations, agreeing certain points, discussing details. My **energy** *was also affected*: I had prepared, studied the company materials, done research to find our common ground. A long flight and twenty-four-hour darkness also took their toll on my energy. And of course we spent **money**, including on preparations (long-distance phone calls, consultations with experts, compiling documents, etc.), flight and hotel costs, and travel expenses within the city. Add all of these components together, and before negotiations had even begun the unit weight of the budget was 6.

But when they told me they wouldn't be holding talks that had already been not only agreed upon but confirmed, the budget of the whole enterprise grew. Because that was when the **emotional** component came into play, in the form of disappointment. I felt that I had been invited, and I had made this long, difficult journey, only to be turned away at the door. But by that point I couldn't back down.

At this point, the key thing to remember is not to give in to your emotions. If you do, the negotiation budget will immediately reach its maximum weight of 10 (1 + 2 + 3 + 4 = 10). Once the maximum budget weight is reached, a person simply can't stand down. And, of course, if they can't get their emotions in check, then they're on thin ice and liable to make a mistake, whether that's getting aggressive and souring their relationship with the client, or hanging on desperately waiting (often longer than a day) for any form of negotiations.

Ask yourself this question: will these negotiations lead to anything? I can on good authority predict that in these situations, there is no way of getting the results you planned.

This is why it's essential to keep tabs on your budget, analysing how much time, energy, money and emotions you are putting into each negotiation process.

Concessions tend to happen once the negotiation budget has already reached its maximum: when that party can go no further; when the process has completely worn them down. Most of the time, this specifically relates to that party's emotional state. So why is it that they start to make concessions, you ask? To get out of the negotiations faster.

**Concessions are due to weakness.** If we apply von Clausewitz's definition of fighting as 'a trial of strength of the moral and physical forces by means of the latter'[12] to this situation, it becomes clear that concessions happen through a lack of moral force or strength of will. A person without this strength will be unable to fight for their benefit, instead moving away from their own interests to partly – or wholly – assimilate their opponent's terms. This happens once their negotiation budget has already reached its maximum.

In cases like these, you would never say that the two sides reached a compromise. One classic definition of compromise is: **a negotiation process through which parties are able to achieve their interests by making mutual concessions.** But this definition in and of itself encourages concessions. Here, the word 'concession' has no negative implications, but if we cast our eyes back to the last paragraph it's clear that concessions are a product of weakness. As it turns out, the classic definition of compromise aims to weaken your negotiating position. Personally, I modify this definition slightly, replacing the words 'mutual concessions' with 'movements towards the other party'. So for me, a compromise is **a negotiation process through which parties are able to achieve their interests by making movements towards the other party.**

**A compromise differs from a concession in that a compromise is a conscious decision.** You can only make a conscious decision if you still have enough reserves of time, energy and money in your negotiation budget and your emotions are under control. Although your negotiation budget is currently high, you feel that you can continue to fight and that as a result you may get more out of these negotiations.

However, you should remember that the final benefit will either be smaller or equal to the additional budget that you will spend on pursuing that fight. When you make an informed decision like this, it is a compromise.

Many authors suggest that compromise is a mathematical value that can be calculated. My view is that it is a psychological aspect of the negotiation process. If a party is satisfied with what has been achieved in the negotiation process and is prepared to implement the terms of the agreement, it can be considered a compromise. If, however, these terms cause discomfort or regret, they should instead be viewed as a concession.

Always keep tabs on the size of your negotiation budget. Before going into negotiations, it is important to replenish your reserves of time, money and energy. Think about what (and where) these reserves are should you need them.

Compromise is possible only during combat (a fight for the benefit) when you understand what benefit your opponent seeks and what they are fighting for. Otherwise your attempt will make your opponent want to get even more from you.

Let's look at a few situations.

A client calls in a blind rage and screams down the line:

'You missed your payment and delivery deadlines! You let us down – we've got a disaster on our hands and it's all your fault!'

An inexperienced negotiator immediately jumps to compensation options.

'You know, we'd be willing to offer compensation for your costs . . .'

'What sort of compensation?'

'How about a discount?'

'And?'

'And . . . well . . .'

This game can go on and on.

What's happening here? This is a manoeuvre. In this situation, neither side knows the benefits at stake. And, when you don't know what the benefits are, any attempt to compromise will simply lead to further concessions.

Now picture two colleagues sitting at their desks, talking.

'Oh, I'm out of paper clips,' says colleague one. 'Have you got any?'

'Yes.'

Colleague two gives colleague one a packet of paper clips. A few minutes pass.

'How about some music?' suggests colleague one, breaking the silence. 'You've got a good playlist.'

Colleague two starts playing some music. He's starting to feel a bit uncomfortable, but he doesn't understand what his colleague is 'fighting' for. As it happens, colleague one is fighting to be the 'alpha', the one who gives the orders.

Obviously, after another few minutes, colleague one says, 'Hey, it's a little stuffy in here, shall we open the window?' He glances at the window key, which is next to colleague two.

Colleague two opens the window. He is feeling even more uncomfortable, so decides to go make some coffee. On his way out, he hears colleague one call behind him: 'Oh, if you're making some coffee, make some for me?'

You can probably imagine what comes next. If colleague two fulfils this command, he'll become the errand boy. It is very important to know what we are fighting for. And as soon as that becomes clear, you need to move from manoeuvring to combat (fight for your benefit).

For example, like this:

'Sure. But when you go to the lunchroom, don't forget to close the window, OK?' (Then let it hang in the air.)

## BUILD A MAGIC POLYGON OF INTERESTS

Although compromise is an emotional state, it should be achieved with the help of mathematics. The magic polygon of interests, which I mentioned at the end of the last chapter, can play a key role in reaching compromises.

We have already seen that when parties negotiate with one sole interest in mind, negotiations will turn not only tough but heated. There won't be enough resources to go around, and this deficit will push parties into heated scuffles. It will only be possible to calm the emotions and reach agreements if both sides can see several interests in front of them. These interests are what make up the faces of our 'magical' shape.

There are five steps to building a polygon of interests.

*Step 1: find your interests*
Think long and hard about what your interests might be when resolving a particular situation. These interests will form the faces of the polygon.

There will always be one key interest that you see immediately, but this will always be accompanied by other interests, however insignificant and unimportant they may at first appear.

A person applying for a job will normally pay a lot of attention to the salary. Besides this, however, the employment benefits, incentives, amount and regularity of annual leave, flexibility in working hours, team spirit, work tasks, responsibilities, experience and knowledge gained, study opportunities and more will all need to be taken into consideration.

Similarly, when a supplier wants to start working with a chain, they will have to consider not only the price and payment terms, but also the possibility of reaching the end consumer, promotional opportunities, heightened brand profile and a stronger reputation.

Note in both cases how many faces (interests) there are, far from all of which are material. The more faces your polygon has, the more flexible your position will be and the more likely that you will be able to reach an agreement with your opponent.

Now, it is very important to visualise your interests – material and non-material – by placing them on the faces of the polygon itself. You should have at least three faces, otherwise the shape won't close.

⚠️
**Always remember:**
the most effective polygons have
between five and seven faces.

*Step 2: monetise the faces*

When I was a student, my classmates and I used to give blood. Of course, I'm sure some of us would have done it for nothing, but the majority of us gladly made the most of the fact that after the procedure we were given either money or food rations. That is to say, our loss was in some way compensated for (and I imagine that those who refused the money and food gained a different, non-material compensation: self-respect, a clear conscience, etc.). I take the same approach to compensation for material bonuses and discounts: to a business, giving a discount is like giving blood. So when you altruistically give away bonuses, it is important to realise that you are draining your organism of blood, and that it will be difficult to recover if you're getting nothing in return.

So now what you need to do is evaluate every face that you identified in the first step *in relation to the key interest*. If the key interest is price, then you should evaluate what the associated payment deadlines, potential recommendations, increase in product awareness, etc. would be worth to you in price. In other words, you need to consider how much you are prepared to pay for increasing your supply volumes, getting new recommendations, establishing a good relationship, etc.

Everything should have a concrete price, from the experience gained to the opportunity to raise the company profile. If you skip this step, your opponent will easily take advantage of your ignorance by overstating the value of any non-material interests:

'You do understand that working with us is essentially free promotion for you.'

'Not everyone gets the chance to work for such a huge corporation.'

Phrases like these seek to provoke the opponent into draining their business of blood for almost nothing in return. But if you have a good idea of what the actual value of the benefit would be, they will have a hard time confusing you.

I myself have experienced one very common example of this. A very large company approached me about doing some workshops with them. After we had met, their HR specialists said they would be happy to commission some workshops on the theme of 'tough negotiations'. They asked me to give them a 20 per cent discount, which they justified by the fact that I would get to put their name on my CV: many were prepared to work with them for free for that very reason. During our fight for the benefit, my position was open and transparent: I would also be prepared to work for free, but I would need to be clear about what I would get in return. As soon as they asked me about the 20 per cent discount, I turned to my polygon of interests. I had valued the 'importance of the client' face as being worth 5 per cent, so that was the discount I agreed to offer.

Every face must be monetised based on the currency of the key interest. Everything needs a price, be it reputation, reviews, or the chance of increased supply volumes in future. When considering this question, it can be very useful to review your own or your company's strategic plans.

*Step 3: work out your desired position*

For this step, start with your key interest. Think about what you would want the value of the key interest to be. So if the key interest is the pay package, then pinpoint a salary figure; if it's the payment deadline, then set a number of days; and if it's a discount, then work out the percentage.

People are often wired to instinctively demand the greatest possible value for their desired position. For example, when being offered a job, an applicant might mistakenly say they want a salary of 100,000 roubles, when they would have been perfectly happy with 70,000 roubles. The latter should be the desired position.

Then, once you have that in place, you need to decide what the value of the other faces should be in relation to it. If I am offered my desired salary, how much annual leave am I prepared to accept? How important is this job title/team spirit, etc. to me?

---

⚠

By completing the following steps, we outline three important positions in negotiations:

1. The red line: the minimum value of the key interest, below which our needs will not be met.

2. The desired position: the value of the key interest that I will be fully satisfied with.

3. The stated position: the value of the key interest that marks the start of negotiations.

---

*Step 4: determine the red line*

Create a new polygon of interests based on your red line. Every polygon has a perimeter. Although the value of the faces may change, this total perimeter must never decrease. This is the most important rule to remember here. In other words, if you reduce the price (i.e. reduce the value of one of the faces), then you need to figure out what other faces you can increase to retain the original perimeter of the polygon.

This rule allows us to meet our opponent halfway without hurting our own interests. For example, if your boss can't give you a raise, you can still protect your interests through increased annual leave, more flexible working hours or additional skills. If a purchasing agent refuses a shorter payment deadline on a matter of principle, you can protect your interests by increasing the price, introducing a new product, or suggesting that they put your product in a more advantageous position.

*Step 5: Figure out your stated position*
Now you figure out your stated position. This is the position that you state at the start of the negotiation process. It should be higher than and clearly different to your desired position.

I am often asked how much higher the stated position should be. This will be down to the individual, although it should of course be reasonable. I often test out the adequacy of the stated position using Henry Ford's rule: 'If there is any one secret of success, it lies in the ability to get the other person's point of view.' I ask myself: 'If I were in my opponent's position and had the information that they have, if my opponent started negotiations from this position would I continue to negotiate or would I walk away?' If I would negotiate, then I have my stated position: I don't fear it and I don't doubt it. If I would walk away, however, then it is worth reducing it slightly and once again putting myself in my opponent's shoes. This is essential, because if your stated position is high even for you, you will quickly surrender it, and in doing so your opponent will see there is the possibility of bringing you down even further.

Two fishermen are sitting on a boat. One says:

'Yesterday I caught thirty kg of carp!'

'Yeah right! I was here yesterday and nothing was biting. BUT I did manage to catch a solid gold, eighteenth-century candlestick! And would you believe it, the candles were still burning!'

'Fine, you've made your point, I'll rein it in by ten kg if you blow out your candles. Deal?'

Why is it so important for us to inflate our position?

Aleksandr, an entrepreneur, has launched an exciting and in-demand software product. Having analysed the market, he came to the conclusion that its market price is typically between 10,000 and 20,000 roubles. However, he decides to 'play fair' and offer his best price (i.e. his desired position) to the market upfront: 9,500 roubles. As a result, he typically achieves a sales price of only 9,000 roubles.

If negotiations were a purely mathematical process performed by robots, then Aleksandr would be leading the way in sales. But the psychological aspect is key here. Don't deny people the opportunity to fight you for a benefit. They value what is harder to earn. As a rule, a benefit that is easily obtained feels less valuable.

Once you have worked your way through the first three steps of this process, you will have created your magic polygon that will allow you not only to consciously regulate the tensions around the negotiating table, but also to fight for your benefit in an informed way. Let's practice this with a worked example.

An IT specialist is looking for a new job. His reasons for wanting this change are that his current job doesn't offer a particularly high salary (50,000 roubles), the working hours are inflexible and the commute is inconvenient.

Let's build his polygon of interests.

*Step 1*

Let's see what faces the polygon has. One will of course be salary, and another two are immediately clear: ease of commute and working hours. Let's add in some other less prominent, but still present, interests: career growth, employment benefits, interesting work. So now we have six faces.

*Step 2*

Now we give each face a value. How? The figures I use here are all examples and should not be used as a template; they will vary from situation to situation. What matters is that these values should be calculated in the 'currency' of the key interest, which in this case happens to be salary. So the question we need to answer becomes: how much am I prepared to pay from my own salary for a job closer to home, flexible working hours, etc.?

And so, in roubles:

Location: max. 5,000.
Working hours: max. 5,000.
Career growth: max. 10,000.
Employment benefits: 2,000.
Having interesting work: max. 5,000.
Perimeter not including salary = 27,000 roubles.

*Step 3*

From here we work out the desired position. As our key interest is salary, let's assume that competitors for this job would accept a salary of 70,000 roubles. Remember: this isn't the maximum they want, it's what they would accept. Next, we need to go back through how we would value the remaining faces if we had a salary of 70,000 roubles.

Location is important, but being close to home isn't essential: 2,000.
Flexible working hours don't matter: 0.
Career growth isn't so important – money is more so: 0.
Employment benefits aren't important: 0.
Having interesting work is important: 5,000.
Total perimeter = 77,000 roubles.

*Step 4*

Now it's time to create a polygon for our red line, remembering to always balance the overall perimeter. This is where our list of face values from Step 2 comes in handy. Remember that the red line is the minimum value of the key interest; under no circumstances is this to be crossed.

> Salary = 50,000.
> Location is important, proximity: 5,000.
> Flexible working hours: 5,000.
> Career growth is important: 10,000.
> Employment benefits are important: 2,000.
> Having interesting work is important: 5,000.

From this, we can see that we would be able to compensate for a lower salary through other benefits. In this example, a 20,000 rouble reduction in salary from our desired position can be balanced through the possibility of flexible working hours, career growth, employment benefits and interesting work.

To check this fact: the perimeter of the polygon comes to 77,000 roubles.

---

**⚠**

Add the values attached to each face (except salary) to find the basis for this position. You can use polygons like these to justify any combination of benefits in a logical, reasoned way, without your demands coming across as an 'I want it because I say so' situation.

---

*Step 5*

For your stated position, I recommend taking the perimeter of the red line as your figure for your key interest. So if our key interest is salary, and the perimeter of the red line is 77,000 roubles, then:

> Salary: 77,000.
> Location isn't important (although we will say it is): 0
> Flexible working hours aren't important (although we will say they are): 0
> Career growth isn't important (although we will say it is): 0
> Employment benefits aren't important (although we will say they are): 0
> Having interesting work is important: 5,000.

⚠️

The process of drafting these three polygons has actually helped us to pinpoint the interest that is truly important to us. Note that in all three polygons, the only face on which we are not prepared to budge is that of 'interesting work'. This interest is therefore our weak link, and we need to try to protect it.

Remember that our fight for the benefit will take place somewhere between the desired position and the stated position. Picture the red line as a minefield: keep as far from it as possible. Between the red line and the desired position, the perimeter must always be protected: if we reduce one face, then we will need to make gains in another to protect it.

**Build your own polygon of interests based on the following situation**

A buyer for a construction company within a major federal holding has made a proposal to a supplier of roofing materials.

The proposed terms include a discount of 20 per cent, a deferred payment period of sixty days and access to a dedicated specialist. The supplier finds these terms unacceptable but they can see that working with this company would give them access to the entire holding moving forward.

You can find my polygons in the 'Answers' section at the back of the book. You can also send me your versions at: igor@ryzov.ru.

When moving towards the other side in negotiations, follow these **five rules**:

- Don't hurry. It should be difficult for the other side to generate any movement.

- As you move towards the opponent's position, think about whether they are actually meeting you halfway or simply giving you that impression. Compromise can only be achieved when both sides are meeting each other halfway.

- Don't give away material benefits in exchange for mythical or non-monetised ones. Everything should have its price.

- Under no circumstances should you make a concession at the start of negotiations in the hope of winning the opponent's favour: you will only embolden them.

- If you offer discounts, put them together like building blocks or weights on a dumbbell: a collection of smaller units rather than one big figure.

Bargaining will fall between the desired and stated positions, whereas between the red line and the desired position it's all about protecting your interests. This is where you should apply the rule of protecting the perimeter.

1. Compromise is a decision made from a place of strength and based on expediency. When our negotiation budget allows us to fight on, we should still weigh up the benefit of the combat against the cost to our budget. Then we will be able to make an informed decision: to fight, or to take the terms being offered.

2. If our budget is running off the scale, then we need to stop, get our emotions in check and minimise expenses. Only after that can we continue negotiation.

3. We only compromise once we understand the concrete benefit to us and to our opponent.

# FIVE KEY TECHNIQUES THAT GET RESULTS IN TOUGH NEGOTIATIONS

*To fight and conquer in all your battles is not supreme excellence;*
*supreme excellence consists in breaking the enemy's*
*resistance without fighting.*

— SUN TZU[13]

This chapter is devoted to some specific techniques that can help us to protect our interests in tough negotiations. These techniques will help you to build up negotiation muscle, boost your confidence and, as a result, improve your negotiation style, as it were. Once again, I should note that only a 'leader' can consciously apply any of these techniques in a fight for the advantage.

So what are these techniques, and how many of them do you need to know? I am often asked this question in my consultations and workshops, and there is no simple answer.

At times it can be the young, inexperienced judo fighters who are the most exciting to watch: in their attempts to grab their opponent, they lurch around trying to put as many moves as possible into action. Watching professionals compete is less interesting in this regard. In these matches, several minutes can pass without anything happening: the fighters slowly size each other up until suddenly, in the blink of an eye, one pulls out a move and combat begins.

Negotiations are exactly the same. So long as you know exactly how and when to use a technique, then just one or two will get you a long way. Of course, it is better to vary your arsenal, because if you always use the same technique it will become your calling card, and your opponent will be well prepared to counter it. In short, if we don't expand our repertoire of moves, we make life easier for our opponent.

A charming young man is a dab hand at giving compliments to win the trust of store managers and goods managers. His modus operandi is to arrive, make a smooth compliment and a bit of small talk and then turn the conversation onto sales. One day he arrives for a meeting with a store manager and, forgetting he was there three days before, starts their conversation with exactly the same compliment. The manager smiles: 'Is that the only one you've got?' she asks.

In this chapter we are going to look at five key techniques that can be particularly effective in a fight for the benefit. These are:

1. Eye contact.
2. Strength in indifference.
3. Saying no.

4. Playing the 'host'.
5. Strength in your cause.

## EYE CONTACT AS A GUARANTEE FOR SUCCESS

Our eyes are a very powerful weapon. By simply looking our opponent in the eye, we can either calm the emotions around the negotiating table, or send our opponent into a rage.

The first meeting is very important. You need to look your opponent in the eye, however hard that may be for you. We often come across negotiators who are stronger than we are, but remember von Clausewitz's words: 'Fighting is a trial of strength of the moral and physical forces.'[14] Well, this is where you size up each other's moral forces. If you look away, it shows that you are the weaker one. As a result, your opponent will naturally try to walk all over you, insisting on their point of view alone. And, in all likelihood, they will be successful.

The initial eye contact is very important, as it lets your opponent see your emotional strength. Now, this is still no guarantee of victory, but it does ensure that your opinion will be considered. At the same time, remember that this isn't a staring contest. Half a second of eye contact is enough; then you can look away.

Eye contact is also important throughout the course of the negotiation process. For example, if your opponent is putting pressure on you or raising their voice, your eyes should tell them: 'I know what you're doing and why you're doing it.' After this, however, it is important to look away; sustained eye contact could be seen as a challenge or provoke a flare-up of emotions.

You may also come across instances of the negotiator playing the underdog.

Everett Shostrom describes this term in his book *Man, the Manipulator*.[15] In summary, in every person there are two dogs: the 'top dog' and the 'underdog'. The top dog puts on the pressure, as though making threats, whereas the underdog begs and demonstrates their own weakness, as though currying favour. Both are tricks. But as Shostrom suggests, in the majority of cases the underdog will in fact win out, because they play on our pity.

I'm sure we've all heard of promoters saying: 'Oh, please, I'm begging you! If you don't take any this month they'll give me the sack, I won't meet my targets . . .'

These are the words of a manipulator. Making eye contact is very effective with people like this: when met with an open, clear gaze, they realise their tricks aren't going to fly.

However, as mentioned, if you look a person straight in the eye during negotiations, there is a risk that it will inflame tensions. Unwavering eye contact can provoke your opponent or rouse a negative reaction, driving the negotiations onto an emotional plane. As such, in constructive negotiations don't get carried away with this technique. Use it only where necessary.

**Eye contact should be used:**

1. At the start of proceedings, where it is important to establish eye contact and demonstrate your emotional strength.

2. If you need to show your opponent that you know what they are playing at and it's not going to fly.

3. If you deliberately want to stir up negotiations.

## SHIELDING YOURSELF FROM 'NEED' AND FEAR

Entire teaching systems are devoted to this technique, which is also described in detail in Jim Camp's books. 'Need' often drives many negotiators – in a bad way. That and fear, or what we can call a sense of over-motivation.

I'm hoping you'll remember the postulates of the Kremlin school of negotiation we looked at in Chapter 1. As we saw, that school is grounded in fear in particular: a fear of losing a client; a fear of walking away with nothing. Over-motivation.

Imagine a person's internal weighing scale during a negotiation. On one side we have their need for a positive response to their proposal, and on the other side lies rejection. When the need side outweighs the rejection side and that person isn't prepared to hear 'no', then they have no other option – they aren't prepared to walk away; they probably haven't even considered it. A person in this situation is very weak, and their opponent will likely be able to get whatever they want from them.

A negotiator is only powerful if their internal weights are balanced. An event that completely changed the course of world history can serve as an excellent example of this method in action.

In July 1945, the USSR, USA and UK were still allies: a bloody war was raging on the Eastern Front against Japan, and President Harry Truman was anxious that Joseph Stalin should keep his word about entering into this war. The heads of state of these three countries all convened at a conference in

Potsdam on 17 July, during which the question of Germany's post-war administration was discussed. At the recommendation of Prime Minister Winston Churchill, President Truman, who had just received an encrypted telegram confirming the successful testing of the atom bomb, informed Stalin that the USA had created a weapon of mass destruction. The leaders of the USA and UK wanted to see how the Kremlin's dictator would react to this message.

But Stalin's reaction was very restrained. He thanked Truman for notifying him and made no further comments on the matter. His behaviour seemed so strange that both Truman and Churchill thought Stalin simply hadn't understood what they had said. Their attempt to put pressure on the Soviet leader at the conference and make him more amenable to their wishes was unsuccessful.

Stalin, as witnesses have testified, understood perfectly well what the news meant. After the meeting, he called Igor Kurchatov in Moscow and demanded that he speed up his work on the Soviet atomic bomb.

I imagine we have all felt over-motivation in our lives. Now, I realise this isn't the first time that I've used an uncommon turn of phrase in this book, so I should probably clarify what I mean by that term. Over-motivation is the feeling you get when you are not only focused on a task, but when it feels like life as you know it depends on getting the result you want. We can compare this feeling to 'need' as Jim Camp describes it, or, quite simply, fear.

For example, let's say a man walks past a car dealership and sees a beautiful car. In that instant, a feeling is stirred in him that he simply can't suppress. He can't eat, he can't sleep, he takes no pleasure in sun-filled days or the smiles of his loved ones: all he can think about is how much he needs that car. You can predict what he does next. He starts to obsess over where to get the money to buy this thing that is suddenly so vital to his wellbeing. In the end, he gets into debt to buy it. And then? After this 'need' has led to him doing something he didn't think through, he will naturally start to justify his choice.

Sound familiar? That's what I like to call **over-motivation**. What would he have done had he simply wanted the car, had it inspired motivation in him but not **need**? He would probably have weighed up his situation against his desire and considered what sensible options he had. And he would have accomplished his goal. But not, you will notice, through hasty actions.

It is a basic rule of our modern world that we dream most about what we need least. In life, we end up in a situation of 'need' when, for example, we get (or paint ourselves) an image of what a happy future means. We begin to imagine it, ponder it, dream about it, gradually feeling those emotions as though that future's already here. And very soon we find ourselves not wanting to imagine anything else. Thus a state of over-motivation or 'need' is born: we feel that we *have to have it*. This state holds us back in many ways – including from achieving that very future we feel we must have.

If we enter negotiations in such a state, then an experienced opponent will waste no time in taking advantage of the situation and squeezing all that they can from us. The following situation may be slightly exaggerated, but it is a great illustration of what over-motivation can lead to:

141

'I reeeallly need to get some sales on your account this month!'

'So?'

'So I'm willing to make some concessions . . .'

'What, exactly?'

'How about a discount?'

'How much?'

'5 per cent.'

'That's not too convincing.'

'OK, I'll offer you the very maximum I can do: 10 per cent.'

'That's better, but I think you can do better still.'

What is driving the seller? 'Need'. He isn't thinking about his client's needs, nor the benefit of the company. The only thing driving him is his own bonus, his need to meet his targets. He's already thinking about the new car he's going to buy, or the holiday he's going to take – anything but the true goal.

And the buyer, of course, having picked up on this 'need', grabs it with both hands. As a result, he gets the maximum discount there is to get.

Skilled negotiators, like sharks swimming towards the smell of blood, are able to detect even the slightest hint of 'need'. As soon as that hint appears, they pounce. A 'need' immediately makes you more vulnerable.

Another technique the negotiation shark uses to submerge their victim in a sense of 'need' is to give a quick 'yes'.

In the early 2000s, one of the managers working beneath me went to negotiate with a major chain. He came back beaming like a diamond and swanned straight up to my desk without even taking off his coat.

'We've got the contract! They're going to stock us in twelve stores, really favourable conditions.'

'OK. Do the sums and we'll take a look.'

No more than ten minutes later he came back to me with the figures.

'Look! The contract would be worth 12 milllion roubles per month. Would we be able to meet that supply? Allocate all of our reserve stock to me. How long will it take for us to bump up our volumes?'

His voice was practically cracking with joy. It's worth noting here that 12 million is twice his monthly target. I could already tell what was going on, but as we know, you only learn from your own mistakes. So I said: 'That's great, go back to negotiate with them.'

The next day, he came into work a new man: in his mind he'd already moved up the social ladder; he was already planning what to spend his future bonuses on. He was wearing a smug smile and the look of a victor. And – of course – he was carrying a couple of catalogues for a famous car brand under his arm. The entire department looked on jealously. After hanging around in the office announcing his upcoming holiday plans and the new car he was going to buy, our hero set off for more negotiations.

When he got back, looking like Napoleon himself, he dropped the draft contract and an appendix with the relevant prices onto my desk. I read the contract carefully, and when I reached the appendix – which put the discount at 20 per cent and featured numerous other terms that made the deal unprofitable – I got out my pen. At this point our hero, anticipating that I was about to sign, leapt into the air. Instead, however, he saw me slowly write: 'Cannot agree to the terms of this deal – will not sign.'

It's hard for me to describe what came next. The entire room shook with shouts and exclamations that were completely inappropriate not only for his level of seniority, but also for all social decency. Once his emotions had subsided – or, rather, when he had tired himself out – I said: 'Dmitriy, I understand your frustration, and in your position I would be smashing things up, but let's take a closer look at the situation.' I walked over to the whiteboard on the wall, took out a pen and started to write. 'According to the agreement, the supply volume would be worth 12 million roubles per month, right?' I confirmed.

'Yes!' Dmitriy cried, looking around the room for support.

'And the discount is 20 per cent, i.e. 2.4 million roubles. Right?'

'Yes, but we'd be getting such a major client, we really need this deal.' He looked around again for support.

Unhurried, I continued: 'Now, according to the clause on marketing, we'll have to make a monthly payment of 5 per cent of the purchase price, i.e. 480,000 roubles (the purchase price after the discount is 9,600,000 roubles).'

'Yes, but we know that products don't sell without marketing.'

'Excellent! Now how much does our logistics company charge?'

'12 per cent,' our hero replied with a groan.

I wrote 1,152,000 roubles on the whiteboard and tallied up the total: 4,032,000 roubles.

One of the other managers in the room said loudly: 'That's a loss!'

'Well . . . I guess there won't be a deal then . . .'

'Why not? Let's go back to the start and work this out.'

Let's think about what led this experienced negotiator astray. Why didn't he go through the terms of the agreement and clarify the details with the buyer from the beginning? Because when he set out for negotiations, Dmitriy was expecting to have to break down the buyer's walls of indifference. The experienced 'shark' detected Dmitriy's blood and pulled out a nice little trick in the shape of a quick 'yes'. He made no resistance, but immediately said, 'Of course, let's work together,' in Dima's mind painting an image of a happy future. And in doing so, he inspired a sense of 'need' in Dima, a fear of losing this client and everything that came with it.

As a rule, a quick 'yes' is always followed by a 'BUT . . .'

145

To Dmitriy's credit, he turned out to be a very good student. Once he and I had done some work on avoiding 'need', he put it into practice with aplomb. And he's still working in negotiation, fulfilling his own desires and those of his family. But more on that later.

We all have our own desires, plans that seemingly descend on us from above, ambitious goals and families, so it's impossible for us to completely escape a sense of 'need'. However, it is entirely possible for us to keep it in check. A healthy level of motivation is a good thing. Desire is important: it allows us to progress towards the goals we've set for ourselves.

So what sorts of behaviours give away the fact that we're feeling a 'need'?

- We talk too much, don't listen, and interrupt others.
- We display too much emotion.
- We get ahead of ourselves and the stage of negotiations.
- We apply 'closing' tactics, trying to finalise the deal as quickly as possible.

## How to contain and control manifestations of 'need'

1. When going into negotiations, it is very important to be able to answer two questions: 'What will I do if they accept?' and 'What will I do if they refuse?' In other words, what will I do in the case of a 'yes' and a 'no'? Dmitriy hadn't known the answers to these questions; had he done so, he would have been well equipped to hear that crafty quick 'yes'. The answers to these questions give us a good idea of what is going on around us. And they mean that we are ready to accept either outcome. When you answer these questions for yourself, you bring your internal weighing scales

into a neutral position: the 'yes' stops outweighing the 'no'. This is a strong position to be in when negotiating. If, despite this, your opponent has been able to force your internal scales and draw you out of a healthy state of motivation, then it is very important to recognise that you are displaying a 'need'.

2. Control your speech. When we feel a sense of 'need', we tend to speak faster and in a higher pitch.

3. Focus only on what you can control: your voice, your way with words, your charm, your skills. Steer the negotiation process. Think about the results, but don't get caught up in them. Interests can and should change during the negotiation process. Contracts at any cost often end up costing far too much.

4. Pause. Pauses and even breaks are a very valuable tool in a negotiator's arsenal. We will talk about the power of pauses later, when we go on to look at emotions in negotiation.

## SAYING 'NO' WITHOUT DAMAGING RELATIONSHIPS

A great number of unprofitable contracts and loss-making deals come about for two reasons:

The negotiator is afraid of saying 'no'.
The negotiator is afraid of getting a 'no'.

There are many definitions of negotiation, a lot of which are fairly cursory and abstract. However, the following definition, used by Jim Camp, fundamentally changed my approach to negotiation:

Negotiation is the human effort to bring about agreements between two or more parties with all parties having the right to veto.[16]

Get used to saying and hearing 'no'.

Kids don't fear the word 'no'. If they don't want something, they will make sure you know about it. But as we grow up, we have it drummed into us to fear both hearing and saying 'no'. Experienced negotiators are able to take advantage of this fear, forcing us to make concessions against our better judgement.

The following is a very common example:

'Vitya, lend me ten grand.'

'What? What for?'

'Well, I want a new phone but I don't have enough cash.'

'Oh, I don't have any cash on me.'

'Tomorrow then.'

'Well, you know, I actually don't have ten grand myself.'

'Then borrow it!'

Sound familiar? At least a little, I imagine. What do we see happening in this dialogue? By entering into this discussion (by asking for more information on what the money is for), Vitya gives the other speaker hope that he's going to lend him the money.

In actual fact, Vitya just fears the word 'no' like the plague. His friend, seeing this, starts to pile on the pressure, and Vitya starts talking himself in circles, making excuses. He can tell where this is going: if he refuses, the other person will be completely justified in feeling somewhat hurt, and, believe you me, he will have no qualms in making the most of it. After all, Vitya has led him on by asking what the money is for. Or it could go the other way: Vitya lends his friend the money and won't see it back for ages, he'll feel uncomfortable constantly reminding him, etc.

But what would have happened had the conversation gone like this?

> 'Vitya, lend me ten thousand roubles.'
> 'No, Slava. I don't lend money to anyone.'

Would Slava have been offended? I don't think so. And if he had, then it wouldn't have lasted long. Vitya hasn't got his hopes up by discussing what it's for or when he'll get the money back; he hasn't even entered the discussion. So what's there to be offended by?

This is just the way we are: we make our decisions emotionally, and only later does our mind switch on, by which point we have to backtrack and justify our decisions.

Saying '*no*' will help you to avoid unreasonable expenses, giving offence and getting quite so offended yourself.

## Learning to say 'no'

*1. Whenever you receive a proposal or request, ask yourself a few questions:*
'When making me this tempting offer or asking me to do this service, what do they actually want from me?'

'Does this conflict with my own interests?'

'Will what they are offering me benefit me?'

'Would it be worthwhile for me to accept such terms?'

---

'So, what payment period can you offer us?'

'Forty-five calendar days.'

'That won't work for us. We work with big volumes so want no less than ninety days.'

'It's company policy. For your region forty-five days is the maximum deferment we can offer.'

'If you don't give us ninety days you won't get a contract.'

---

At this point, when you ask yourself whether this is worthwhile to you and find an answer to that question, you are acting from a place of strength. If the answer is 'yes', then look at the details and move on in the chosen direction. If the answer is 'no', then move on to point two, below.

*2. If the proposal isn't worthwhile, just say 'no'*
This 'no' should both *be* and *sound* like a final, unshakeable answer, one that doesn't require any clarification.

'Hey guvnor, spare some change!'
'No time, leave me alone.'
'So when you have time, you will?'
'Leave me alone.'

This sort of back-and-forth can go on forever. But had the answer been: *'No, I'm not giving you any money. You're wasting your time on me,'* then it's unlikely that the cheeky lad would have continued his grumbling.

Don't give false hope. If you don't want to do something, just say 'no'. Even if the product isn't of interest to you, as soon as you ask about price you are giving the other person the right to keep talking to you. If you ask when volunteers would be needed, then you are indirectly agreeing to help out. If you ask how much time your relative needs babysitting for, you are agreeing to play nanny. Only a resolute 'no' will get you out of needless resentment and unnecessary gestures.

I once went on a trip to Italy, and one of my colleagues (with whom I wasn't particularly close) called me to ask me to buy a phone for him while I was there. Of course, I felt uncomfortable turning him down, so I said, 'I don't think I'll be able to, but if I have time . . .' To be completely honest, I then forgot all about this. When I came home, however, it turned out my colleague hadn't interpreted my probable 'no' as a 'no': he'd been waiting impatiently for the phone and was upset to learn I'd forgotten him. Had my answer been 'No, I'm not going to any special shops, and I won't be able to make the purchase online,' then his feelings wouldn't have been hurt.

⚠

In our culture (by which I mean the wider, Russian-speaking world), it is very important to explain why you are refusing someone. But this explanation should be clear and straightforward, and not give rise to any further discussion.

In short: don't try to be cooler than you are. Don't try to be good to everyone: say 'no' and give people the right to refuse you, too. When we are prepared to hear 'no' in negotiations, we put ourselves on the level of our opponent; we don't fall into a dependent role.

And always remember: you cannot win or lose in negotiations. You can only figure out what stage you are currently at, what is going on and what your next step should be. 'No' is not the end of a relationship; it is simply a reason to reflect and make your next step.

## THE POSITION OF 'HOST' SPELLS SUCCESS

We are already familiar with the importance of this role in negotiation.

Clearly if we don't have to travel for negotiations, but let someone else travel to us (especially if from far away) while we sit waiting in our office in our comfortable chair, we have an advantage. We are the hosts. There's a reason that we talk about a home advantage in sports. Any sportsman will tell you it's easier to win on their home turf. In football, away goals are even given more value than home ones.

However, sometimes we can't avoid negotiating on our opponent's turf, and our opponent may try to make us feel not altogether comfortable. We may have a long wait in the lobby or even the office itself, listening to detailed phone conversations before our 'host' even gives us the time of day. And then the questioning begins. All of this is done to further reinforce a role of 'host'.

The 'host' asks the questions, and the 'guest' can't refuse to answer them. The 'guest' makes proposals, the 'host' picks and chooses. Picture how someone sits on a chair when they are the 'host'. They will be sitting confidently, leaning back into their seat with their feet firmly on the floor or their legs crossed. Their movements will be smooth and decisive. The 'guest', on the other hand, will be almost frozen, sitting like a student on the edge of their seat, waiting stiffly and hesitantly to be called up to the board.

Wherever you are (be it in your office or that of an important official, buyer or doctor), it is crucial to adopt a comfortable position – not imposing, but comfortable. During negotiations you need to move, not freeze.

This move is based on the Chinese stratagem 'exchange the role of guest for that of host'. This is nicely illustrated by a Russian folk tale: a hare has built a little hut made of wood, whereas the fox has built one made of ice. In spring, the fox's hut melts. The hare lets the fox come and stay with him, and the fox eventually drives him out.

In negotiations, there is only one way to take on the role of 'host': by taking your time to answer questions, especially if you are unsure of their intent. Ask counter-questions or ask for clarification if you aren't completely sure where the question is going.

Sun Tzu has a very effective saying for this situation: 'The skilful fighter puts himself into a position which makes defeat impossible.'[17] Or, as Vladimir Tarasov puts it: 'Get closer to the deer and you won't miss.'[18] Reducing your distance to your target can compensate for a bad aim. Anything that is easy to check, check yourself. If a buyer tells you that your competitors are cheaper, don't take them at their word: get closer to your target and check it yourself.

In my opinion, the best example of 'getting closer to the deer' took place on 11 March 1992, following the introduction of a new Russian law. This law, known as 'the law on commodity exchanges and exchange trade', prohibited the exchange of real estate on the stock market. All firms trading in real estate duly wound up their activity. Only the owners of Moskovskaya Tsentralnaya Birzha Nedvizhimosti, the Moscow Central Real Estate Exchange (MTBN), who had carefully studied the specific text of the law, saw that it regulated the activity of exchanges alone: other business structures in the real estate sphere would not be affected. So they set up a closed joint-stock company under the name of Moskovskaya Tsentralnaya *Burzha* Nedvizhimosti. You see, the law didn't prohibit the trading of real estate through a *burzha*, only through a *birzha*, the word for 'exchange'. Through this loophole, realtors at the *burzha* were fully entitled to work as exchange brokers. And so MTBN, through their meticulous reading of the text of the law, approached the deer and easily hit the mark.

Remember those great words of wisdom: read the fine print. If someone is shouting and waving an order in front of you, telling you that you're prohibited from doing something effective immediately, take it and have a good look at it. It might just be that it isn't applicable to you. Or perhaps that it *recommends against* rather than *prohibits*.

Getting closer to the deer is simple: ask questions. Step by step, these will lead you to your true target. By asking questions, you will eventually win over the role of 'host' in negotiations, in doing so taking control of the process.

If we don't get closer to the deer, we risk putting ourselves in uncomfortable situations.

In Andrei Gromyko's book *Memories* there is a fascinating episode as recounted by Che Guevara. This is what the legend and *comandante* of the Cuban Revolution says:

'After Batista was overthrown and power transferred to the people, we leading activists were meeting with Fidel [Castro] so he could distribute responsibilities among us. When we got to who should handle the economy, Fidel asked: "Tell me, friends, which of you is an economist?"

'Che paused. "I thought he had said, 'Which of you is a *communist*?', so straightaway I said, 'I am,' at which he said, 'OK, you handle the economy.'"

That's how Che Guevara became president of the National Bank of Cuba.[19]

Let's go back to our example in the section 'Shielding your-self from "need" and fear', and my subordinate, Dima, who had a major comedown after what he thought had been very successful negotiations.

Dmitriy told me about the negotiations in detail, and we established that the figure of 12 million roubles hadn't actually been put to paper anywhere: all the buyer had given were verbal assurances. So we decided to 'get closer to the deer'. Our lawyers put together a protocol of disagreements, which stated that the supply volumes should come to a value of at least 12 million roubles. I had a long talk with Dima about the question of 'need', and a few days later he set off for further negotiations, accompanied by a trainee. Who, you might ask? Me.

Now, if you are a manager, please listen to me when I say: if your subordinates are leading negotiations, you should only ever accompany them in one guise – that of 'trainee'. Your role is to listen, keep your mouth shut and provide silent support to your colleague. If you decide to step into the negotiations, you can be sure that your opponents will squeeze even better terms out of you.

But back to the story. The negotiations began:

'Oh! Dima, how are you? Good to see you!'

'Hello, Vladimir.'

'So, where are we with the agreement? Have you signed it?'

'Of course, but we drew up a protocol of disagreements.'

'All right then, let's take a look.'

He read it carefully and his facial expression turned. His friendliness vanished into thin air.

'What's this?'

Dima made a well-timed pause.

'What, you want to tie us to a set supply volume?'

More pausing.

'Do you even realise how many people we have queuing up to work with us?'

'We just put to paper what you and I had agreed verbally. Everything here is as we stated: the price, terms and volumes.'

'Yes, but I was giving a maximum volume.'

He buried his face in his computer screen and studied something carefully. We said nothing.

'Plus that's our total supply volume across all suppliers – do you really expect us to purchase that from you alone?'

'So what sort of figure are you planning to spend on our products each month?'

'I have no idea how they're going to sell. And I don't want to get into a systematic supply arrangement.'

'So how do you predict how a product will sell?'

'We do test sales for a two-month period.'

'Great! So let's not worry about volumes for now. We can do some test sales instead. If our product meets your expectations then we can come back to these points.'

The chain's first order was for a value of 240,000 roubles, after which our sales grew to 800,000 roubles – on our terms. We gained extremely valuable negotiation experience. And Dima truly was our hero: he was able to overcome his 'need' and seize the role of 'host' to take our negotiations forward.

A bear is walking through the woods. Suddenly he sees an angry lion.

'Hey, who's there?' the lion asks.

'Bear.'

'Let me make a note: Bear. Come back here tomorrow and I'll eat you. Any questions?'

The bear walks away, sobbing.

A wolf appears. Suddenly he sees the angry lion.

'Hey, who's there?' the lion asks.

'Wolf.'

'Let me make a note: Wolf. Come back here the day after tomorrow and I'll eat you. Any questions?'

The wolf walks away in despair.

A hedgehog appears.

'Who's that?'

'Hedgehog.'

'Let me just make a note: Hedgehog. Come back here in two days and I'll eat you. Any questions?'

'Yes. What if I don't come back?'

'That's fine. I'll just cross you off the list.'

Actions that help you to win the role of 'host':

A comfortable, relaxed position at the negotiating table.

> Don't rush to answer questions: clarify, ask counter-questions and 'get closer to the deer'.
>
> Use pauses.

## FINDING YOUR CAUSE

> Whenever Napoleon arrived at a populated area, the law had it that he was to be welcomed by the chime of bells. However, upon his arrival in one village there were no bells to be heard. Furious, he summoned the village leader and asked: 'Why did you not ring the bells?'
>
> 'Well, you know, we didn't know you'd be coming. And our bell ringer's ill. And we don't have a bell . . .'
>
> Napoleon commanded the poor man be put to death.

History tells us that as soon as a person starts to justify or defend themselves in some way, in the eyes of those around them they are immediately in the wrong.

Recently I saw some very interesting negotiations.

The sales manager of a food supplier was negotiating with a buyer. Essentially, stock that the supplier had delivered had since passed its use-by date and was now accumulating in the buyer's warehouse. The buyer was, in no uncertain terms, demanding to return the products.

'Your product is no good! Take it back!'

'We shipped the items to you at your request, and they weren't defective on arrival, they've simply passed their use-by date. Look, at the end of the day, we're partners, and you owe us money.'

'So then act like a partner. Take back your junk.'

Of all of the arguments offered, the buyer easily found the weakest one and directed their blow at it. That's where a desire to justify yourself gets you.

I have already written many times that confidence and a belief in your cause are your most important allies in negotiations. A negotiator who lacks confidence in their own cause – like the village leader or the sales manager in the previous examples – will scrabble around for lots of arguments, which they will then try to dump in front of their opponent in quick succession. They think that the more arguments they have, the better.

Is that true?

Before answering, let's unpack where the line between argumentation and self-justification lies. It's really very simple. A person who is justifying their own actions is asking their opponent to accept their conclusion, so they will try to offer many arguments. Self-justification is an act of weakness. A person who has confidence in their position lays out each argument in a consequent manner. They have nothing to prove, and every word they say oozes self-assurance. Had the head of the village been confident in his reasons, then one argument would have been enough: no one took the trouble to inform us of your visit. Yes, he would have been punished, but he might have kept his life.

And so, while you need to have several arguments at the ready, it is very important to be confident in your own cause and not put all your cards on the table. Be a little greedy: always keep the trump card in your hand, and use it only when you need to. A good example of the use of one – strong – argument is the dialogue between Professor Preobrazhensky and the manager of the cultural department of the house, Vyazemskaya, in Mikhail Bulgakov's novel *The Heart of a Dog*:

Vyazemskaya: I want to ask you . . . to buy a few of these magazines in aid of the children of Germany. Fifty kopecks a copy.

Professor: No, I will not.

V: Why not?

P: I don't want to.

V: Don't you feel sorry for the children of Germany?

P: Yes, I do.

V: Can't you spare fifty kopecks?

P: Yes, I can.

V: Well, why won't you, then?

P: I don't want to.[20]

This is art, of course, and there is an element of exaggeration to it, but you'll agree: in what way is 'I don't want to' not an argument? Had the professor started defending himself and looking for insincere reasons why, he would most certainly have been caught out and made to buy magazines he didn't need.

When preparing your argument, it is crucial that you choose only those arguments you believe yourself. During negotiations, try to use them sparingly, and only bring a new argument to the table when you have exhausted the preceding ones.

It is also important to note that it is only possible to give your arguments if the negotiations are in a rational mode. When emotions are raging, even the strongest argument will seem like justification. It is always worth remembering Lucian's ancient saying: 'Jupiter, you are angry, therefore you are wrong.'[21]

Only once you have brought negotiations into a rational framework can you start sharing your arguments. And that is what we will be learning to do in the next chapter.

# 4.

# NEGOTIATING IN
# TOUGH CONDITIONS

*Do not surrender your mood to one who would insult you.*
*Don't let yourself be drawn onto the path they would have you walk down.*

— MARCUS AURELIUS

Negotiations can follow many modes, two of which are key. These are:

1. The emotional mode.
2. The rational mode.

I'm assuming you remember our matrix of behaviour models when fighting for gains, as described in Chapter 1. There we saw that emotional negotiations are most typical of a 'tank'. A 'tank's' constant objective is to draw their opponent into an emotional mode of negotiation, i.e. to put them into an emotionally unstable state. Why? Because in this the 'tank' sees a guarantee of success. If they succeed in drawing us onto an emotional plane, we will begin to make rash decisions and, as a result, fatal errors.

To be more precise (and drawing on what we have already explored in this book): the negotiation budget goes off the scale, causing the person to make rash and thoughtless moves, after which they will try to justify themselves. How often have we seen the following in negotiations: an experienced negotiator pushes us, we find ourselves unable to answer a question, due to which we either make a serious error, offer terms we hadn't planned (but that we will later justify to ourselves), or storm out of the negotiations slamming the door?

How do we justify these actions? 'You know, he's so tough, there's no negotiating with him,' or: 'You know, she represents such a big organisation, you're not going to argue with her.' Or even: 'Oh, he's horrible, he makes constructive conversations impossible.' These are all excuses. Our mind will always find a suitable excuse for our own mistakes. But why do these mistakes happen? Because we get drawn into an emotional mode of negotiations.

As negotiators dealing with a tough opponent, our main objective is to figure out how to shift negotiations back from an emotional to a rational mode. The negotiation techniques that follow are aimed at doing precisely that. In short, these are techniques that get results.

To begin with, let's explore two behaviour models of emotional negotiations: the 'barbarian' and the manipulator. How do the two differ?

## PROTECTING YOURSELF FROM PRESSURE AND MANIPULATION

Within each of us is a set of strings that react to certain words or actions. An exhaustive list of these strings would be impossible, but for our purposes we are mainly interested in the following:

1. Pity.
2. Fear.
3. Greed.
4. Lust.
5. A sense of duty.
6. Curiosity.
7. Vanity.

So what happens? A manipulator will probe each of these strings individually. Why? To see which one resounds, causing us to do something that will favour them.

We can define manipulation in the following way:

**Manipulation** is when an opponent's emotional strings are played in a way that encourages them to do something that is in the manipulator's interest.

Of course, there are a number of possible definitions for the term 'manipulation', but in my opinion this one most fully gets to its core. Robert Cialdini's book *Influence* offers an excellent metaphor of manipulation, in the form of the click of the button and the whirr of the tape.[22] That is to say, the manipulator presses the 'play' button, and the tape – our response – begins to whirr.

**James A. Garfield's principle.** Influence over others is not an end in itself. Any scheming is done with the intention of satisfying our interests – be those interests a desire or security.

Ably plucking the emotional strings, a manipulator will often get their opponent to react in exactly the way they intended. Even experienced politicians and diplomats can fall into a master manipulator's trap. The following is an example of a piece of manipulation that got the better of German Emperor Wilhelm II some hundred years ago (as recounted by Yuri Dubinin, a Russian Soviet-era diplomat).

In August 1914, Russia, the UK and France were already at war with Germany, but Japan's allegiances still remained uncertain. The German chancellor paid a visit to the Japanese embassy on the subject of some outstanding weapons orders Japan had placed with German suppliers, as a new German law prohibited the fulfilment of any deliveries to foreign countries after the outbreak of war. The Japanese ambassador asked the chancellor to rectify this unfortunate misunderstanding, as his country was 'preparing to wage war with a great power', these words accompanied by a meaningful smile. The ambassador's request was immediately granted, on the assumption that a Japanese attack on Russia was clearly imminent.

A few days later, Japan gave Germany an ultimatum demanding that they immediately withdraw from occupied territory in China. Wilhelm II was enraged by the Japanese diplomat's stunt. But all that the ambassador had said was that Japan was preparing to go to war 'with a great power'. And wasn't Germany a great power?[23]

The emotional strings are often targeted by not altogether honest entrepreneurs.

In the early 1990s a firm offering to predict the sex of its customers' unborn children enjoyed long-term success. Ultrasound imaging wasn't widely available, and many people wanted to know whether they were expecting a boy or a girl.

After performing a few simple procedures, the firm would give the parents-to-be the happy news over the phone. They would then enter the exact opposite results into their records. If their 'prediction' was correct, their customers wouldn't ask any questions. If it wasn't, however, and the client came to complain, the firm would simply fish their records out of a safe, search for the surname and read their 'results', which would, of course, be correct. A very simple piece of trickery: by logging the opposite result in their records, they ensured that one of the two answers – spoken or written – would always be correct.

What strings are these manipulators playing? The answer can be found at the back of the book.

To avoid falling into a manipulator's trap, you need to recognise which emotional strings spark undesirable reactions in you.

**Influence in action**

The 'click' is something that the manipulator says or does that causes a string (or multiple strings) to vibrate or 'whirr' within us in response. As a knock-on effect, we take some form of action that is profitable not to us but to our opponent – the person plucking the strings.

It should now be clear what the 'manipulator' model in emotional negotiations is. But what about the 'barbarian' model? How does the 'barbarian' differ from the simple manipulator?

In principle, the actions of both the barbarian and the manipulator seek to force their opponent to do something that is in their interests. That is their goal: to play their opponent's emotional strings.

Let's return, once again, to the film *Anger Management*. More specifically, I'd like to look at a scene that takes place on a plane, when the hero is seemingly endlessly provoked until he reacts angrily. Someone takes his seat, the man sitting next to him is laughing obnoxiously while watching a film, and then the flight attendant repeatedly ignores his request for a headset. To top it all off, when he confronts the flight attendant, a musclebound air marshall appears and starts escalating the matter. Finally, the man flies into a rage, lets rip and gets himself tasered. He is found guilty of assault and battery against a flight attendant. These provocateurs were in fact deliberately trying to bring out this reaction in him, and they passed with flying colours.

If you have a chance, watch this scene and ask yourself: what strings did each of his provocateurs try to play? You will quickly see that one is plucking the 'sense of duty' string, another 'curiosity', another 'vanity' and more.

But where does this get us in our question of the difference between the manipulator and the barbarian?

Unlike the manipulator, a barbarian doesn't aim for one string: they take a club and strike at them all.

When I got my first job as a sales manager, I was fairly young and ambitious, managing other youngsters who were just as ambitious as I was. My boss, however, was an authoritative old-timer. When it was time for our monthly reports, he would call me into his office and ask for that month's figures. I would present our reports with enthusiasm and gusto – our indicators were always on target or better – but he would listen stony-faced and then say: 'So what, you think you're a star? That if you exceed my targets, you're my hero? If I fired you today I could get ten others just like you.'

This is typical 'barbarity', because it hits many strings. Which ones, do you think? Essentially all of them. And ask yourself the question: what was his aim in doing this? What did he actually want from me?

His main aim was to make something 'whirr' within me from his 'click'; to make me run off and do something that would put me in a worse position and him in a better, more advantageous one.

He wanted me to strain myself even more, so as to achieve even more than planned. But I, being quite rightly proud of my record, started to defend my own interests. I wanted time for holidays, to see my family, etc. He just wanted me to work, work, work.

This is how a 'barbarian' works. A manipulator's behaviour is slightly different. They are more artful.

As we have seen, manipulators aim for just one string. But how?

I travel to Arkhangelsk for negotiations with a major chain. A young man appears, well dressed, an expensive watch on his wrist. He takes a seat and, without even looking at me, says: 'Could you tell me whether you'd be willing to work with us on a ninety-day payment period?'

I know this isn't in my interest.

'No, we aren't.'

'Why not?'

'Because our board of founders took the decision not to work with anyone on that basis.'

'Tell me, what is your position within the company?'

'Managing director.'

'Now tell me, can a managing director really not make up his own mind on such a simple question?'

This is elegant, skilful manipulation, targeting my vanity. This immediately tempts a reaction, at which point the other person is acting in the grip of their emotions. But the barbarian and the manipulator both have the same end goal: in these examples, my opponents both want me to do something that benefits them. In this particular instance, that is for me to give him terms that benefit him, not me.

If we are to look at this within the framework of the negotiation budget, we can note that the actions of both the barbarian and the manipulator seek to immediately increase this budget. We already know that as soon as emotions come into play, the negotiation budget grows. And that when our emotions come into play, we are far more prone to make concessions that we would never even have considered before.

Remember Postulate 3 of the Kremlin school of negotiation: when you introduce your own scale of values, your opponent is shifted into an emotional mode of negotiations and their emotional strings are plucked. This is, of course, barbarism.

I'm going to repeat the list of the key strings that exist in each of us, but remember: these strings don't all reverberate the same way in each person.

1. Pity.
2. Fear.
3. Greed.
4. Lust.
5. A sense of duty.
6. Curiosity.
7. Vanity.

Before going any further, we need to figure out which emotional string 'resounds' most in you. To do this, complete the exercise on the next page:

1. Think of a phrase that has provoked an angry or undesirable reaction in you in the past few days/hours. This is a trigger: the thing that makes the string vibrate within us. Write this down in the left-hand column.

2. In the right-hand column, write the string (or strings) affected.

I would recommend doing this exercise every day for at least a week. This should be enough time for you to get a clearer picture of your own strings and how they sound.

## THREE IMPORTANT MEASURES FOR CONTROLLING YOUR EMOTIONS

Now, dear readers, when a manipulator or barbarian starts flicking or plucking at your emotional strings, you will immediately be able to recognise this as an attack on your internal state. And you will be armed and ready to take some sort of action. But what?

First and foremost, take your time. Don't under any circumstances let yourself be rushed.

Many methods for working with barbarian negotiators demand a fast, unequivocal response. However, I find that fast, unequivocal responses can lead you deeper into a game I know as negotiating ping-pong. Essentially, you'll stand there exchanging verbal attacks. But our primary task – as results-driven negotiators – is to shift negotiations from an emotional to a rational mode. To do this, we must first get our own emotions in check. Only once this is done can we select one of the techniques we will later discuss.

So, first, get ourselves out of range of these emotional blows.

Yes, blows. Or else: a sharp change in world view. Vladimir Tarasov has described the term 'world view' in detail in his books, but in essence it is how we perceive our life's maze.[24] It's how we move through life, and how we view our life itself: what's good or bad, ethical or unethical, cheap or expensive, etc. Everyone has different views on all of these points, and everyone navigates their mazes differently. We find secret passages; we meet dead ends. World view is how we understand the consequences of our actions, words and decisions.

However, our world view is often found wanting: we've drawn ourselves a route but life hasn't gone to plan; we've come up against the unexpected. It is in these clashes with the unexpected that we are dealt blows.

These blows may come in the form of an unexpected question or statement that sharply changes our world view, or through our emotional strings being plucked (or beaten).

The deputy director of a major company once again visits an official's office to ask him to sign a document permitting the construction of a store. They have gone through all the formalities and have even gathered signatures of local residents in favour of the project. However, in response, the director gets the following blow:

'I know what you're like, you money-grabbers, I'll bet you were up all night forging signatures. Or lining pockets.'

'We haven't forged anything.'

'Well, feast your eyes on this: I've received a petition from some unhappy residents.'

Let's take a closer look at this blow, and why it caught the young deputy director off guard.

In his mind, the deputy director has envisaged the following route through his maze: they've got the signatures and have made the necessary agreements, so he'll simply go there, show the papers and the official will have to sign, even if there is the odd grumble. After all, the majority is on the store's side. That's his world view.

But the official makes a surprise attack and strikes the first blow, playing on the director's emotional strings of vanity and fear. He can't parry the blow and instead starts getting defensive, at which point the official delivers a second blow.

In this match, the official has an information advantage: he has searched for the businessman's opening, and that's where he deals the finishing blow. As soon as we let the first blow fly, our opponent will immediately deliver a follow-up series of well-aimed blows, making use of Sun Tzu's rule: 'strike at what is weak'.[25]

**From Andrei Gromyko's *Memories***

In 1955 a meeting of the heads of government of the USSR, USA, Britain and France took place in Geneva. Sharp exchanges occurred revealing serious differences between the former allies. Eisenhower, Eden and Edgar Faure fiercely argued that NATO was a force for peace, especially in Europe, while in fact their plan was aimed at swallowing up East Germany into West Germany, and whitewashing the remilitarisation of West Germany in peace-loving propaganda.

In an effort to deprive the three Western powers of their notion that the Soviet Union was not doing its part in consolidating peace, the Soviet delegation, consisting of Khruschev, Bulganin, Molotov, Marshal Zhukov and myself, announced that the Soviet Union was willing to join NATO. We argued that, since NATO was dedicated to the cause of peace, it could not but agree to include the USSR.

It is hard to describe the effect this announcement had on the Western delegations when it was made by Bulganin, as President of the Council of Ministers. They were so stunned that for several minutes none of them said a word. Eisenhower's usual vote-winning smile had vanished from his face. He leaned over for a private consultation with Dulles; but we were not given a reply to our proposal.[26]

Thorough preparation for negotiations can serve as an effective preventive measure against such blows. In Chapter 7 of this book we will look in more detail at preparation techniques. However, what we're interested in doing now is dodging these blows.

One very effective way of doing this is a simple pause. Don't rush to respond; don't jump headlong into the next blow: pause, still those jangling strings and only afterwards continue negotiating.

'**A pause** is an effective instrument that helps you to compose yourself, bring your emotions under control and take back the initiative. **Silence** is an aspect of communication that very few have mastered, and very rare are those who know how to use it in a focused, conscious manner.'

**Karsten Bredemeier**

A boy is born. For fifteen years the boy doesn't say a single word, until one day, while eating breakfast, he suddenly pipes up: 'The toast is burnt.'

'Why haven't you said anything before?' the parents asked, shocked.

'Well, everything's been fine until now.'

Even an awkward pause is much better than an emotional response that risks drawing you into an exchange of fire from which you will either leave with nothing or a big loss.

## How to pause during negotiations

*1. Find a simple distraction*
We're all human, all subject to getting something caught in our eye or a tickle in our throat. There are a great many, albeit unoriginal, things we can say to win a quick pause in negotiations:

*'I've got something in my eye.'*

*'I need to take some medicine.'*

*'I've got a tickle in my throat.' (Then drink some water.)*

*2. Step out briefly from the negotiation space, under a plausible pretext*
If the blow dealt is hard enough, then it's common for the recipient to get stuck in one position, like a statue. It is very important to change your pose, and to do so in a major way. Get up, walk around, get some papers from your briefcase. In the difficult situation I had in Murmansk that I have already mentioned, I found it helpful to get out of the room the negotiations had been scheduled to take place in. I excused myself, saying I had a phone call to make, and then simply went for a little walk to cool down.

Once in negotiations I was observing for one major chain, I even saw a supplier knock over his cup of coffee after taking a particularly powerful blow. That little break in proceedings allowed him to get out of an unpleasant situation.

Now, knocking over your drink is perhaps a bit excessive; you can get by with something much more commonplace, like:

'Excuse me, I've realised I need to get some papers from my office.'

'Excuse me, I just need to take this call/reply to this message. It's urgent.' *(Here, if you don't want to risk any hard feelings from your opponent, say that the call/message is from someone the attacker themselves wouldn't want to dismiss, like a son, daughter or parent. That's a very plausible pretext.)*

'I'm sorry, you'll have to excuse me for a minute.' *(Or whatever euphemism you prefer for going to the toilet.)*

*3. A more philosophical pause can come in the form of a rhetorical question or abstract statement:*

'What is truth?'

'We're all subjective . . .'

'Nothing is more permanent than the temporary . . .'

It's only once we have paused and brought our emotional state back under control that we can start to reply.

• • •

The next two chapters are both devoted to responding to attacks. However, none of the techniques described will be effective if you don't follow the right order of how to use them:

Spot an attack.
Dodge the attack.
Respond.

# 5.

# SEVEN TECHNIQUES FOR REACHING AGREEMENTS WITH A TOUGH OPPONENT

*Friends! Stride purposefully down the path leading to the temple of agreement, and surmount any obstacles you meet along the way with the courageous meekness of a lion.*

— KOZMA PRUTKOV,
fictional nineteenth-century author[27]

So, as soon as you have recognised an attack and dodged it through a pause, it is essential that you respond. Remember that negotiations are not ping-pong: the aim of your response is to shift the negotiations back into a rational mode. An agreement can only be reached in a rational mode.

In this chapter, we will explore and perfect seven techniques:

1. The reverse (to clarify intentions).
2. The partial agreement (to set up a smokescreen).
3. Connectors.
4. The Marcus Aurelius.

5. The predator.
6. Share a smile.
7. Show some humour.

When deflecting manipulative or 'barbarian' attacks, the main thing is to take your time before responding. Remember the three crucial steps:

1. Spot an attack.

2. Dodge the attack. Pause.

3. Respond in a way that brings the negotiations back into a rational framework. If at all possible, this response should let you walk out of the negotiations with the door still open.

## HOW TO PARRY SMALL JABS AND FIGURE OUT YOUR OPPONENT'S POSITION

Not every question or remark requires a response.

As humans, it is in our nature to try to give lightning-fast responses to questions we are asked. When negotiating, we need to drop this human quality and instead follow a different principle: not every question requires an answer, especially if it is not clear what lies behind it.

Imagine you are walking down the street and bump into someone you know, and he tells you your tie is always crooked. When he makes this comment, what is his intent? You don't actually know. The simplest answer would be that your acquaintance, meaning well, wants to let you know that your tie looks a mess (the use of 'always' here is, admittedly, confusing). Or it could be that this person wants to assume the right to judge you.

Judgement is a very dangerous thing. When you give someone else the right to cast judgement on you, know that you are giving them the right to do that every day. Today they judged your wonky tie, tomorrow it'll be the quality of your work, and the day after your professional capability as a whole. Giving someone this right is very dangerous indeed.

This is why the best technique in these situations is the 'reverse', a clarification technique.

In English, the word 'reverse' has a number of possible meanings, all of which stem from the Latin *revertere*, meaning to turn back or return. In general terms, a 'reverse' is something that is directly contrary to something else: in technology, it is the gear that causes an engine to perform its action in the opposite direction; and in numismatics it is the opposite side of a coin. The same word also denotes the other side of a medal, which can imply a certain level of mystery: what's the flipside of that award?

It is in the latter meanings that the word has come to be used in negotiation techniques. What lies behind an opponent's comments? This, reader, is what we have to find out. Alternatively, you can simply ask the person for some concrete advice. In the situation described, you could simply say: 'What would you advise me to change? How would you advise me to do up my tie?'

This is a very good way of transitioning from the emotional to the rational plane. Firstly, if a person is in a constructive frame of mind – if their comment is well-meaning – negative criticism is not their goal and they simply want to offer assistance on the finer points of doing up a tie, then this forces them to either show you or teach you how. And if they aren't in the frame of mind for a constructive chat, then the onus is on them to figure out a suitable response. You might well get a response along the lines of: 'Do I look like a walking tie consultant?' But in most cases they will simply step back from this emotional exchange, which is also a good thing. So it's a win–win for you. As I've said before, the aim of these techniques for dealing with barbarism and manipulation is not to get into a game of ping-pong, but to move on to rational discussion.

At a recent workshop on this topic, a woman jumped in and said that she had employed this technique.

I recently got my driver's licence. I know I'm a young and inexperienced driver, so when I drive I get my husband to come along, as a sort of safety net. But the last time he kept on making these sarcastic remarks about the way I was driving, how I braked, how I changed gear . . . Anyway, I kept on getting emotional and losing track of what I was doing. I was nervous, my hands were shaking, and so I was making even more mistakes. Eventually I stopped, looked at him and said, 'Darling, please teach me how to brake properly; show me how to do this, etc.' From that moment on, the fault-finding stopped. Because it's one thing to attack someone with a purpose, and another thing to teach them. Teaching is always harder. I realised that my husband was in a destructive frame of mind – he wanted to hurt me. He wanted to show me that I was a bad driver and that I didn't deserve to drive. But he wasn't at all prepared to teach me.

For this very reason, when you use the 'reverse' technique you are guaranteed of one thing at the very least: you will gain a more accurate understanding of other people's intentions – whether they mean you well or want to do damage.

It is important to evaluate the framework for each technique: when should it be employed? In this case, when you are unsure of your opponent's intent. When you're hearing comments like these:

- 'For some reason I can't see what it is you want.'
- 'I don't like what you're proposing.'
- 'How unattractive.'
- 'I don't get . . .'
- 'I'm not interested in . . .'

The following sorts of questions can help you to clarify your attacker's intent:

- 'What would you recommend I improve?'
- 'What would you recommend I change?'
- 'What should I pay particular attention to?'
- 'What would be the best action to take?'

Don't expect your opponent to suddenly open up and begin to talk after the first question asked. In general, you will have to repeat the question (or variations thereof) two or three times. If after this your opponent still doesn't settle into a rational discussion, then the conclusion to draw is unambiguous: it's time to end that round of negotiations.

'Your tie is always so crooked! Will you ever learn?'

'What would you recommend I change?'

'Well, that knot is all wrong on you.'

'Then recommend one that suits me better.'

'So now I'm supposed to give you knot advice?'

'In that case I suggest we stop discussing my tie and move on to the matter that has brought us here today.'

By the way, bear in mind that the 'reverse' technique isn't suitable for all situations. Don't turn to it if the attack feels personal, or if you (your company, your friends or family) are being slighted in any way. I'm sure you can see that a remark like: 'What the hell are you on about?' is probably not best met with an: 'Advise me what I should do.' Or that if you are told: 'I heard your company's gone bust,' then asking for advice on how you should act is illogical to say the least. This will simply lead to the ping-pong described above, and all you're going to hear is something like: 'You know that it's time to get out of there.'

An important variation on this technique is to use appeals instead of questions. Like questions, appeals allow you to:

- Get an explanation.
- Continue the conversation.
- Calm your opponent.
- Promote action.

Appeals have one important advantage over questions: instead of inviting recommendations, you are presented them on a silver platter. So, instead of asking for advice on the remarks given earlier (where the opponent's intent is unclear), you could respond with the following appeals:

- 'Please tell me what to improve.'
- 'Be more specific.'
- 'Tell me what you think.'
- 'Please elaborate.'
- 'Please let me know your thoughts.'

A large company approaches a well-known photographer to do a photographic portrait of the manager for the company's anniversary. The photographer accepts and completes the work, but the client is unhappy with the results. They do another sitting, but the response is the same. Then it happens again. By now at breaking point, the photographer is prepared to drop the commission completely, and the client is clearly not desperate to pursue their collaboration, either.

This is when the photographer came to me. I recommended he use the 'reverse' technique. Here's how their next conversation went.

'Ivan – well, we don't like the shots.'

'What would you like me to do differently?'

'Ivan, you're the photographer here! Or do you just say you are?'

'Show me what you would like to change.'

'Well . . .'

'I'm waiting for your feedback.'

'Change the background. Our boss can't stand green.'

When using questions and appeals, it's always worth remembering that there are two sides to every coin. Don't use only appeals or only questions. Appeals serve as prompts, whereas questions nurture the sharing of information.

To prevent yourself from getting caught up in a game of ping-pong or a banal exchange of emotional remarks, it is important to remember to look away immediately after responding. When people use manipulation or make an attack, they tend to look you in the eye as they do. If after giving your response you don't break eye contact, they will read it as a challenge to take another shot. As a result, your opponent will instinctively enter combat with you, even if they were initially trying to be constructive. For this reason, once you say something, look to the side or at your papers. Do not stare down the opponent.

Now, reader, it's time for you to try your hand at employing this first technique for negotiating with a tough opponent. At this point I'll mention that this chapter features exercises on all seven techniques. Feel free to either write your answers onto the pages of the book or use a notepad or computer program to keep track of them. To ensure the exercises form a coherent whole, I have numbered all of the exercises in this chapter sequentially, starting with number one here and ending with thirty-seven at the end of the chapter. The following five questions are devoted to the 'reverse' technique.

**How would you respond to the following statements using the 'reverse' technique?**

1. 'There's something about your proposal I don't like.'

**Question:**

**Appeal:**

2. 'For some reason your presentation style bothers me.'

**Question:**

**Appeal:**

3. 'I don't find your proposal very constructive.'

**Question:**

**Appeal:**

4. 'You aren't looking very festive.'

**Question:**

**Appeal:**

5. 'I'm not sure – do you think it's worth being so rash?'

**Question:**

**Appeal:**

The 'reverse' technique should be employed when the intent of an attack is unknown and when you still have the opportunity to understand the attacker's true motives: are they trying to be constructive, or not? When posing a question, don't repeat a negative message. If our opponent tells us they don't find our proposal very constructive and our response is: 'What don't you find constructive about my proposal?, then we are simply reinforcing our opponent's opinion. It is much better to send positive messages, such as: 'What about my proposal could be improved?' If your opponent offers a constructive recommendation in response, then that means they are in the frame of mind for constructive negotiations. But if the response is 'You decide, I don't know what more I can say', then it's time to realise that constructive discussions are not on the horizon. In this situation, it is better to take a break so that they have a chance to cool off and think. Say something along the lines of: 'Thank you for your time. In that case I will try to make some changes. But if you could give me an idea of what to focus on I would be grateful.' It might just be that after this your opponent will nevertheless start to open up and move away from a modus operandi of destructive attacks.

## TURN BATTLE INTO CO-OPERATION

The more we criticise others' opinions or attempt to contest their point of view, the less chance we have of finding common ground on which to take our ideas forward. The following is an extract from the memoirs of the famous American psychologist and educator Dale Carnegie, one of the creators of the theory of communication.

Years ago Patrick J. O'Haire joined one of my classes. He had had little education, and how he loved a scrap! He had once been a chauffeur, and he came to me because he had been trying, without much success, to sell trucks.

A little questioning brought out the fact that he was continually scrapping with and antagonising the very people he was trying to do business with. If a prospect said anything derogatory about the trucks he was selling, Pat saw red and was right at the customer's throat.

Pat won a lot of arguments in those days. As he said to me afterward, 'I often walked out of an office saying: "I told that bird something." Sure I had told him something, but I hadn't sold him anything.'

My first problem was not to teach Patrick J. O'Haire to talk. My immediate task was to train him to refrain from talking and to avoid verbal fights. Mr. O'Haire became one of the star salesmen for the White Motor Company in New York. How did he do it? Here is his story in his own words:

'If I walk into a buyer's office now and he says, "What? A White truck? They're no good! I wouldn't take one if you gave it to me. I'm going to buy the Whose-It truck," I say "The Whose-It is a good truck. If you buy the Whose-It, you'll never make a mistake. The Whose-Its are made by a fine company and sold by good people." He is speechless then.

'There is no room for an argument. If he says the Whose-It is best and I say sure it is, he has to stop. He can't keep on all afternoon saying "It's the best" when I'm agreeing with him.

'We then get off the subject of Whose-It and I begin to talk about the good points of the White truck.

'There was a time when a remark like his first one would have made me see scarlet and red and orange. I would start arguing against the Whose-It; and the more I argued against it, the more my prospect argued in favor of it; and the more he argued, the more he sold himself on my competitor's product. As I look back now I wonder how I was ever able to sell anything. I lost years of my life in scrapping and arguing. I keep my mouth shut now. It pays.'

As wise old Benjamin Franklin used to say: 'If you argue and rankle and contradict, you may achieve a victory sometimes; but it will be an empty victory because you will never get your opponent's good will.'[28]

Before getting into a scrap, it's worth asking yourself if it's really necessary. What will it achieve? This question is key when it comes to our second technique for dealing with tough opponents, the 'partial agreement' technique.

When we agree with our opponent, we give them no reason to keep on arguing with us; we don't allow them to proliferate the conflict. When you are unsure of the intent of an attack, or when you don't particularly want to get caught up in conflict and are unsure where engaging in an emotional exchange with the attacker might lead, then it is best simply to agree in part with their conclusions. In doing so, you will stop their attacks short, allowing you to discuss the burning issues in a rational way. But you need to agree with something that you do not consider to be a fundamental issue. This is a technique of the three paths: some things we can take as fact, others we can accept, but some things we will not agree with on principle.

You can rattle on for hours about how much worse your competitors' products are and still come to nothing. Or you can agree that their products are good, but that you also know what's what, and let your opponent make up their own mind.

A young man is walking down a hallway at work. A manager from another department is walking towards him. The manager looks at him and says: 'Your boots are dirty.'

The young man is immediately cast into an emotional frame of mind. He replies in the same way: 'Who are you to be commenting on my boots?'

'Oh, right, I've heard you can't handle criticism.'

What happens next? They squabble. And at a meeting later that evening, our hero stands up to give a report, but the same manager interrupts him and says: 'No, no, stop. Your figures are all wrong.'

The young man knows that his figures are correct.

'No, I'm certain that these figures are absolutely correct.'

In response he hears: 'See, what did I say earlier? You can't handle criticism.'

Everything has worked perfectly for the manager: the label has now been attached. And our hero, without even wanting it, has ended up in a situation where there's no room for logic, only a sense of righteousness. But that very same righteousness suddenly turns out to be on the side of the person applying the label. Why? Because they got there first. The string is plucked a second time. The young man gets riled up again – this time in front of everyone – which leads them to believe he must be the one in the wrong.

How else might he have responded to the quip about his dirty boots? He could have agreed! Which isn't to suggest he should call himself a dirty slob who doesn't look after his boots. All it would have taken was a simple agreement: 'Yes, they are. It's raining outside!'

Nothing else required. And what is this actually saying? That it's raining. He doesn't start to get defensive, doesn't put a chokehold on his own interests. He simply confirms that it's raining, in doing so disarming his opponent.

To be honest, when I first read Dale Carnegie's story many years ago, I didn't really get this technique. For some reason, I didn't immediately understand or accept it. I mean, how can you agree with something you don't actually think is true? But one event helped me to see how it works.

You will probably remember that the company I worked for had a very close relationship with a Moldovan producer. In good times, our supply volumes from this factory represented 60 per cent of their total output. As a result, we knew virtually all of their factory processes. Including the technical ones.

Anyway, one day I flew to Krasnoyarsk for negotiations with a major regional distributor, and during the talks themselves I put a sample on the table. The distributor's representative looked at it, turned it around in her hands and – very sceptically! – brought out a bottle of wine that a competitor had given her. The bottle, as it happened, had been produced by the same factory as my sample. Then she said: 'You know, your competitor's wine tastes much better than yours.'

I was stunned. That was impossible: we were supplied by the very same factory, and – there's no point hiding it – even from the same containers. So of course I tried to explain as much.

The fascinating thing is, the more I tried to convince her, the more she dug her heels in. Which brings me back to something I've already mentioned: *He who proves isn't right. He who is right has no need to prove.*

Well, at this point my mind supplied me with the technique I needed. So I put it into action:

'You're absolutely right, tastes can vary. But whose design do you prefer?'

'On design . . . Yours.'

Why did she agree with me? The answer is simple: I stopped arguing with her. I agreed with her and in return she agreed with me.

It's important to learn how to pinpoint when to fight with your opponent and when to work with them. When you express agreement, no matter the topic, you are essentially showing that person that you are with them. Think of Mowgli from *The Jungle Book*: 'We be of one blood, ye and I.'[29] Co-operation is always much more effective than combat. However, on this point it's also worth remembering that the road to co-operation may run through a fight. It's important to know how to be an ally and – when you need to – a challenger.

### The Benjamin Franklin principle

I made it a rule to forbear all direct contradiction to the sentiments of others, and all positive assertion of my own. I even forbid myself, agreeably to the old laws of our Junto, the use of every word or expression in the language that imported a fix'd opinion, such as certainly, undoubtedly, etc., and I adopted, instead of them, *I conceive*, *I apprehend*, or *I imagine* a thing to be so or so; or it so *appears to me at present*.

When another asserted something that I thought an error, I deny'd myself the pleasure of contradicting him abruptly, and of showing immediately some absurdity in his proposition; and in answering I began by observing that in certain cases or circumstances his opinion would be right, but in the present case there *appear'd* or *seem'd to me* some difference, etc.

I soon found the advantage of this change in my manner; the conversations I engag'd in went on more pleasantly. The modest way in which I propos'd my opinions procur'd them a readier reception and less contradiction; I had less mortification when I was found to be in the wrong, and I more easily prevail'd with others to give up their mistakes and join with me when I happened to be in the right.

And this mode, which I at first put on with some violence to natural inclination, became at length so easy, and so habitual to me, that perhaps for these fifty years past no one has ever heard a dogmatical expression escape me.

And to this habit (after my character of integrity) I think it principally owing that I had early so much weight with my fellow-citizens when I proposed new institutions, or alterations in the old, and so much influence in public councils when I became a member; for I was but a bad speaker, never eloquent, subject to much hesitation in my choice of words, hardly correct in language, and yet I generally carried my points.[30]

As we see, Franklin teaches us that agreement is by no means a concession; it is a serious opportunity to remove ourselves from emotional arguments and conflicts and to move on to rational discussion. Not all attacks need to be answered with attacks. Very often a simple agreement is enough.

## The limits of the 'partial agreement' technique

It's not by chance that my discussion of the limits of this technique is accompanied by a rule. Yes, the following examples and situations should be viewed as *rules*. But let's not forget: the exception proves the rule. So:

*1. Can you employ this technique if you don't (or hardly) know the person attacking you?*
The answer is yes. You can also use this technique if you are not completely sure of the attacker's intent. But only on one important condition: there is no threat to your reputation or that of your company, or to the dignity of you or your loved ones.

'You're too tough a negotiator.'

'I agree, that's my style.'

However, after this, you need to add a comma and suggest returning to the topic under discussion:

'Now why don't we get back to our discussion?'

'You're often tough on people.'

'I agree, but I'm working on it. Now let's take a look at my proposal.'

'You aren't being constructive.'

'Perhaps not, but I think it's important we don't get distracted from the subject of these negotiations. How about we go through this again in detail?'

To prevent negotiations from turning into a game of ping-pong, after responding to your opponent's comment you should add a comma and finish your sentence by returning to the topic being negotiated, or: pause, respond, comma, return, look away.

*2. This technique is very useful when your opponent starts talking about other people – in particular what other people have said about you.* For example:

> 'You know, Ivan is always saying what a sloppy dresser you are.'

Before reading the rest of this example, have a look at this anecdote.

Bagheera the panther walks up to Kaa the snake and says: 'Hey, did you hear that Mowgli said mean things about you?'

'Yes, I did. The whole jungle heard it.'

'Yeah, but did you hear that he called you a dirty yellow snake?'

'Well, if the shoe fits!'

This little joke teaches us an important lesson. What do you think Bagheera was trying to get out of Kaa (in the anecdote, of course)? Clearly he wanted the snake to do something bad to Mowgli. And had Kaa fallen for this, what do you think would have happened? And who would have been guilty? The snake, of course: Bagheera would have been sound asleep on the sidelines, to all appearances completely uninvolved.

Ask yourself: would you have fallen for a trick like this?

> **⚠**
>
> It's worth noting that this technique is very effective if a man is baiting a woman at work, particularly if they are rivals:
>
> 'That's such a woman thing to say, so flippant and emotional.'
>
> For women, especially those in the business sphere, this will work on their vanity string, and they may start to react emotionally. Here, it is instead important to agree:
>
> 'I agree. I mean, wouldn't it be absurd for me to act like a man? I'm a woman – how else should I act?'

*3. There is one other instance in which it is worth applying the 'partial agreement' technique: when you really have done something wrong or been at fault in the past and are being reminded of it.*

I once ran an in-house workshop for a coffee supplier. One of the salespeople asked me: 'What should we do if we are told we did something wrong? One chain stopped working with us because the coffee wasn't good. Now I'm going around trying to prove that tastes vary.' I asked him if the coffee really was bad. He confirmed that the coffee had been disgusting, and that they had discontinued that line and brought in a whole new range of flavours.

So what was stopping the manager from admitting his own error and saying: 'Of course, you're right, that coffee was disgusting. That's why we've discontinued it. Our product is different now – try it for yourself.'

The answer: the echo of his vanity string. Admitting to our mistakes and rectifying them, now that's the real secret of success.

If you hear something like: 'Management probably doesn't trust you enough,' and if you also feel that way, then it's better to agree that trust is a complex thing than to argue that you have their complete trust.

Now I would like to suggest a few ways of using this technique. I'll give you two or three sentences for each situation, but I suggest you add to these lists yourself.

## A few ways of expressing partial agreement

*1. True agreement*: you admit that part or all of what the opponent has said is right.
- 'You know, I have to agree with you there, although for me it's not quite so black and white.'
- 'I agree with you . . . in part, at least.'

*2. Apparent agreement*: you admit that what the opponent has drawn your attention to is of interest to you and could be valuable for future discussion.
- 'Yes, at first glance it might seem that way . . .'
- 'Indeed!'
- 'I think about this a lot myself, but I haven't come to any particular conclusions.'

*3. Agreement gratitude*: you express gratitude to your opponent for bringing an issue to your attention, raising an important topic or putting forward a powerful argument.
- 'Thank you. That's a really important point.'
- 'I really appreciate you bringing this matter to our attention.'

It's also worth remembering that in practice there are many instances in which agreement is expressed through interjections or short exclamations. What's key here is that they are made with a friendly intonation that conveys acceptance of the other person and what they have said.

- 'Oh wow!'
- 'Well, I'll say!'

The 'partial agreement' technique is suitable when attacks are made towards you, but only if these attacks don't concern you personally or your company, or undermine your, your company's or your loved ones' dignity. This technique is particularly effective when there is something that you can agree with that might work in your favour. In short, the formula is as follows: agree with what's advantageous to you, but immediately deny anything that could harm you. Think of it this way: if you and a tiger are playing tug-of-war and the tiger wins, give it the rope before it gets to your hands. You can always get hold of another rope.

Now, let's get back to our exercises on applying these techniques for dealing with tough opponents. This time, the exercises all relate to the 'partial agreement' technique.

**How would you respond to the following statements using the 'partial agreement' technique?**

6. Don't you think you're being too cocky?

7. What you're saying is arguable.

8. That's a very female assumption to make [when addressing a woman].

9. How can it take so long to explain?

10. You're too slow!

11. What you're saying gives me doubts.

12. Petrov told everyone you're a slob.

13. I don't think your management trusts you all that much.

## USE CONNECTORS TO UNEARTH A MANIPULATOR'S MOTIVES

At its bare bones, the '**connector**' technique is the following: not every question or remark is worth a response. Often a simple 'and . . .' is enough. Then wait for your opponent to keep on talking.

'Doctor, you really aren't helping me at all.'

'Please explain what you mean.'

'Well, I don't feel like I'm making any progress.'

'And . . .?'

'I find it hard to do the exercises you recommended.'

'I see. What do you find most difficult about the exercises?'

When in skilled hands, a long, drawn-out 'and . . .' can be a deadly weapon. This technique is as effective as it is dangerous.

Now, the first thing to say is that I recommend this technique only to those who already know how to sustain a pause. If you pause after a drawn out 'and . . .' but still end up breaking the silence, then the battle's as good as lost.

Secondly, this technique should not be used with opponents who are higher than you in position or status, or with whom you simply feel in a 'dependent' position. You risk putting your foot in it.

'I don't appreciate your answers.' [Manager to a subordinate.]

'And . . .?'

'And get out of here.'

However, in discussions between two equals, this is a very powerful tool. It is even more so when used by someone who is superior in rank or status to their opponent.

A new manager calls his subordinate into his office and returns a report to him with the demand he redo it. The subordinate is indignant: 'I've been doing these reports for five years, and this is the first time I've been asked to redo one.'

'And . . .?'

'Well, everything went smoothly before, and everyone was happy with the reports.'

[Still pausing.]

'So have the rules changed or something?' [Questioningly, quieter.]

'Exactly.'

'Then I'll familiarise myself with the changes and correct it.'

Not all attacks need to be answered. Often, a pause or a long, drawn-out 'and . . .' are more than enough. However, this should only be used with equals or subordinates, and only if you know how to maintain a pause. In other circumstances, it is best to use other techniques.

## DISPUTING THE RIGHT WAY, WITHOUT PROVOCATION

Renowned political figure, philosopher and Roman Emperor Marcus Aurelius had the following basic life principle: 'Do what you must, come what may.'[31] It is this principle that forms the basis of the following technique for dealing with manipulation, so it is fitting that it bears his name: the '**Marcus Aurelius**' technique.

This technique is particularly effective in a few distinct situations. It is not unheard of for negotiation opponents to attempt to constrain you by applying certain conditions. One such condition, for example, is for them to add time constraints. Such ploys are their right; let them do it, *come what may*. But this is precisely the point at which you need to bring the Marcus Aurelius technique into play.

How many times have you heard something like: 'You've got five minutes – give me your pitch and then go', 'I'm pushed for time', 'I don't have time to listen to you' and more? What does this aim to do? Let's take a closer look.

Why might a person tell you they have no time?

Reason one: they really have no time. Even if you have arranged this meeting in advance, prepared yourself, observed every formality and arrived on time, unforeseen circumstances can always come up that require your opponent's urgent attention. Your opponent's child or wife might be unwell, for example, or at that very moment they might have been called in to see their boss. Lots of things can happen in the blink of an eye! So what should you do if this happens?

You should postpone negotiations, of course. Otherwise, rest assured: if you start making your pitch as planned it won't have any impact. Your opponent will be in a hurry, you won't have their full attention – their thoughts will already be elsewhere, com-
pletely absorbed by their sudden change in circumstance. None of this serves the matter at hand. In such situations, rescheduling is essential, but make sure to reschedule to a time that is convenient for you both. By doing so, you are showing them that you are equals, that you understand their need at this particular time and are meeting them halfway.

I can confidently say that the next time this person meets you, they will be paying attention to you and your proposal.

Now, that doesn't mean that they will gladly accept it; they will still need to examine it closely. But it does mean they will feel a greater sense of loyalty to you, because you also showed that loyalty to them. It's all very simple: this is where Niccolò Machiavelli's principle – 'Men, when they receive good from him of whom they were expecting evil, are bound more closely to their benefactor'[32] – kicks into action.

However, there are instances where the phrase 'You've got five minutes – give me your pitch and then go' is simply a deliberate and targeted play being used by the negotiator. For what? Many schools of negotiation that were popular in the nineties taught us to 'break' our opponent's negotiation rhythm in exactly this way.

Even today, many still use this as a managerial move, and it works. When a negotiator hears a phrase like this, a timer immediately starts ticking in their head.

In actual fact, when a phrase like this is said, it really is nothing more than words. Only once in my entire career have I seen someone say, 'You've got five minutes – give me your pitch and then go,' and actually put a watch on the table. This was a very bold move, aimed not so much at showing their lack of time and forcing their opponent to limit themselves to those five minutes but as a way of getting inside their opponent's head.

When facing a tough negotiator like this, use the Marcus Aurelius technique and say to yourself: 'Do what you must, come what may.' Under no circumstances should you get bogged down in declarations ('I'm sure two minutes will be all you need'), and don't assure them how concise you'll be: in that situation, you really only have twenty seconds to capture the other party's imagination, and that's precisely what you need to use that time for.

The only way you will pique their interest is through your own confidence, which is in this context the same as being results-oriented. If they see a confident, results-oriented opponent, they will still stop and listen. But if the person before them is faltering and constantly checking their internal timer to keep to their alloted time, they aren't going to want anything to do with them. That, or only under terms that are maximally advantageous to themselves.

All of this brings us to one more gambit: 'Honesty is the thief's best weapon.' Honesty and directness. And fearlessness, when faced with losing a client.

So now we have seen what to do when the timer starts ticking. Another situation in which the Marcus Aurelius technique can be effective is when, during negotiations, attacks are directed at you personally, your loved ones or company. When people say phrases like: 'I heard your company's gone bankrupt', 'I heard you never stand by your words', or 'This is all junk.'

How should we react to remarks like these? First and foremost, when attacks like this happen, you should never under any circumstance ask where your opponent got that information.

Firstly, by repeating a negative message, you reinforce that person's belief that they should have nothing to do with you.

During the Soviet Union a certain Nikolai Stepanovich, a party official, took his wife to the theatre. There, to everyone's great dismay, her fur coat was stolen, causing a scandal. Six months later, two high-ranking party officials were deciding whom to appoint to a prestigious position. One of them said: 'Let's give

> it to Nikolai Stepanovich.' To which the second replied: 'No, not him, never. He was linked to some unpleasant business – either he stole a fur coat, or someone stole one from him.'

Secondly, every word you say will simply confirm and reinforce the attitude that has already formed in your opponent's mind. These attitudes hold a great weight and significance.

As soon as you become associated with an attitude in a person's mind, you need to change it. The equation for dismantling such attitudes is: denial + positive message.

⚠

> 'I heard your company's gone bankrupt.'
>
> 'Quite the opposite, our company has a stable market position. But why take my word for it: we work with companies like . . .'
>
> If listing names of other companies, they need to have a strong reputation. If a person thinks that companies A, B and C can do no wrong, it then follows that if they are working with you then everything must be fine: your market position is strong. After saying this, make a short pause for breath and move on to the planned discussion topic.

**Formula: denial, positive message (e.g. your connections to other companies), move on to the subject at hand.**

In the case of non-constructive attacks based on rumour, personal opinion or hearsay, deny these with the phrase **'quite the opposite'**.

In any other circumstance, you should respond to attacks with a succinct, pre-prepared phrase. This phrase must distil the essence of your message. But whatever you do, don't repeat the negative allegation! By repeating it, you give it weight.

'What the hell are you on about?' your opponent attacks.

'It's a shame you didn't catch my main point,' you reply. 'Let me repeat it: our company produces high-quality equipment that will save your resources . . .'

After a consultation, one student of mine shared her story:

'I'm a lawyer at a major holding company. I have ten years' experience and I know my profession. Once, at a meeting with my boss, I showed him that the deal his deputy was proposing was fraught with possible issues. Of course, his deputy cut me off with the phrase: "Nonsense! Do you even know the legislation?"

"'It's a shame you overlooked the key point of my report," I replied. "There I showed that if we go through with this deal as our counterparts are proposing, we run 100 per cent risk of losing our licence. Because it violates articles [here I listed the articles] of the relevant legislation.'"

This lawyer did a fantastic job of navigating a complex situation. Had she started to assert her qualifications or prove her legal knowledge, she would inevitably have been told something like: 'Oh please, don't tell us how to do our jobs. We know you lawyers. Always trying to hold the show up . . .'

When you go into negotiations with a proposal or pitch, you need to be able to distil its essence and benefit into one syntactical construction or succinct phrase. This should contain who you are, your relationship to the company and how your proposal could benefit the people you are presenting it to.

And don't forget our rule about eye contact: once you have said your piece, turn your gaze away from the opponent – don't look them in the eye. Don't challenge your opponent: I've said my piece, now it's your turn.

But now let's take a look at a situation in which your tough opponent doesn't react to your proposals or actions. The Marcus Aurelius technique also features another interesting play. This is to repeat a variation on your basic idea.

'You aren't listening to me; you aren't listening to my questions.'

'I'd be happy to listen . . .'

'You don't want to listen, and you don't understand.'

'I'd be happy to listen to your questions again.'

'Fine, let me ask you one question.'

'You have my full attention, and I'll be pleased to answer it.'

As a rule, the third time is when someone tells the truth, or asks the question they want to ask, the one they really need an answer to.

In her book, well-known coach and psychologist Elena Sidorenko describes this technique as the 'English Sergeant' method. The sergeant gives his command once to get the attention of the soldiers, twice to make sure that the soldiers have taken it in, and three times to make sure he himself understands the full scope of the command. Often, in negotiations, people stop listening. This is when it's important to bring their attention back to the matter at hand by stating the same idea and variations thereof three (or more) times.

One other type of situation in which the Marcus Aurelius technique is particularly appropriate is when your opponent has taken an extremely destructive stance. When they are pelting you with accusations, not letting you speak and not listening. Any word that you say will simply give them fodder for further, more sharpened retorts.

In situations like these, you have to stop the attacks. But

you must also be prepared to get up and end the negotiations. You face a choice: either become a training apparatus for your opponent to further hone their tough technique on, or be a serious specialist who won't let yourself or your business be pushed around. There is always a choice.

A great example of how to successfully cut off a 'barbarian' is Russian Emperor Alexander I of Russia's reaction to an aggressive outburst from Napoleon Bonaparte at the Congress of Erfurt, as described by Armand de Caulaincourt, one of Napoleon's aides.

Both emperors had taken up the habit of walking up and down the Emperor's study while discussing important international affairs. At one point, Napoleon, unable to get a satisfactory answer from Alexander I, tried working himself up into a rage. He threw his hat onto the floor and started to stamp on it. Tsar Alexander stood still and watched him with a smile. When he saw Napoleon's outburst was starting to lose steam, he said: 'When you become violent I just become stubborn. With me anger is of no avail. Let us discuss, and be reasonable, or I go.'[33] Napoleon was forced to concede. After this, they resumed their discussion in a calm manner.

Let's summarise the key points of this lesson. Knowing how to stand up to a 'barbarian' influence is crucial, otherwise you face a considerable risk of losing face. But you need to do so in a civil, courteous manner, without sinking to similar methods.

## To interrupt an attack choose one of two methods: tough or gentle

*Tough interruption:*

'These allegations aren't constructive. As you are opposed to our decision, your behaviour is clearly aimed at frustrating these negotiations. I would ask you to stick to the subject at hand, otherwise I will have to bring these talks to a close.'

*Gentle interruption:*

'Unfortunately it seems we have got caught up in mutual recriminations, which will make it hard for us to meet our goals. I suggest we get back to the main topic under discussion.'

**Rules of use:**
- Clearly and directly tell your opponent that you do not appreciate the way they are speaking or behaving.
- Address them politely.
- Change your physical position: lean back into your seat, give a deep sigh, or it can even be effective to stand up and take a few unhurried steps. What is important here is that your movements are smooth and confident – no bursts of energy or jerkiness.

**Basic rules of use:**

'Do what you must, come what may.'

Don't react to an emotional message. Simply pursue the matter that has brought you to the negotiating table. Don't justify yourself, act defensively or repeat negative messages. Project an image of positivity alone.

Don't ask who told whom what. Questions like that simply give credibility to rumour. Distil the main point of your message into one succinct phrase.

Use the negator 'quite the opposite'. Keep your movements calm and cut off attacks using either a tough or gentle interruption. Repeat your point calmly and non-confrontationally. Not everyone understands (or wants to understand) your message first time round.

Now let's return to our exercises on how to apply these techniques for negotiating with a tough opponent. As you might have guessed, this time our exercises relate to the Marcus Aurelius technique.

**Respond to the following negative messages using the Marcus Aurelius technique:**

14. 'I've heard you're always late on payment.'

15. 'They say your employees are all jumping ship.'

16. 'Your proposal is complete rubbish.'

17. 'Come on, get to the point!'

18. 'You aren't listening to me.'

19. 'What nonsense!'

20. 'Your market reputation is terrible.'

21. 'Given your persistence, I take it you're not particularly competent.'

22. 'Ugh, enough of your so-called innovations!'

## DODGING RUDENESS

I f you've ever switched on the Discovery Channel and seen lions and tigers on the prowl, you'll have noted how the predator (hunter) always keeps its focus on its prey's movements. It follows them intently, analysing and tracking every step its future target makes: which direction it will take, the way it jumps, how it's going to react. It predicts their behaviour.

This is what separates the predator from the prey. The potential prey isn't thinking about the predator; all it is thinking about is itself. It is through its self-preservation instinct alone that it decides its best route to survival.

It's chalk and cheese: the predator thinks about its prey, whereas the prey thinks about itself. This is a very important principle in negotiation. And this is precisely what forms the basis of the 'predator' technique.

In negotiations, two roles are easily distinguished: predator and prey. When we 'hunt' in negotiations, we shouldn't be monitoring our own emotions or thinking about whether we'll get angry or not; we should instead be watching our opponent, always keeping one step ahead. We should not react to emotional messages, but to the essence of what that person wants to achieve by them. Very often, consciously or not, a person will hide the point that they are trying to make behind negative statements about us.

'Can't you see that what you're saying is nonsense?'

Let's say you hear this outburst during negotiations. What does it make you think? What is the first thought that comes into your mind? Probably something like: 'I said something that made them angry', 'My stories and pitch really got under their skin', etc. If thoughts like this did run through your mind, then you turned your thoughts on yourself – in doing so turning yourself into the prey.

Wild animals have a certain number of responses. They can fight, flee or play dead, or peacefully graze in a clearing, soberly evaluating the situation and reacting to what is happening.

When your opponent says something like this, what are they actually trying to say?

'Can't you see that what you're saying is nonsense?'

Try to put their sentence in other words. For example:

*'I don't quite understand what my opposite number is saying.'*

This is their true message. This is what you need to react to.

*'So if I understand correctly, you don't fully agree with my conclusions?'*
  *'No.'*
  *'OK. Then let's take a closer look at each one.'*

We can give the following formula for responding to remarks like these:

Figure out the true message.

Ask a question that clarifies the true message.

Once this has been confirmed, move the conversation on to a detailed discussion.

If your clarifying question is met with denial, keep on trying to pinpoint the true point of what they said.

Let's see this formula in action.

**Variant 1:**

'Enough of all this foot-dragging!'

'Am I right in understanding that you would like to take these negotiations forward?'

'Yes.'

'OK, then let's run through the key points.'

**Variant 2:**

'Enough of all this foot-dragging!'

'Am I right in understanding that you would like to take these negotiations forward?'

'No!'

'Then could you please explain what's concerning you?'

'I don't like it that you aren't interested in my conclusions.'

'I do apologise — tell me what they are.'

Use this technique if you understand your opponent's true message.

Here, with my apologies to the reader, I'm going to break with our established order of exercises on how to employ our techniques for negotiating with tough opponents. In the preceding sections, I have included the exercises towards the end of the section. But here I would like to seize the moment and propose doing exercise 23 straight away.

23. In the table below, try to write down what you interpret the true message hidden in the attacker's words to be, and what you feel would be the appropriate response.

| Phrase | True message | Reply |
|---|---|---|
| I'm tired of listening to your empty arguments. | I want to hear an argument that will convince me. | If I've understood you correctly, you want to hear some strong arguments? |
| I've had enough of this twaddle. | | |
| How many times must they send these simple clerks to negotiate! | | |
| Your arguments are ridiculous. | | |

| Phrase | True message | Reply |
|---|---|---|
| Aren't you too young and inexperienced for this? | | |
| I know your 'Italy': I bet everything's made in China. | | |

When we are willing to truly understand a person's concerns, we not only become the 'predator'; we gain wisdom. We don't let ourselves get worked up by even the most negative message; we react only to the essence of the issue. By doing so, we move negotiations into a rational sphere.

I was once giving a talk in front of an audience. There were roughly two hundred people in the auditorium, and they represented a wide variety of companies. Now, I was already some way into my talk, and the audience and I had developed a good rapport: we were already speaking the same language and using our own in-jokes — we understood each other completely. At this point a very imposing middle-aged man walked into the auditorium, and I could sense his immediate discomfort. Without the preceding context, our idiosyncratic terms were leaving him a bit at sea. I could see he was about to say something unflattering, and that's exactly what he did: he stood up, thrust his hand up and shouted:

'Gibberish!'

You couldn't make this stuff up. It was a good thing I was prepared for this: I had 'played the predator', and what was important to me was his point rather than his emotion.

'Am I right in sensing that the terms I'm using aren't clear to you?'

'Yes!'

'Then come see me at the break — I'll explain everything.'

The audience burst into applause.

It is very important to take on the state of the 'predator'. Only then will you be able to understand a person's message rather than react to the shell they are hiding behind.

Let's remind ourselves that the fundamental aim of these techniques for standing up to manipulation or 'barbarism' is, where possible, to shift the discussion into a rational sphere and move on to a constructive discussion of the issues that led to the meeting being set.

If the attacks continue and you want to cut the meeting short, then you need to call it off in a way that allows you to leave with your head held high.

Nowadays, many negotiations happen over email. The predator technique allows you to avoid fatal errors that could otherwise arise when you react to an emotional message.

Read the following email correspondence. I'd like to propose you try to analyse it by pulling apart where the supplier and buyer went wrong and what they could have done differently. You won't find any 'correct' answers for this exercise at the back of the book, but you can send your responses to me at igor@ryzov.ru, and I'll make sure to get back to you with my comments.

The correspondence is between a sales manager at a trading company and a buyer for a federal network. In the preceding email, the sales manager has informed the buyer that, due to an increase in prices from their manufacturer, they will have to pass on a price increase to their clients.

Please excuse the style and punctuation of the emails, but this is how the correspondence really looked. I felt it was important to retain the same style, as this could help to decipher both parties' true message. ☺

|  | Email text | True message |
|---|---|---|
| Buyer | Andrei, You have to give us a discount for product 1! This promo should be discounts<br><br>Kind regards, Buyer. | |
| Supplier | As of 1 December, our manufacturer has increased prices by 5 per cent. | |
| Buyer | Hello,<br><br>Andrei, it feels like your factory is raising prices every month. Before you, we discussed an increase in prices with Ivan. We accepted that, and factory costs were also part of the reason for that increase. Ivan told us that your company had managed to agree to a small increase of 3 per cent, and we also took on that increase. But now another???????<br><br>PLEASE CONFIRM THE PROMO FIGURE AS THE DISCOUNT!! Or we'll cut the goods and I'll find a replacement.<br><br>Kind regards, Buyer | |

|  | Email text | True message |
|---|---|---|
| Supplier | Elena, I'm afraid I haven't made anything up, it's just that Russian suppliers are taking advantage of the current situation on the border with Ukraine. They really are raising prices every month. No one in our procurement department is in at the moment, but I'll send you the letter we have confirming the increase in price tomorrow.<br><br>However, if this issue is so categorical then of course we'll find some way of giving a discount at our end and repeating the promo price that we gave you (2 per cent discount)<br><br>Thank you. |  |
| Buyer | Andrei, according to our contract our minimum promo discount is 5 per cent. Please find a different manufacturer. Speak to factory X.<br><br>I imagine they would be happy to supply goods to our network. |  |
| Supplier | Fine. |  |
| Buyer | FINE – huh???????<br><br>???????? What does that mean?<br><br>What have you actually agreed to? J |  |
| Supplier | Hello Anna,<br><br>Sorry for this slow reply. The absolute maximum discount that we are able to offer for product 1 is in fact 2 per cent, but we can offer 5 per cent for everything else. Please find attached the letter confirming these price increases. |  |
| Buyer | Find a replacement manufacturer.<br><br>Or I'll find a new supplier.<br><br>Kind regards, Buyer. |  |

We have seen that when using the predator technique it is very important to establish or deduce the true message behind what might well be an overly tough phrase from your opponent. However, it is no less important to clarify the manipulator's true aims. When you are unsure what lies behind negative remarks, or when you find it difficult or even impossible to identify their true message, then clearing up your opponent's true aims could be key. How is this done? By asking questions.

In theory, this play also has its own name: **questioning the manipulator's intent**. But the main thing to know is that you don't just throw this question in their face; instead, you pose it in such a way that your point is nevertheless clear.

In particular, the construction 'what for' makes the true aims of the manipulator clear, and it is therefore very important for us. When faced with this question, the opponent will either reveal their intent or step back from the exchange. Either option works well for us. If the opponent is open to constructive negotiations, then this will lead them off the emotional plane and allow us to continue negotiating in a rational one. If, however, they are in a destructive frame of mind, then they will simply stop pursuing their point, which is also good. At the very least, this will lessen our negotiation budget.

If someone exclaims: 'What rubbish!', what is it they really want to achieve? What point are they trying to make? We know that our words aren't 'rubbish' by any stretch, that we are expressing ourselves clearly and that our arguments have some weight. And it isn't as though our opponent is stupid – they're quite capable of keeping up. So what are they injecting into this comment by using the word 'nonsense'? Clearly they haven't just blurted it out by accident; it's serving some sort of aim. This is exactly the moment at which it is important to pose the question of intent. Of course, you could simply fall back on something along the lines of: '*Are you always this aggressive in your negotiations?*' But asking this question would be responding to toughness with toughness. It keeps the conversation moving in the same emotional direction your opponent has set. Essentially, if we ask this question it is as though we have already figured out our opponent's intent and made the corresponding decision.

Your question will be much more effective if it seeks to clarify their intent, particularly if it is delivered in a manner that allows for a return to a rational mode. For example:

'What makes you say that?'

Or:

'What did I say to make you draw that conclusion?'

In his article '*Model Dinamiki Aktivnosti Zhivykh Sistem*' ('A Model of the Dynamics of Activity in Living Systems',[34] Sergei Kharitonov, research fellow at the Federal Institute of Mediation, describes a model that negotiations practically always follow: security – goals – partnership.

In my experience, negotiations often get stuck in the 'security' phase. Opponents are unable to progress beyond this stage as they are unsure whether what their opposite number wants is a completely safe option for them. Let's take an example: a salesperson is attempting to convince a buyer to change supplier, but the buyer keeps on hiding behind excuses. Here, we have to understand that, to the buyer, the salesperson represents danger: with them comes change, and if their product doesn't sell, then what will management say?

Getting past this stage is crucial. And knowing how to shift negotiations into a rational mode makes it easier to do so.

By being a predator and thinking about your opponent, you will be better able to understand what they actually want. Most of the time, behind negative remarks lies either a certain aim – a desire to get something – or a concern of some kind. The objective of any good negotiator is to recognise which is the case and act accordingly – that is to say, to approach the target or step away from the exchange, if partnership isn't possible at the given time.

⚠

It is worth clarifying what the person's motives are, and by this I mean **what** they actually want, rather than **why** they are saying what they are. The question 'why?' has two very important drivers behind it: why as a reason and why as a purpose (for what). It is very important not to confuse the two. When asking about your opponent's true motives, you can phrase the question any way you like, but the drive of the question should be: for what?

Let's take a few examples.

A dialogue between two colleagues.

One turns to the other and says:

'Your desk is always a mess. When will you learn to clear up after yourself?'

The other replies:

'What are you actually asking me?'

Or:

'What do you actually want to talk about?'

If the attacker is not in the frame of mind for dialogue, then they might well evade this question, but they will also stop their attack. Note: it is not worth pursuing them with follow-up questions like: *'Come on, tell me!'* This will only strain relations.

So, by this point we have (hopefully) achieved our aims and stopped the attack. If, however, our opponent continues to attack us with remarks like *'Well, it's a mess, and that annoys me'*, then you can ask one more question: *'Why did you decide to speak to me like that?'* Again, the drive of this question is: What did you hope to achieve by saying this to me? What is your aim?

Should yet another attack follow, then simply repeat this same question calmly and clearly. But don't get carried away. If the opponent stops their attack, then we stop too.

I was once taking part in negotiations with one partner on my side, against four people on the opposing side. The negotiations were primarily being led by the deputy CEO on the opposing side, and by a lawyer on our side. We were discussing certain clauses of an agreement, and the lawyer was explaining that if amendments weren't made to it then it would inevitably spell problems for both sides. However, making the amendments would require time.

At this point, the deputy CEO interrupted the lawyer to exclaim: 'Come on, that's a bunch of crap, are you trying to ruin our deal or something? Jerk.'

I'm sure you can imagine that after such an outburst it is very hard to carry on as normal. Of course, my colleague was fuming, but I was able to step in and take the blow myself. I could see that we were stuck on the security phase of our interaction, and we were somehow unable to get past it. Whatever the lawyer said, no matter how rationally, the other side saw it only as a threat to the deal.

I paused (this is very important) and then said: 'Would you mind explaining what you mean by the word "crap"?'

'Surely that's clear.'

'You and I might mean different things by the word.'

There was a ten-second pause. Then the attacker answered my question: 'You know, I just think that any foot-dragging will break this deal.'

'OK. But if these amendments don't take much time and don't affect our schedule, would you be prepared to explore them?'

'I think so.'

I turned to the lawyer: 'Andrei, how long would it take for you to prepare these amendments?'

'An hour.'

'So why don't you do them while we discuss the commercial points of the agreement?'

I turned back to our opponent: 'Do you agree?'

'Yes.'

We got the deal.

If you aren't entirely sure what someone intended, then you urgently need to get to the heart of the matter. You will find that this effort reaps rewards.

As a practising negotiator, my toolkit is full of expressions that can be used to **question intent**. Here are just a few of them:

- 'What makes you say that?'
- 'What is it that you're trying to ask?'
- 'What do you mean by the words . . .?'
- 'What are you actually asking me to do?'

For extra practice, try to come up with some of your own questions. But don't forget, you are questioning *purpose*, so the drive of the question should be 'for what?'

Questioning a manipulator's intent can also be a very effective line of defence against false choices that force you to play by someone else's rules.

If you have ever had the dubious fortune of holding talks with the criminal underground and with officials, you will probably have noticed the similarities in the tactics they use when defending their views and interests.

Both will start by pulling the rug out from under their opponents' feet in exactly the same way, to demonstrate that talks with them won't follow the accepted rules. Crooks will appeal to certain *understandings*, while officials will appeal to laws – or to specific interpretations of these laws that suit their interests.

From the very beginning, both will draw conclusions with the greatest yardstick of truth, but based on very specific rules and values.

No matter what the situation, they will always be right, because you can never play as equals on their field and by their rules. As a result, the behaviours or rules of the game that favour the opponent will be imposed on you, and you will have no choice but to follow them.

This tactic is used to humorous effect by Karlson, the hero of Astrid Lindgren's beloved children's book, *The World's Best Karlson*:

Miss Crawley interrupted him in her stoniest voice:

'Answer yes or no, I said! It can't be that hard to answer yes or no to a simple question!'

'So you say,' retorted Karlson. 'I'll ask you a simple question, and then you'll see. Listen! Have you stopped drinking brandy first thing in the morning?'

Miss Crawley gave a gasp and seemed to be about to choke. She tried to speak but couldn't get a word out.

'Come on then, tell us,' said Karlson. 'Have you stopped drinking brandy first thing in the morning?'

'Yes she has,' said Smidge eagerly. He was really trying to help Miss Crawley, but she blew her top.

'I most certainly have not,' she cried in fury, and Smidge was petrified.

'No, no, she hasn't stopped,' he corrected himself.

'I'm sorry to hear that,' said Karlson. 'Drunkenness leads to nothing but misery.'

Miss Crawley gave a sort of gurgle and sank down onto a chair. But Smidge had finally worked out the right answer.

'She hasn't stopped, because she never started – as you well know,' he told Karlson sternly.

To top it all off, Karlson declares:

'Silly you, now you can see that a yes or no answer won't always work . . . give me some drop scones!'[35]

The most effective way of reacting to these false choices is to question your opponent's true intent. Miss Crawley could have asked Karlson something like:

*'Why are you trying to put me in a difficult position?'*

Or:

*'What do you mean by asking me a question like that?'*

Once, while I was participating in judicial proceedings, one lawyer decided to provoke the other, and his opponent started to play by his rules. He turned to his opponent with the question, 'Now tell me: do you think your client has the exclusive right to break the law?'

However, his opponent turned out to be well-equipped for these negotiations. After a moment's pause, he replied: 'Why are you asking me that question when the answer is obvious?'

The attack was unsuccessful, and the point went to the other side.

**Rules for using the predator technique and questioning intent**

Do not react to emotional messages. Do not think about your emotions; think about your opponent. It can be very useful to put yourself in their position and get a sense of what they are actually trying to say.

Only react to the core of the message. Don't react to the words, but to the idea that lies behind them. If you are unsure what this is, then ask a 'what for?' question.

It is also very important to ascertain the attacker's true motives if you are given a false choice.

And now, as we have done before, let's take a look at our exercise to tie up the predator technique. This time I am going to ask you to prepare two responses for each of the statements.

**Try to formulate your own questions in response to the following attempts to draw you into an emotional mode:**

24. You'll never be able to finish this task, you're too dim!

**Questioning intent:**


**'Predator' question:**


25. I never realised you were so sharp.

**Questioning intent:**


**'Predator' question:**


26. I'm sick of all this empty chat.

**Questioning intent:**


**'Predator' question:**


27. Are you always this insistent?

**Questioning intent:**


**'Predator' question:**

28. You're being very provocative.

**Questioning intent:**


**'Predator' question:**


## A JOKE AND A KIND WORD – GUARANTEES OF SUCCESS WITH EVEN THE MOST AGGRESSIVE OPPONENTS

When a person attacks you, their aspiration and desire is to provoke a negative, aggressive reaction in you – to pluck one of your strings and induce an undesirable emotion. Their main motive is to do what they need to do to turn you into the aggressor. All in order to later prove that because you're angry, you must be in the wrong.

When sending these tough or negative messages, your opponent is in no way expecting positives in return. What do I mean by 'positives'? Compliments, well-meaning comments. If these are what you offer, this will disorient the attacker.

When looking at the four behaviour models back in Chapter 1, we already saw the sorts of things people do to provoke negative reactions. And the basic technique for dealing with these is to eschew rudeness in response to rudeness in favour of a positive, pleasant response.

The following example is from negotiations I had in a Russian city.

I had been given an appointment with the buyers for a major regional chain. I flew in to the city and arrived at the venue at the appointed time. Our negotiations, it appeared, were going to take place in a large space divided into smaller cubicles by plasterboard partitions.

In the unforgettable Soviet comedy *The Twelve Chairs* (1971), there's a great scene set between the walls of a cramped, grey dormitory, in which all of the residents join in the conversations going on on the other side of the paper-thin walls. Well, the space we were negotiating in reminded me of that scene.

After I'd arrived, I was led to one of the plasterboard cubicles and asked to wait. So I waited. Suddenly the door flew open as though it had been kicked. A woman came storming in. And I have to say, the sight was something to behold: her hair was everywhere, her eyes were ablaze, and when she opened her mouth she practically screamed: 'What the hell are you doing here? Who invited you?'

This was one of the few occasions on which I was able to faultlessly put this technique into play. I replied to her with a sincere, pleasant 'Oh, I'm so pleased to meet you!'

This completely threw her, and she sat down immediately. The room went silent – an unplanned pause. Then the woman said: 'You have my attention. Let's talk.'

She and I talked. We came to an agreement that led to a fruitful collaboration.

Many years later, at one of my workshops on working with purchasing agents for major chains, I used this example. Naturally I didn't mention any names, nor even where the meeting took place. But one participant put up his hand and said, 'I know where that was. It was chain X, in city Y.'

He was absolutely right – he really had recognised the buyer. How? By her signature. The thing is, every one of us has our own signature negotiation style, and it is recognisable. If a person consistently uses the same plays and techniques, maintaining their individual signature, then as a rule this means only one thing: that their negotiation model is successful, and that it has helped them to succeed and achieve their goals in previous negotiations. So, every time that woman provoked someone, what was she actually after? She wanted her opponent to either get angry or start justifying themselves.

In both instances, this would allow her to seize the initiative in the negotiations and steer their subsequent progress. And you can bet that she would get much more from her opponent than what they had planned on giving.

This play was successful until it came up against a different behaviour model: responding to rudeness with a positive (a smile and a compliment).

For this, however, you need to know how to give a compliment. In my point of view, the best formula for giving compliments was presented by Leonid Kroll, Professor of the Higher School of Economics, in his book *Peregovori s Drakonami* ('Negotiating with Dragons'):[36] *I'm looking at you – I see you – I'm interested in what you have to say.*

Don't think in terms of typical evaluative categories. It is very important to give a compliment about what you genuinely like about that person. In other words, you have to be sincere.

Take a lesson from the lead character in the Soviet animation *Vlyubchivaya Vorona* ('The Amorous Crow'). In this short film, which sees the crow fall in love with an unlikely string of characters, she demonstrates a striking ability to make compliments.

'Hare, you're not skew-eyed, your eyes just swivel!'

'How big and clever you are, bear.'

If you ever get the opportunity to watch this film, you will see how precisely the crow homes in on what evokes a sincere and unbreakable interest in her. If you like your opponent's watch, then point that out. Your sincerity will reap rewards.

Insincerity, however, will lead to problems.

One of the participants in a workshop I gave recounted the following story:

Once I got myself into a tricky situation. I was always taught to give compliments, whether sincere or not. One beautiful day, an acquaintance of mine came to my office for negotiations in a small car. I went out to greet him and, remembering I ought to give him a compliment, I said I loved his car. He went purple with rage. It turned out that the car belonged to his wife, and that he really hated it.

So there you have it – truly not the planned result. This man didn't actually like the car, so why did he make a song and dance about it? Because he was taught that's what you're supposed to do. Now let's say he actually did like the car. In such an instance, had his acquaintance shot back with 'Well, if you like it then why don't you drive it!' he would have been able to respond: 'You know what, I would happily drive that car, it really is nice.'

A different, inadvertently more successful example comes courtesy of another one of my audience members:

Two years ago I went to meet with a company. From my perspective, my aim was completely mercantile: I wanted to make money out of them by selling our services at a high price. But they weren't really willing to buy anything, not even on the cheap. Somehow, by hook or by crook, I'd managed to get a meeting with the main decision-maker – their sales director.

When I arrived there, I was certain I'd be meeting with a man. But that was only because my colleagues had always spoken about the sales director with such fear and panic, using terms that never once made me think that they might be describing a woman. They never mentioned her by name, and for some stupid reason I'd never got round to finding out her name prior to our meeting. I dropped the ball; that was my bad.

So there I was, waiting for the sales director for our little discussion. Suddenly a woman burst into the room. She was young but tough, extremely clever, really into her work and rules and dressed to the strictest of dress codes. The smile slipped from my face in shock. Then she, as they say, started to pile it on, sticking out her hand for a handshake. I was so thrown I couldn't figure out which hand to give her.

241

In short, I was completely bowled over by this unexpected turn of events, and felt, well, pretty pathetic. Then she looked at me and said: 'Svetlana, I've only got five minutes. I'm listening.'

Now, even before this dishonest little trick I was feeling my tongue start to dry up; I'd realised I wouldn't be able to sell anything to this woman. The meeting was a waste of my time. But my brakes failed. Stupidly – but honestly – I just blurted out what I was thinking: 'Tell me, do you really only have five minutes? Or are you just saying that to throw me off?'

She just looked at me. Clearly it had been the right move. I could see her starting to come unstuck, because she hadn't expected to hear that. Which made me start to feel better, get a bit of my confidence back.

Taking advantage of her momentary confusion, I continued, smiling like an idiot: 'Well, you didn't even need to do that. Did you see how thrown I was when you walked in? I was sure you were a man. My colleagues spoke about you with such deference and fear that for some reason I was sure you were a charismatic man, a born leader who has no problem keeping everyone in line. But it turns out that it's a woman who has all of these qualities. You can't imagine how pleasantly surprised and proud of my sex I am!'

I have to say, I said all of this purely out of frustration, because I knew I had nothing to lose. But by saying that I unexpectedly hit the mark. She actually liked hearing herself described in such professional terms! Anyway, it broke the ice and we spent an hour chewing the fat. And it might not have happened in that first meeting, but we did eventually put together a contract.

It is very important to look at the person and really notice them. But if you are in any doubt as to whether the compliment will go down well, then it's better not to say it. If, however, that compliment is honest, sincere and polite (as Larry King recommends) and follows the formula '*I'm looking at you – I see you – I find you interesting*', then it will always spark positive emotions. And let's not forget that what we are concerned with right now is bringing our opponent back into a rational framework. By giving compliments in negotiations, we stand a better chance of doing just that. But remember: after giving a compliment, leave a moment's pause and then get straight back to the subject of your negotiations. It is essential to follow a compliment up with something along the lines of: 'I'd like to draw your attention to . . .' or 'I'd like to focus your attention on . . .'

Where it isn't easy to respond to negative attacks with a positive, if you practise, the results will surprise you.

A manager shouts at his subordinate:

'You're so slow! When are you ever going to pick up the pace?'

'Nikolai Stepanovich, I've always admired your ability to get your colleagues moving.'

An official to a visitor:

'Surely it isn't hard to fill out a form correctly – even a child could do that.'

'Maria Ivanovna, thank you for drawing my attention to that error. You're so good at picking up on these things! I'll make sure to correct everything. But could you tell me, what in particular do I need to change?'

I'll admit it: I'm not very good at giving compliments. So I'd also like to put forward a simpler, but no less effective way of cutting short an attack: **quotes**.

To use this technique in negotiations, you'll need to have a selection of quotes to mind that can help you to stave off manipulative attacks.

Once, at negotiations in my office, my opponent looked me in the eyes and said: 'You know, other coaches do lots of workshops on a range of topics, but you only focus on negotiating. It makes me wonder if you might be a bit narrow-minded?'

How can you respond to an attack like that?

Immediately the words of Sergei Korolev, the lead Soviet rocket engineer, came to mind. So I quickly replied: 'Sergei Korolev once said that if you do a lot, but badly, people will forget that you did a lot and remember that you did it badly. But if you do little, but well, then people will forget the little part, but not the fact that you did it well. I subscribe to that principle in my life. Which is why I specialise in negotiation. Would you be interested in learning more?'

This approach will require you to gather and memorise quotes to form your own quote library. Now, these don't have to be the quotes of great thinkers; I often cite people I respect.

For example, an opponent once showed me some statistical data to prove their position. I had my doubts about these figures, and I said as much to my opponent, who replied: 'What, don't you trust statistics?'

'You know, my father is a trauma surgeon. And he says that, after medicine, statistics are the most precise science.'

We laughed it off, and our negotiations moved past security and onto our goals.

'If one does not know to which port one is sailing, no wind is favourable.' – Lucius Annaeus Seneca

'Do not surrender your mood to one who would insult you. Don't let yourself be drawn onto the path they would have you walk down.' – Marcus Aurelius

'You do not have to agree with a person to find a common language.' – Margaret Thatcher

'. . . Artists who draw landscapes get down in the valley to study the mountains and go up to the mountains to look down on the valley . . .'[37] – Niccolò Machiavelli

'If there is any one secret of success, it lies in the ability to get the other person's point of view.' – Henry Ford

'I often had to say no, to prevent myself from being manipulated by others.' – Andrei Gromyko

'We only truly possess what we can share.' – Vladimir Tarasov

'Do what you must, come what may.' – Marcus Aurelius

'If you think you know the truth then offer it to another in the same way you would a coat – so that they can put it on more comfortably – rather than shoving it in their face like a wet handkerchief.' – Max Frisch

'Silence is an aspect of communication that very few have mastered, and very rare are those who know how to use it in a focused, conscious manner.' – Karsten Bredemeier, business trainer

'Ironically, the most solid, unshakable beliefs are the most super-ficial ones. Deep convictions can always change.' – Leo Tolstoy

'People are not thinking about you as much as you worry about what they think.' – Susan Newman

'Books serve to show a man that those original thoughts of his aren't very new at all.' – Abraham Lincoln

So now we have looked at the 'compliment + smile' technique. To practise it, I would like to set you a very simple assignment: write down at least two quotes that could help you in complex or tough negotiations.

Give compliments using the formula: 'honesty – politeness – sincerity'. And don't forget: 'I'm looking at you – I see you – I'm

interested in what you have to say.' Don't encourage rude behaviour. Respond to rudeness with politeness, and in doing so disorient your opponent.

Keep a set of quotes. These don't have to be from great thinkers or famous people. But remember the 'comma' rule: after staving off a manipulative attack, bring the negotiations back into a constructive mode.

## THE 'HUMOUR' TECHNIQUE

Humour is a most powerful weapon. But if not used correctly, we can shoot ourselves in the foot. Humour can become a pistol that turns back on us.

On a visit to Paris, the Pope was once asked by a journalist: 'What is your view on brothels?'

The Pope hesitated, unsure what to say. Understandably: if he were to say something positive, he would lose a considerable chunk of his audience. And if he were to say they were bad, he might come across negatively in others' eyes. So he decided to make a joke: 'What, do you mean to say there are brothels in Paris?'

Everyone laughed. But the next day, the headlines read: *Pope arrives in Paris, asks for the brothels*.

And here's a suicidal joke used at a job interview:

---

**HR manager:** 'So, tell me, how many times have you changed job in the past five years?'

**Candidate:** 'Three.'

**HR manager:** 'Oh, you like to move around.'

**Candidate** (deciding to make light of it): 'Oh, that's me, once I get a good tailwind I'm off.'

**HR manager:** 'Well, in that case this'll be a short layover. We aren't looking for a temp.'

---

Jokes like these force negotiations down a blind alley, turning the conversation against you.

But for all of these dangers, you shouldn't underestimate what a good joke or story can do if negotiations begin to get emotional. An audience-appropriate, clear, unambiguous joke will immediately deflate any tensions. But the key thing to remember is that as soon as you crack the joke, you must return to the original topic of conversation. We can make the following formula: '(audience appropriate) joke – return to the original topic of conversation'. Something like the following examples:

*'Oh, buddy, I see you're wearing glasses now. Is age finally catching up on you?'*

*'All the better to see you with, my friend – but what was it you wanted to talk about?'*

*'Your replies are so slow – why do you keep putting on the brakes?'*

*'On a slippery road like this, it's better to drive slowly than end up in a ditch. Now let's take another look at this in detail.'*

Many people think that the ability to crack jokes is a gift – which is partly true. But it's still very important to try to develop this ability in yourself to some extent.

Cracking quick jokes is a trained habit. So keep on working at it, whenever you've got five or ten minutes to spare. Remember something a tough opponent has said to you in the past that plunged you into an emotional state, and then try to bat it away with a joke. If you think the joke works, then write it down somewhere. And try it out on someone who puts you in a similar situation.

Now that we've unpacked the humour technique, have a go at the following exercise (the last of this chapter):

**Respond to the following attacks using a joke or humour, but don't forget the formula: 'joke – return to original topic'**

29. You're hiding something – is this a deliberate stunt?

30. Are you having a laugh?

31. You're too sharp for this job.

32. Do you even realise how risky your proposal is? Where's your head?

33. What you're saying is arguable.

34. You are wrong and should agree with me.

35. Think before you speak.

36. I shouldn't be having to chase you – you should be the one chasing me.

37. Why are you looking at me like that?

Now, when I said that exercise was the last in this chapter, I might have been getting ahead of myself: I've got one more up my sleeve. View it not so much as an exercise, but as training. Now that you've acquainted yourself with all seven techniques for negotiating with tough opponents and how to put these into practice, it can't do you any harm to get used to using them.

Remember how at the start of Chapter 4: Negotiating in Tough Conditions we talked about the emotional strings a tough opponent will try to pluck? I proposed an exercise where you created a table, with the provocative phrases a tough opponent might use in the left column, and the emotional string that these phrases might act upon in the right. Now, having mastered seven new techniques, let's add a third column to that table and write how you would parry that attack using three different techniques.

I recommend doing this exercise for a minimum of ten to fifteen days in a row. You'll be pleased with the results.

# 6.

# GENTLY AND DISCREETLY
# CHANGE YOUR OPPONENT'S
# POINT OF VIEW

*We should take others' interests into account,*
*for only in this way can we influence them.*

— ANDRÉ MAUROIS

H aving completed the previous exercise, you will now recall the strings a tough negotiator will do their very best to pluck. In addition, I hope that with the help of these exercises you will by now be more aware of what your most sensitive strings are. Still, I feel I ought to reiterate: psychological influence is exercised through this emotional instrument.

You might remember me mentioning this principle before: described by Robert Cialdini in his book *Influence*, it is known as the 'click' and the 'whirr'. That is to say that the person who wants to influence us will pluck our sensitive strings and in response we will begin to 'whirr', reacting in a way that the manipulator has anticipated, but that we have not.

Let's list the main strings once again:

1. Pity.
2. Fear.
3. Greed.
4. Lust.
5. A sense of duty.
6. Curiosity.
7. Vanity.

Having probed an opponent for their sensitive strings, the manipulator will use these to obtain a great deal. This chapter is entirely devoted to the principles of influence in negotiation. By knowing these principles, not only will you be better able to withstand your opponent's influence; you will be able to influence them yourselves.

As a side-note, I am often asked how ethical it is to use techniques of influence in negotiation. My attitude is ambivalent.

On the one hand, there is nothing unlawful or illegitimate about these techniques. We are all human, emotional beings (indeed, our emotional often prevails over our rational), and as such it would be foolish not to acknowledge or use this fact. The only question is, to what aim? If you are in the middle of a competitive fight and want to gain the upper hand over your opponent without causing them any damage – to simply nudge them towards a sensible decision – then using these techniques is quite ethical and legitimate.

However, if you seek to use the principles of influence to deceive or mislead others, then I would fiercely object. But, incidentally, this is why I am going to describe them in detail; so that you can both use, and resist, this influence.

I should also note that applying the principles of influence is no 100 per cent guarantee of success. However, I can say that they are a powerful weapon. The important thing is knowing how, when and with whom to use them.

Before turning to a detailed examination of these principles, I will first present to you a list of tenets based on Robert Cialdini's evidence-based principles of influence.

## Principles of psychological influence

*1. Reciprocity.* According to this principle, we are obliged to try in some way to repay the treatment we receive from others. As Niccolò Machiavelli noted, we strive more to *do* good than to *receive* it. Virtually all societies are united by a shared concept of gratitude. This feeling prompts a person to respond to politeness with politeness, a gift with another gift and a concession with a concession.

*2. Consistency.* People strive to be consistent in their words and deeds. Having given their word, they will endeavour to keep it. Striving to be consistent, a manager who has made a decision will see the matter through, even if their actions will have negative consequences. This desire to appear consistent frequently prompts us to act against our own interests.

*3. Social proof.* According to this principle, we decide what is right and what is not based on what the people around us think. There is a strong tendency to consider an action 'right' if many people act in the same way. In short, 'herd mentality'. Constructions like 'The majority of our suppliers were open to us deferring our payments' or 'Practically the whole team agreed to do some work on Saturday' are used to prompt us to make the 'right' decision.

*4. Liking.* As a rule, we are more willing to agree to the demands of those we know and like. This isn't simply a question of pleasantness; a 'similarity' factor is also involved. We like people who are like us – be that physically, psychologically or socially. Here Mowgli's principle is important: 'We be of one blood, ye and I.'[38]

*5. Authority.* We have a deep-rooted need to show *obedience to authorities.* From the cradle onwards, it is ingrained in us that we should listen to our parents; that mentors and teachers are always right. 'You should act more like your grandfather,' etc. This system of authority is highly developed, allowing for many other systems of relationships to be developed and reinforced within it.

*6. Scarcity.* Virtually everyone is, to some degree, liable to be influenced by this principle. In essence, *the value of something we view positively significantly increases if its availability decreases.* The thought of potentially missing out on something influences us much more than the thought of obtaining it.

## SHOWING YOUR OPPONENT THE BENEFIT OF YOUR PROPOSALS: A PLAY ON CONTRASTS

would like to open this section with a rather long quote from Robert Cialdini:

There is a principle in human perception, the contrast principle, that affects the way we see the difference between two things that are presented one after another. Simply put, if the second item is fairly different from the first, we will tend to see it as more different than it actually is. So if we lift a light object first and then lift a heavy object, we will estimate the second object to be heavier than if we had lifted it without first trying the light one. The contrast principle is well established in the field of psychophysics and applies to all sorts of perceptions besides weight. If we are talking to a beautiful woman at a cocktail party and are then joined by an unattractive one, the second woman will strike us as less attractive than she actually is.'[39]

Let's do a quick experiment. Go into a supermarket, take a basket and, as you pick up products, guess how much your shop is going to cost. If you predict that basket will set you back 5,000 roubles, then when you reach the checkout and see the total is 4,000 roubles you will feel good – you've saved money! However, if the total comes up as 6,000 roubles, you'll get something of a sinking feeling and think that you've overspent.

Moshe comes to the rabbi and says, 'Rabbi, life is so hard: I've got ten kids and we all live in one room, we're broke, our house is filthy to the point of reeking, the kids are always screaming and jostling each other, there are dirty nappies everywhere . . . it's terrible!'

The rabbi says to him, 'Buy a goat.'

Moshe says, 'What do you mean, a goat? Why? How will I get it into our room?'

The rabbi repeats, 'Buy a goat.'

Moshe thinks and thinks, and in the end he buys a goat. He takes it back home.

One week later he comes back to the rabbi, who asks him, 'Well, how's life?'

Moshe clasps his hands together and shouts, 'It's even worse, that goat in one room with ten people – it takes dumps everywhere, breaks everything, snatches things and butts everyone. Then the kids start riding around on it, they're even wilder now. And everything reeks . . . it's awful!'

The rabbi says, 'Sell the goat.'

Moshe is shocked. 'What? Then what did I buy it for?'

The rabbi says, 'Sell the goat.'

Moshe thinks and thinks, and in the end he sells the goat.

One week later Moshe returns to the rabbi and says, 'My God, rabbi, life is great!'

This method can be used to good effect in negotiations concerning a material benefit.

Negotiators often make the mistake of naming their lowest price early on in negotiations. Don't ever name your lowest price straight away. You have to resist this urge. We're all aware of the inexplicable pull a person feels to focus on low cost right off the bat: they think that if they name their lowest price straight away then they can avoid haggling. Nothing of the sort. No matter what price you name, even your very lowest, people will try to haggle with you. The only difference is that in this case any deal will become completely unprofitable to you.

I recently wanted to change my TV and internet plan at home. A young man came to see me and made a short presentation of the services his company could offer. After listening carefully to what he said, I thought it sounded good, so naturally I asked about the price. The price I was quoted (249 roubles) was absolutely fine for me. But then it turned out that I would have to pay additional fees for the connection unit, touchscreen controls, installation and more, quickly driving the total up to almost 550 roubles. And my desire to subscribe to this service vanished. Why? Because the contrast principle kicked into action. I had heard the lowest price – 249 roubles – first, so the price of 550 roubles simply filled me with frustration and distrust.

So what should you do in a situation like that? Bearing the principles of influence in mind, it is important to always begin with the most expensive proposal. It is rare that you will escape any attempts to haggle on price. If you are providing a product, service or package proposal, then you should reveal your most expensive offer first.

Take a lesson from the salespeople at famous car dealerships, who always present to their clients the most expensive cars first. When you refuse that option and go on to look at other models or specifications, anything even slightly cheaper will begin to look much more appealing.

On holiday in Israel, my wife and I decided to take a group tour to the Dead Sea. On the way there, our coach was scheduled to make a stop at a cosmetics shop. Of course, everyone was sceptical about this little diversion, but what can you do? Anyway, on our way there, our guide – who, by the way, was a very skilled negotiator – told us that this shop sold this incredible specialist skincare set. He did a great hard sell of this product before mentioning the price, at which point he slipped up and admitted that it was very expensive. This miracle set cost 2,500 shekels (25,000 roubles), or in other words, it was ridiculously expensive. A wave of disappointment flooded through the tour bus.

But when we reached the shop, what did we find? That precious, big-spender set – and a huge selection of other creams. All of which, when compared to the set, were very reasonably priced: 700–800 roubles. Of course, many people made purchases, because on a subconscious level the contrast principle had sprung into action.

In negotiations, it is crucial to introduce your own comparison system. But to ensure that the options you are proposing appear maximally attractive to your opponent, you need to think about what *they* will consider most beneficial – a discount described as a percentage or as a sum of money? And what should you compare it with – the previous year or the previous month?

Note: an experienced estate agent will always show prospective buyers the most expensive property first. Conversely, if the clients are renters, they will show them the worst, least attractive option first. A discount of 5 per cent might not sound like much when a big transaction is being made (1 million roubles, say), but saying that the saving is 50,000 roubles makes it immediately more compelling. The opposite is also true: when selling an item for 100,000 roubles, telling the buyer that they can save 5,000 roubles won't hold much weight, whereas a 5 per cent discount might give them the push they need to buy.

**Try to come up with a pitch that uses the contrast principle:**

You represent a gym. You are eager to sell subscriptions for 50,000 roubles per year. How can you present your proposal to the buyer in the most favourable light?

> **Try to re-write the following copy so that it uses the contrast principle:**
>
> Three patients out of ten who are treated in our clinic feel results almost immediately.

## A TRUSTY WAY OF NUDGING YOUR OPPONENT TOWARDS THE 'RIGHT' DECISION

The principle of reciprocity (or, more specifically, the principle of reciprocal concessions), when combined with the contrast principle, can be a supremely powerful force.

Encouraging a person to accept your proposal requires a thorough, considered approach. It is also important to introduce your own comparison system that builds on the principle of contrasts.

A buyer demands a 10 per cent discount from their supplier, taking a fairly tough and unflinching position to do so. Then, having ceded slightly (to 8 per cent), the principle of reciprocity and the contrast principle kick into action. Their opponent will now view this shift from 10 to 8 per cent as a concession from the buyer, and they will instinctively want to respond with a concession of their own. In reality, however, 8 per cent was the discount the buyer intended to get from the supplier from the outset.

An American is walking down a busy New York street with his friend from India. The Indian suddenly exclaims: 'I hear a cricket.'

'You must be hearing things,' the American replies, looking around at the noisy street brimming with rush-hour commuters. There are cars zipping around everywhere, builders operating heavy machinery and aeroplanes passing overhead.

'But I really can hear a cricket,' his friend insists. He then steps over to a sliver of flowerbed in front of a large building, bends down and pushes some leaves to one side. There, a cricket is indeed chirping away happily.

'I can't believe it,' his friend replies. 'Your hearing must be fantastic.'

'Oh no. It's just what you're tuned in to,' he explains.

'I find that hard to believe,' says the American.

'Here, watch this,' says the Indian, and he drops a handful of coins on to the edge of the sidewalk.

Passers-by immediately turn their heads and reach into their pockets to check whether they've lost any money.

'You see,' says the Indian, his eyes shining, 'it's just what you're tuned in to.'

So people tend to be drawn to compromise. From this, there are a few different strategies that you can employ in negotiations.

1. *Concede.* That is to say, immediately try to strike a deal on the compromise. This is a bad strategy, and experienced negotiators will avoid it. Why? Because in denying your opponent the chance to haggle with you, you are also denying them any psychological participation in the decision-making process. You are immediately imposing options on them, and in a visible way. On the whole, attempts to move straight to a compromise will lead nowhere.

2. *Choose one position and stick with it to the end*, without any give-and-take – i.e. demonstrate no leniency. This behaviour model often provokes resistance. Newton's law kicks into action – every force has an equal and opposite force. So your opponent will start to push back. And if you stand resolutely by your initial plan and insist on having things only your way, your opponent will start to resist simply to frustrate you.

3. *Assert your proposal for a long time, but when the opponent shows signs of pushing back take a slight step down* from your initial demands. This is the strategy often employed by skilled negotiators. For example: in negotiations with a potential tenant, a landlord names the rent as 100,000 roubles, and does not budge from this figure. However, when it's clear that the potential tenant is walking away, the landlord makes some sort of movement in their direction. But what is the right way of doing this? Give and take: 'OK, you've talked me into it, I'm prepared to decrease the rent to 90,000 roubles if you pay me two months' upfront.' And here, as we see, we have a compromise.

It should be noted that the latter strategy is the most widely used negotiation model in Russia. Even as far back as Soviet times, American diplomats noted that Soviet diplomats would always overstate their position and firmly stick to it, only slightly softening their demands at the very end of negotiations.

In negotiations, you can make use of a person's desire to reach a compromise, combined with the contrast principle, to put forward your demands effectively.

Let's take a look at an example:

'We would like to propose a collaboration.'

'On what terms?'

'The first delivery needs to be paid for in advance.'

'That won't work. We only work on a deferred payment basis.'

'For us it's important that the first delivery be paid for in advance.'

It's clear that these negotiations have reached a dead end. Let's try to construct a dialogue based on the aforementioned principles.

'Would you be prepared to start doing business with us?'

'Yes. But the terms would be important.'

'We propose three collaboration models.'

'What are they?'

> 'Advance payment and a 1 per cent discount off the base price.'
>
> 'We're not interested in that. We don't do advance payments.'
>
> 'The second option would be a deferred payment, but with a 2 per cent charge added to the price.'
>
> 'That won't work. We don't want to pay added charges.'
>
> 'Then I'd like to propose a compromise. Payment upon delivery, at the price we have agreed.'

In this dialogue, the seller prepares and presents their opposing number with three packaged proposals one after the other, in doing so creating their own comparison system (making use of the contrast principle) and activating the rule of compromise.

Here, to get results, you need to come up with three packaged proposals. By 'packaged', I mean proposals that bring together a number of interests into one bundle. For example, price and payment terms, pay and annual leave, etc. (By the way, when putting together such packages, the polygon of interests that we looked at in Chapter 2 will come in handy.)

The first proposal should always look as disadvantageous as possible to your opponent. The aim of the first proposal is to introduce a comparison system that we can use to activate the contrast principle.

> 'Honey, let's go fishing with the guys this weekend. Relaxation, a few beers, a tent, a campfire . . . what's a few mosquitoes and a bit of rain? It just adds to the romance!'

Similarly, the second option should also seem fairly unattractive to the opponent. The aim of this proposal is to add a new dimension to the contrast and demonstrate a desire to meet your opponent halfway.

'Well, if you don't want to go fishing, then . . . why don't we get a film, and then you can cook us dinner and we'll watch it on the TV?'

Finally, the third option is the compromise that you would like to encourage your opponent towards. Remembering our polygon of interests, the third proposal should be around the area of your stated position.

'Hey, why don't we get out of town with our friends? We can rent a house, do a barbecue . . .'

If you package these proposals up properly, you can feel confident that your opponent will more than likely plump for your third proposal.

A travel agency was selling spaces on a wine tour in the French wine regions. The price of this trip was around 180,000 roubles. When the manager of the travel agency presented this tour, everyone would listen enthusiastically to begin with, but when she came to the question of price then almost everyone would refuse. The agency came to me to ask for assistance on selling this trip. That is to say, to develop a sales technique that would help them to actually make these tours happen.

We changed their sales technique, applying the principles of influence. So, instead of costing 180,000 roubles, the first tour the agent presented cost 300,000 roubles. We artificially increased the price to its maximum. Of course, the clients were stunned. They would say the price was too high, at which point the agent would give them the reason: the flights were all business class, the hotel rooms luxury, and guests would be personally accompanied by a sommelier. The majority of clients would then say that they didn't need all of those services or bonuses. That they would be happy to fly economy class.

Then the second option would be proposed, costing 180,000 roubles. But the agent would point out that that package would involve them staying in a shared room (two to a room). And once again, the majority of potential buyers would agree to fly economy class, but not to share a room.

At which point all that remained was to propose the third option, costing 220,000 roubles. And what do you think? The majority of packages were immediately sold, even at 220,000 roubles! The tour agency was then faced with a quite different problem: they didn't have enough single rooms, and so they had to come up with another plan to sell more doubles.

By then I had done my bit: the agency solved the other problems on their own, after thanking me for the knowledge I'd shared.

Now I would like to encourage you to do a similar task, but one involving a different package that is closer to your own experience.

How to increase the price of a package costing 180,000 roubles?

Now let's talk about how we can resist plays like these. What should you do when you are pitched packaged proposals encouraging you to choose the compromise?

It is crucial that you always keep your own benefit in mind. Ask yourself the question: does the option I am being offered fall within my zone of interests, or does it contradict them?

As Eliyahu Goldratt, originator of the Theory of Constraints, states in his book *The Goal* (which I have already mentioned in this book),[40] it is important to be 'paranoid' in the good sense of the word. This really helps us to ask ourselves the questions we need to ask to stay out of troublesome situations that harm us above all. It is also worth making use of a polygon of interests. When you are being pushed into making reciprocal concessions, you need to see how much that will cost you in your own system of interests. Particularly if you are being asked to exchange a relationship for material benefits.

Not so long ago I bought a car from a dealership. As soon as I walked inside the showroom, the salespeople of course showed me the most expensive model and configuration. When they realised that they would need to show me other options, they led me straight to the cheapest models and specifications, knowing full well that those cars wouldn't cut it. After that, they suggested another option – with a mid-range configuration. On the face of it, a compromise. I was almost ready to buy.

But then I asked myself: what is my benefit? My benefit was not to overpay! And, naturally, to buy a nice, new car with the functionality that I needed. Nothing more, nothing less. So then what did I do?

Remember the predator technique? Well, 'getting closer to the deer', I asked them to show me the different packages and specifications in detail. As a result, I saw that the difference in price between the cheapest and mid-range configuration was 200,000 roubles, but that the difference in functionality was virtually non-existent: a navigation system was all that separated the two.

Now, for some people a navigation system may be so valuable as to justify an additional cost of 200,000 roubles. But for me, that's a very expensive map. So I made an informed decision and bought the car model and configuration that matched my benefit.

So let's sum up what we have seen.

If we want to encourage people towards a certain decision, we need to bundle up our proposals into packages. Ideally, there should be three. Don't forget to package your options in the following way and to present them in the correct order:

1. Unfavourable proposal. Immediately sweep this aside yourself: oh, that option isn't great for either of us.
2. The cheapest, but also less attractive option, to offer a contrast.
3. Finally, the contrast option. A compromise for both sides. Only by doing this will you achieve your benefit.

In negotiations, the best tactic is to choose a position, maintain it for a fairly long time and then make a slight stepdown while asking for a reciprocal concession from your opponent.

The antidote and resistance are one and the same – always remember your benefit, and stick to it. Keep within the polygon of interests that you have constructed and remember that you can only exchange one material value for another. So if you are being asked to exchange a material value for a non-material one, you need to know exactly what it's worth.

**Read this case and do the exercise below:**

Anna and Sergei have been married for six years. Anna has a seven-year-old daughter. The girl's biological father doesn't pay child support and isn't particularly interested in raising her. He has a new family and lives in another city. Sergei treats the girl as his own and very much wants to adopt her so that she takes his name at school. 'Head-on' negotiations with the biological father have led to nothing.

**Think about how, using the contrast principle and compromise plays, you might be able to encourage talks to progress. Prepare three packages.**

## DON'T FALL FOR A QUICK 'YES'

I would like to begin this section with an example, particularly as this, much like the preceding one, is about a car purchase.

An acquaintance of mine, an influential man who is moderately well-known in the city he lives in, decided to buy a car. He went to the main multi-brand car dealership in town and was immediately drawn to a high-end brand of off-road vehicle. The dealer showed him the car and told him the price: almost 2.5 million roubles. *A lot.*

By now he was having second thoughts: he still wanted the car, but he had no desire to spend that much money. Picking up on this, at exactly the right moment the dealer suggested another option: he could look at a slightly less well-known brand. The car was still a high-performance off-road vehicle, but it came in at a significantly lower price: 1.7 million roubles.

My acquaintance looked at the car, assessed it and decided to make the purchase. He paid an advance of 100,000 roubles, and he was told that the car he had chosen would be built to his specifications for collection in three months' time. However, two months later, the manager of the dealership called him and started apologising profusely. He asked my acquaintance to come into the dealership so that they could give him a refund. As he put it, the situation was as follows: the car factory had made a mistake, and a car was waiting for him in the dealership but with the wrong specifications. It had higher-end features and as such was more expensive, coming in at 2.6 million roubles.

So what do you think: how does this story end? In an incredibly banal way: my friend bought the less prestigious car brand for 2.4 million roubles.

How often do we get hit below the belt by a quick change in terms? This happens everywhere. Everywhere.

My wife and I were recently looking to buy a plot of land near Moscow. We were told the price and agreed to it. However, the next day, when we arrived at the office to pay the deposit, the sales manager told us that the price had gone up since the previous day. When we asked why we hadn't been told, she was all surprise: what do you mean you haven't been told?

Upon which she started to blame the associate we had dealt with the day before, who had taken us through all the details of the deal. The new manager tried to persuade us that her colleague had had no authority to withhold that information and that she would be punished. Now, by this point even we were starting to feel somewhat responsible for the situation; that we should agree to the new terms for the associate's sake as much as anything else. This is what I term a 'blow below the belt' in negotiations.

It often happens that, instead of a 'no', a well-trained negotiator will open the negotiation game with a quick 'yes': yes, I am prepared to work with you; yes, I am prepared to buy from you. Do you remember my story about Dimitriy – my sales colleague we met in Chapter 3? This is the blow that buyer had so cunningly prepared for him. In that story, we were able to ward off that powerful, painful blow. But this isn't always the case.

The play we're about to look at is based on a few principles of influence, namely reciprocity, social proof, consistency and scarcity. And, as is so often the case, a stratagem lies at its core: 'Invite your enemy onto the roof, then remove the ladder.'

**'Invite your enemy onto the roof, then remove the ladder'**

The enemy is urged on with the promise of a large benefit and easy success, only to discover that all is not as it seems. This benefit should seem very achievable, otherwise it won't entice.

The 'blow below the belt' play works in the following way: once someone has reached an agreement with their opponent and taken that step towards collaboration, they will be filled with positive feelings and expectations that cause them to expose themselves. This continues until the cunning negotiator is sure that enough parties are implicated – the negotiator, managers, friends – to make backing out difficult. And that all of these parties – even those who are only indirectly affected – already have great expectations.

Then, all of a sudden, an obstacle will appear that completely changes the course of the deal: competitors have come along with better offers, for example, or it emerges that the supplier can't supply the item the buyer needs because the original offer was only applicable when paired with another, redundant item. But by this point, pulling out would be difficult. After all, plans have already been finalised, and that particular buy or sale has already been incorporated into those plans.

In the case of my acquaintance, in his own mind he had already started driving his new car, and he had already celebrated the buy with his friends. When it became clear that there were new terms, he, wanting to be consistent, started to sell the new car to himself: 'Well, it's still an excellent car, and the specs are great.'

Company A holds a tendering process to select an equipment supplier. They receive a range of proposals and, on the results of all of the indicators measured, they choose company B. Their proposal meets company A's needs most fully – including their technical specification – and it is also the most attractive proposal, price-wise. When the agreement is signed, company B starts to claim there has been some sort of misunderstanding: the price proposed was for basic equipment. Meeting the exact technical specifications will require additional charges for a number of items. By this point, however, the results of the tender have already been announced, so the buyer at company A is faced with a choice: they can either cancel the results of the deal-making process (which would be labour-intensive and reflect badly on them) or convince their own management that these additional charges are necessary. They decide to go with the latter.

To this, many of you will probably say that this sort of deal will be a one-off: there's no way the buyer would go near a company that had pulled a move like that again. Of course, that may be true. But my experience has told me time and time again that we keep falling for the same bait; we are pulled, as though by magnetism, to step on one and the same rake.

Once upon a time there were three mice who wanted to become hedgehogs, so that they would have spines to defend themselves against fox attacks. They went to ask the owl for advice. The owl said: 'Travel to the west of the forest and find the tallest oak. Next to the fattest root of this oak, you will see a green cucumber. If you eat it all, then you may be able to grow spines. If you start to feel a prickling in your mouth as you eat, don't be afraid. That simply means that your spines are growing.'

So the mice went to the west of the forest and found the tallest oak and its fattest root. Lo and behold, there was a cucumber standing there, a big, spiny one. The mice each took one bite, then two, and their mouths started to prickle. But when they remembered what the owl had told them, they sank their teeth into the cucumber with added gusto, painful though it was.

And so was born a legend about three little mice who ate an entire cactus because they thought it would give them spines.

However, a word of warning: be very careful when employing this method. If your opponent knows how to react to it, how to put up a block (i.e. how to block a 'blow beneath the belt'), then their response will be both strong and very painful. If you are preparing to use this play, it needs to be planned down to a tee and packaged up both beautifully and flawlessly. Another one of the Chinese stratagems can aid you in this.

**'Point at the mulberry but curse the locust'**

This stratagem is all about hiding the true offenders or the true cause of an event by pointing at false or imaginary culprits. It is the stratagem of the buck-passer, and it is what the car dealer in the example above does. He elegantly passes the buck towards the factory, in doing so hiding the true cause.

**Resistance**

When someone suddenly changes their terms, you should ask yourself a very important question: **if I knew what I now know about this deal or agreement, would I have agreed to these terms?**

Remember that a desire for consistency is one of the methods of psychological influence. As Robert Cialdini points out: a desire to appear consistent often causes us to act against our own interests. Or, as American philosopher and public figure Ralph Waldo Emerson put it even more sharply: 'A foolish consistency is the hobgoblin of little minds.'

My wife and I asked ourselves the same question about the plot of land. Would we have bought it had we known it would cost 5 per cent more? Yes, we would have. In that instance, we assessed the situation and grasped what was going on, and we decided to take the negotiation process further. Of course, I tried to haggle some better terms, but I knew that the decision we had made was a conscious, informed one.

But to the bigger question. Let's get back to my example about my acquaintance's car. When he decided to buy his off-road car for 1.7 million roubles, would he have made the same decision had he known it might cost 2.6 million roubles? If you are unsure, then don't shoot from the hip. Instead, pause.

I'm not suggesting that you necessarily pull out of a decision you've already made. I'm simply saying that you should think it through again: do I really need a car right now? And do I really need all the specs that this one has? In short, you need to weigh up the pros and the cons. And it is very important to ask yourself this question not in the now, the point at which you are today, but to take all of your knowledge with you and cast your mind back to the point at which you made the original decision. If you ask yourself whether something is favourable once the change in terms has occurred, then you are more likely to tell yourself it is, because the rule of consistency will have come into force. You will even start to persuade yourself.

If you have been caught by a blow below the belt, then take your time and keep your emotions in check. You need to tell yourself to stop and make a clear-headed assessment of the situation. Take another look at your polygon of interests. If the new offer is still favourable, then move forwards in the negotiation process. But if not, then go back to the drawing board and look at everything afresh: the goal posts have changed, which calls for more negotiations, plain and simple. Otherwise you will simply keep on letting blows past you.

Every time someone tries to deliver a blow below the belt – i.e. suddenly change the terms – in negotiations you are participating in, it is then your job to reassess the situation and cast your mind back. In fact, casting your mind back can be a very useful thing in general. It will immediately give you answers to a wide range of questions, from whether to hire a candidate to whether to work for a company or enter into collaboration.

Casting your mind back to the initial point of agreement is crucial. If you are certain that your interests aren't being met, then it is very important to go back to the drawing board with negotiations based on this new information.

## THE ANSWER TO THE HARDEST QUESTION

What makes you better than the rest of the pack? What is your USP? How are you different to your competitors? These questions have the power to stump many negotiators. They will begin to search for assets that the opposing side will then easily dismiss.

'You have talked me through everything, but I still have one question: what makes you unique?'

'Well, you know, we have a unique personalised approach.'

'Which is?'

'You will be guided by your own dedicated expert.'

'Well, that's not unique.'

By attempting to prove how unique and reliable you are, your arguments, no matter how weighty, will activate a resistance in the opponent. And for every one of your arguments you will hear a very ponderous 'So what?'

A Georgian and an Armenian are sitting on a train. Suddenly the Georgian says: 'Georgians are better than Armenians!'

The Armenian says nothing. The Georgian repeats: 'Georgians are better than Armenians!'

Still the Armenian says nothing. The Georgian repeats again: 'D'you hear me? Georgians are better than Armenians!'

The Armenian can no longer contain himself. 'In what way?'

The Georgian: *'Way better!'*

This is where the principles of social proof and authority can help you to come out on top.

If you have to talk about yourself, then use some sort of intermediary where possible. Your opponent will trust information coming from a third (disinterested) party far more than from an interested one.

'You have talked me through everything, but I still have one question: what makes you unique?'

'You know, if I start singing my own praises it probably won't hold much weight. Better that I let my actions and achievements speak for themselves. Or, where necessary, reviews from our clients. By the way, you're welcome to contact Mr/Ms XX personally to hear how they found working with us.'

## TO CATCH SOMETHING FIRST LET IT GO

One of the questions I am most often asked at workshops and consultations is how to win the opponent's interest. How to get them to even look at a proposal. Reader, I can assure you that if you build a dialogue along the following template, you will be unlikely to see any results.

'I wonder if you might take a look at my proposal?'

'OK. Leave it with me.'

'When should I expect a response?'

'I don't know. If we're interested, I'll call you.'

'I hope to hear from you soon.'

I'm not sure what a proposal would need to contain to make someone interested in looking at it after that damp squib of an introduction. The same goes for commercial proposals sent via email. Most people don't even read them.

This next principle of influence will allow you to significantly increase the responses you get to proposals, emails and cold calls.

This move is based on the following Chinese story:

Representatives of the northern state, Wei, persuaded the leader of the southwestern barbarian tribes, Meng Huo, to lead a rebellion against Wei's main rival, Shu Han. Zhuge Liang, regent of Shu Han, marched against Meng Huo, but his goal was not simply to seize the territory; it was to win over the hearts of the southern rebels themselves. Zhuge Liang defeated Meng Huo's allies one by one, but instead of putting the rebels to death, he magnanimously released them. And when he captured Meng Huo himself, he simply released him. He knew that he would never win the hearts of the people by putting the rebels to death – that would only happen if the rebels themselves submitted.

Meng Huo once again gathered his forces against Zhuge Liang, but he was captured once again and – you guessed it – released. This happened seven times. Zhuge Liang even pardoned Meng Huo when the rebel's own fellow-fighters tied him up and personally delivered him to the regent.

> In the end, upon his seventh capture, Meng Huo showed remorse for his actions and swore eternal obedience to Zhuge Liang. After that, peace reigned in the southern frontiers of the Shu Han state.

The play we're about to look at builds on a few principles of influence: reciprocity, social proof and scarcity. It goes as follows.

We give our opponent the opportunity to refuse us. We give them the very thing they have always had: the opportunity to say 'no'. According to Jim Camp's definition, negotiation is the human effort to bring about agreements between two or more parties with all parties having the right to veto. At the core of this play lies yet another Chinese stratagem: 'To catch something first let it go.'

You see, it is very easy for people to reject us, or to fail to read or get the point of our proposal. They are not burdened by any responsibility for their rejection; they can simply say, 'we aren't interested', 'no good', etc.

Interestingly, it's quite a different matter when we reinforce someone's responsibility for their decision. We put the ball into their court and say: 'your turn'. This is when the real decision-making takes place. It means that they have to make a conscious decision, with all of the consequences that entails. That's less simple to do.

A workshop participant told me the following story:

One day, my ten-year-old son came home from school and said: 'I'm not going to school tomorrow, it's boring.'

I tried to talk him around, but he wasn't having any of it. Then I decided to try a different tack: 'Ivan, it's your decision. If you don't want to go, then don't.'

The morning after, Ivan didn't go to school. He wandered around our apartment in silence for a whole hour, then he got his things and ran off to class. That evening he came up to me and said: 'Mum, I'm not going to skip school again.'

This example is a very clear indication of the importance of letting people make their own decisions. When going into negotiations, you need to know that the opponent has every right to refuse you. But if we make a show of giving them that right, we are a) demonstrating our assertive position and b) encouraging them to take a closer look at what we have to offer.

For months Roman, a young entrepreneur, had been unable to break off his burdensome ties with a business partner. I should note that this business partner was much older and more experienced than him; the sort of man who was active in Russia in the nineties and who had a shady and complicated past. Whenever Roman tried to cut the final ties and dump this extra weight he was carrying, his 'partner' would deal him a blow that would take them right back to square one.

Roman came to me. We analysed the situation closely, and this is what we found. In their conversations, the nineties man kept using phrases like: 'Well, if you've made a firm decision to part ways, then go on, but remember – it's your decision'; 'Look, if you want to stop working together just tell me, no problem'; or 'If you think our company doesn't need me, then just say.' Every time he heard a phrase like these, Roman would make a complete turnaround.

His partner was exploiting psychological mechanisms that forced Roman to take full responsibility for himself, something he found hard to do. There is only one thing for this. You need to learn to pursue your interests and say no. One fine day, that's exactly what Roman did. He cut the tie and strode forward, to great success.

Using the following phrases in negotiations will significantly increase your effectiveness.

**In emails/letters:**

'Of course, I hope that we will be able to do business together, but should you decide that this isn't of interest to you then please let me know. I would really value any feedback that you are able to give on whether my proposal is of interest to you or not.'

'I don't know whether this proposal is of interest to you, but if not please let me know. If, however, you would like to find out more, I would be happy to answer any further questions.'

'Of course, you have every right to turn down this proposal. Please let me know in either eventuality.'

**Face to face:**

'Do feel free to give me a "no". Really.'

'It's your decision, and I'll respect it either way. Just let me know.'

**On the phone:**

'I'd like to make you a very interesting offer. Though, of course, I don't know if it'll be of interest to you or not. Let's just say that if you aren't interested, then you can hang up, and I won't bother you again. Is that fair?'

'I don't want to waste your time. So if you aren't interested in what you hear, then just say "no" and we'll end the conversation. OK?'

> ⚠️
>
> By giving your opponent the opportunity to reject you, you aren't actually giving them anything at all. They already have that. But by doing so, you take a slight step back, which makes them intuitively try to get closer to you. If people want to lumber you with a sense of added responsibility by giving you a right that you already have, then simply weigh up the pros and cons of their offer carefully and, if it goes against your interests, give them a firm 'no'.

## DO I NEED TO RECIPROCATE GIFTS?

Some two thousand years ago, the great Roman poet Virgil wrote in *The Aeneid*: 'Beware of Greeks bearing gifts.' Well, in short, in two thousand years little has changed!

Negotiators will often encourage reciprocity. You scratch my back and I'll scratch yours. Of course, reciprocity is natural. Machiavelli noted that people don't like to feel indebted; that when people do us some kind of service or favour, we try to respond in kind to avoid that very feeling of indebtedness. But many negotiators exploit this desire of ours to not feel 'indebted'. So they will give us some small service or insignificant gift, in the hope of drawing some quite significant pampering from us during the negotiation process in return.

This is a good point to bring in another quote from Robert Cialdini:

. . . [T]he power of the reciprocity rule is such that by first doing us a favor, strange, disliked, or unwelcome others can enhance the chance that we will comply with one of their requests. However, there is another aspect of the rule, besides its power, that allows this phenomenon to occur. Another person can trigger a feeling of indebtedness by doing us an uninvited favor.

Recall that the rule only states that we should provide to others the kind of actions they have provided us; it does not require us to have asked for what we have received in order to feel obligated to repay.[41]

The regional manager of a major trading company earned a reputation of being a real go-getter, capable of winning over even the most unaccommodating buyer. He had a secret technique for this. Instead of forcing his way in and talking himself up to potential partners, at the beginning of the business relationship – during the first meeting or by post – he would give his opponent a very interesting gift.

Now, when I say interesting, read: valuable. Sparing no expense, he would commission quite pricey market research on the development tendencies in the branch in which his opponents operated. Then he would go through the reports and pull out the key findings.

This gift would be so valuable to the buyer that he would of course be in their good books immediately.

There is no doubt that the majority of negotiators apply this rule and (rather 'altruistically') give gifts to their opponents. However, their gifts can also blow up in their face.

## What basic errors do negotiators make?

*Error 1: giving a gift and expecting an immediate reaction*
Once, just before the winter holidays, I happened to be in the sales department of a trade organisation. The sales executives were busily gathering gifts and talking among themselves, the gist of which was: 'I'll wish them happy holidays and then I'll immediately try to get a supply agreement out of them.'

This, reader, is completely the wrong approach. If you give gifts in this way, you immediately reveal the self-interest that lies behind them. The opponent will see right through it. Better to simply wish them happy holidays and leave it at that. Then, in the New Year, you can come back to talk business.

*Error 2: insincerity*
When we give gifts in a contrived and insincere way, we turn the process into a charade and our opponent against us. If you must provide a service or give a gift, then at least try to do it sincerely.

*Error 3: giving to the wrong people*
One company's sales department decided to distribute gifts to mark 23 February, Defender of the Fatherland Day. They divided these gifts into categories based on the recipient: VIP, business and normal. As you might expect, the VIP gift was intended for owners and directors, business was for heads of departments,

and normal was for your average associates. After the gifts were distributed, the managers went to see their business partners in person. It soon became clear that many of these people had started to cool off towards the company: they were buying less, paying less regularly, and more. What had happened?

What had happened was that, because the company's managers had no direct access to the upper management of their partner companies, they had given the VIP and business gifts to their opposite numbers to pass on up the ranks. But their opposite numbers, being only human, are not immune to resentment or a sense of being belittled. Of course, when they saw that they had been given the 'worse' gift, they had felt cheated. And you can guess what comes after that: retaliation.

In a situation where you would like to single people out, then it's best to give the gift personally. If you aren't able to do so, then give identical gifts or one large shared gift.

*Error 4: thinking about themselves*

When preparing a service or gift, negotiators often fall into the trap of thinking of what they, rather than the recipient, would appreciate. In general, many negotiation errors come down to this same lack of understanding of what is valuable to their opponent.

My wife and I decided to get a juicer. So we went to a home appliance store, where a young man approached us and asked if we needed any assistance. We gladly accepted his offer. He started to tell us about all of the models in stock, listing each one's revolutions per minute. We listened to this fascinating little tale and promptly went home empty-handed. Why? Because we still didn't know what we needed: we had no idea what that information meant in practical terms. A month later, while in the USA, we went into a similar store. With a quick look at the display cases, everything was clear. The price labels didn't say anything about revolutions. Instead, in normal, everyday English they said: two glasses of juice per minute, three glasses of juice, etc.

It is important to remember that value varies from person to person. But it can always be calculated by the equation: value = benefits − cost (equation courtesy of Neil Rackham). To return to our example of the go-getting regional manager who had success with gifts, he was clearly thinking, first and foremost, about what his opponent would find valuable. And it paid off.

If you would like to give someone a gift and force them into some back-scratching, then follow these rules:

1. Show sincerity and expect nothing in return.

2. If you are giving gifts to more than one person in an organisation, the gifts should be of equal value. If you would like to single out one individual, then it is best to do so personally to prevent others from finding out.

3. When choosing a gift, work from your opponent's benefits, not your own. For many people a smile, compliment or attention are more valuable than an expensive material object.

**Resistance**

To prevent yourself from becoming a victim of 'professional' gift-makers who know how to use this play, remember these two rules:

1. Always consider what might be expected in return from someone who 'altruistically' offers you an enticing service or gives you a gift. Sincere gifts require no response, and you do not need to feel 'indebted'. If someone has given you a gift and is demanding something in return, then they were deliberately manipulating you. This also requires no response.

2. Do not accept a gift if you are certain you will have to settle your tab later.

In his *Memories*, Andrei Gromyko offers a clear illustration of how to behave in such situations:

Shortly after the signing, I had a meeting with Foreign Minister Scheel, who in a free moment told me: 'You know, Mr Gromyko, we've had an addition to the family. We have a daughter and we're going to call her Andrea, in your honour. My wife and I agreed on this.'

I must agree I was somewhat embarrassed, so I decided to make a joke of it: 'That is a decision, you realise, that remains entirely the responsibility of yourself and your wife. In this you have 100 per cent sovereignty. And I am very happy to hear the news.'[42]

But what should you do if you have accepted a gift from an opponent and realise there's a possibility they might start hinting at reciprocity? In such a situation it would be only natural to feel a certain unease, and a desire to repay them. In such matters it's best to get pre-emptive – even prior to negotiations.

I once had a similar experience in Armenia. I arrived in the country to a very warm welcome, but I knew that any gifts would have to be met with gifts in kind, so I was very careful about how I behaved. Still, there was one situation I wasn't able to get out of. On my way back to the airport, one of the partners held out to me a big basket full of the most beautiful, mouth-watering fruits, with the words: 'For your wife and child.' I had no choice but to take the gift and go. Back in Moscow, I thought long and hard about what to do, and made the decision to send a gift back to them. Because I was born in Belarus, I bought a souvenir bottle of Belovezhskaya Pushcha, a Belorussian liqueur, and sent it to them as a gift. With this, I relieved myself of the responsibility of being 'indebted'.

# 7.

# BUILDING A
# NEGOTIATION ROADMAP

*If one does not know to which port
one is sailing, no wind is favourable.*

— LUCIUS ANNAEUS SENECA

The attentive reader turning the pages of this book will have already noted that all of my recommendations on negotiating feature the concept of preparation in one way or another. There is an opinion – one which I readily subscribe to – that success in negotiations is 70 per cent preparation. No matter how many techniques we know for deflecting blows, it is far better to be prepared so that we can dodge the blows completely.

There are many negotiation preparation techniques out there. Over my eighteen years of experience, I have studied a great many books on negotiation and countless techniques, and I have accumulated a healthy library ranging from bestsellers to specialist tomes on diplomacy, the secret service and more. I have tried to bring together all of the knowledge I have gleaned from these various books, articles, dissertations, videos and films and distil these through my and my students' many years of experience to create a method that I will present below.

The preparation technique that I would like to present is not about scripting negotiation scenarios. Instead, it is based on the ability to draw yourself a roadmap (a very popular term of late).

The main thing that distinguishes a script from a map is that when a negotiator has a pre-scripted scenario in mind – even one with a number of possible offshoots and variants – it is unlikely to correspond exactly to that of the opponent. This lack of overlap can lead to aggression on both sides: after all, both will try to stick to their script.

A roadmap, on the other hand, has a starting point and a destination, which can be reached by a variety of routes – even adopting the opposing side's script. With a roadmap we are able at any time to evaluate where we are, what is going on, and what our next step should be.

Remember: negotiations cannot be won or lost; it is only possible to determine exactly where you are and what your next steps need to be.

Another advantage of a roadmap is that we are prepared to hear a 'no' from our opponent and make a clear-headed assessment of whether we really are on the right track, moving in the right direction. Should anything happen, we are also in a better position to change our route or even our destination. This allows us to be flexible in negotiations without bending over backwards.

A roadmap takes into account both the strategy and the tactics of the negotiation process. Before moving on to the algorithm for building this map, I would like to unpack these concepts of tactics and strategy.

## WHAT GOVERNS NEGOTIATIONS? THE ROLE OF STRATEGY AND TACTICS

In order to dig down into strategy and tactics in the context of negotiation, I would like to draw your attention to an example from 1905 (recounted in a lecture given by Yuri Dubinin, a Soviet-era diplomat).

Peace talks were underway between Russia and Japan, in which Russia was represented by its then prime minister, Sergei Witte, and Japan by its minister of foreign affairs, Baron Komura. At one point the Japanese negotiator lost his temper and snapped at Witte as he negotiated: 'You're behaving as though Russia won the war, not Japan.' He appeared to have good grounds for his indignation: Russia had suffered a crushing defeat both on land and at sea, losing its entire Far Eastern army and sea fleet and leaving Siberia defenceless. Yet Witte was not only rejecting the Japanese demands; he was making his own. This was a defiant move, one too much even for Japanese restraint. [43]

Let's jump forwards a bit to see how these negotiations ended. Japan was forced to give up many of its claims. It even had to withdraw from the northern part of Sakhalin Island, which it had occupied.

What weapon did Witte employ? The ability to keep to his strategy and employ smart tactical thinking in the negotiation process. Incidentally, this ability was duly rewarded: Witte was given the title of count. The failures of the head of Japanese diplomacy had a similar, albeit converse, bearing on his fortunes: the results of his negotiations, which were codified in the Treaty of Portsmouth, were perceived as a humiliation by the Japanese public. There was a major citywide riot in Tokyo, and Komura was forced to leave his post.

But what were the levers that Witte used to overcome his opponent? How was this even possible given Russia's clear defeat, let alone the fact that negotiations were taking place in the USA, with mediator President Theodore Roosevelt constantly favouring the Japanese side? In his memoirs, Witte shares his version of these events.

Before setting off for these negotiations, Witte developed his own tactics. First, they were to give no indication that Russia wanted peace. They were to behave in such a way as to give the impression that the Emperor had agreed to these peace talks (which were a US initiative) only because practically every country wanted to see an end to the war, but that Russia itself was indifferent. As an observation, we have already seen this play of 'strength in indifference' in Chapter 3.

Second, they were to behave as befits a representative of Russia – that is to say, a great empire that had run into some minor unpleasantness. And Russia was, at the time, a great global empire – that much is evident from Japan's long-held pride in its victory over a superpower, and this may have held some bearing on its decision, thirty-five years later, to attack a different superpower. Again, we are already familiar with this play – that of being the 'host'.

Third, given the enormous role of the press in America, Witte planned to make sure he was always obliging and avail-able to all of its members, so as to win them over. In addition, in order to appeal to the hard-working, ordinary American public, he was to behave in a frank, democratic manner, without airs or conceit. And, given the perceived sway of the Jewish population in New York and the American press, to spurn any hostility towards them. This, as Witte writes, also tallied with his own personal views on the 'Jewish question'.

With these, the strategic aim of defending Russia's interests in these talks was furnished with tactical tools that, if used correctly, were fully capable of seeing that aim realised.

Here is how the events progressed from there. It makes sense to present this extract directly from Witte's own memoirs:

As we approached New York we were met by a virtual flotilla, filled with people who wanted to greet and see Russia's chief plenipotentiary. Among these people were several American journalists, who came aboard. To them I expressed my joy at being in a country that had always been on the most friendly terms with Russia. From that moment on, until my departure from the country, I was under the eyes of newspapermen.

In Portsmouth, possibly by design, I was given two small rooms, one with windows so placed that everything I did in that room could be seen . . .

From the day of my arrival in America the curious were constantly taking pictures of me with their Kodaks. Everywhere I went I was asked, particularly by women, to let them take my picture, to give them my autograph, or both. In addition, I received constant requests from all over the country for my autograph. I fulfilled all such requests in a friendly spirit. And when I travelled by train I made it a point at the end of a trip to seek out the engineer, thank him, and shake his hand. The first time I did this all the newspapers expressed approval and made much of this. This was so because Americans had come to expect ambassadors and other prominent personages from Europe to be standoffish, yet here was a man who, despite the fact that he was the chief plenipotentiary of the Emperor of Russia, the chairman of the Committee of Ministers, state secretary of His Majesty, behaved unaffectedly, being more accessible than the very democratic President Roosevelt, who makes good use of his democratic simplicity.

In short, I acted an equal among equals. This meant that I had to bear the heavy burden of constantly playing a role, one that helped me gain public support . . . As a result of my efforts to influence the powerful American press, public opinion gradually shifted away from Komura and his country toward me and my country.[44]

The shift in public opinion is demonstrated by the telegram that Roosevelt sent to Japan toward the end of the negotiations, in which he stated that under no circumstances would Witte agree to such Japanese demands as the one calling for an indemnity and that if the negotiations should fail because of Japanese obduracy, the American public would be less sympathetic toward Japan than it had been.

As for the Japanese, they, as Witte remarked, helped to turn public opinion in Russia's favour. 'Although [Komura] had been educated in America, he not only shunned the press but also made it difficult for the press to learn about the course of the negotiations. I took advantage of his coolness towards the press.'[45]

And what was the result? President Roosevelt 'was fearful that American public opinion was moving toward Russia and would turn against him and the Japanese if negotiations were broken off',[46] and so he sent a telegram to the Japanese emperor advising them to agree to the proposals of the Russian negotiator, which he did.

As is visible from these extracts, Witte demonstrated the effectiveness of a well-thought-through and in many senses groundbreaking style of negotiation, based on recognition of the influence of public opinion. This played a decisive role in his success. He proved – convincingly – that the art of negotiation (diplomacy) is no less important to the success of a state than the art of war; a skilful negotiator no less important than a skilful commander.

So what are tactics and strategy in negotiation? Strategy is the answer to questions of *what to do*, whereas tactics are the answer to questions of *how to do it*. As you enter the negotiation process, knowing your answers to these questions is key.

But that's not enough. As Igor Mann has rightly noted, you also have to get in there and do it. In the West, tactics are positioned as the maidservant of strategy. The Russian mentality, on the other hand, holds these two as sisters that should go hand in hand.

## BUILDING A ROADMAP AND WHAT YOU WILL NEED

Before going into negotiations, you need to ask yourself seven key questions. Once you have answered them, you can be sure that you will have a clear and understandable roadmap ready to hand. Some relate to strategy and begin with question words like 'what' and 'where'; others reveal tactics and begin with the word 'how'.

A word of warning:. these questions must be answered in order. It can often be tempting to jump on ahead, but I advise against this: if your answer to just one question is unclear (or absent), then your map will not be up to the job and you will run the risk of getting lost.

Use the following procedure: move on to the next question only once you have a clear answer that you can recount for the previous one.

Once again, I would like to focus your attention on this point: in negotiations, that Napoleonic principle so loved by us Russians – 'We'll engage in battle, and then we'll see' – does not work. When you enter into combat, you put your benefit at risk. It is far better to work from Sun Tzu's principle: 'The victorious strategist only seeks battle after the victory has been won.'[47] Or, as we say in Russia: 'Measure your cloth seven times before you cut.' Incidentally, this is also the reason why I have devised seven questions: our very own magnificent seven.

## Seven key questions for preparation

1. What do I have at the start of my journey?
2. Where do I want to get?
3. Is it realistic?
4. How will I progress towards this goal?
5. What will I be happy with?
6. What will I do if I get a 'yes'?
7. What will I do if I get a 'no'?

*Question 1: What do I have at the start of my journey?*
This question isn't as naive as it might at first seem. Of course, more often than not people are adamant they know where they are. Which is true, to some extent: even if we're lost in a forest, we will know which forest we're lost in, the bus stop we got off at on the hunt for wild mushrooms, the turns we made along the way and, finally, which way is north and which way south. But by the same token, if we're lost, we will also have some difficulty setting out the rest of our route.

When you start negotiations, you are setting out on a specific route that you will need to travel from start to finish while gathering those very mushrooms you have set out in search of. To prevent yourself from getting lost, you need to know the entire route; you also need to have a very clear idea of where your path started. This is particularly important in mountaineering, for example, where, in order to conquer the summit safely, you need to pinpoint the start of your route. Experienced mountaineers will know that your chances of success are directly dependent on your choice of starting point.

'Would you tell me, please, which way I ought to go from here?'

'That depends a good deal on where you want to get to,' said the Cat.

'I don't much care where—' said Alice.

'Then it doesn't matter which way you go,' said the Cat.

'—so long as I get somewhere,' Alice added as an explanation.

'Oh, you're sure to do that,' said the Cat, 'if you only walk long enough.'[48]

Picture negotiations as a steam engine: in order for them to get anywhere, they need to have a departure point. The better idea the engine driver – i.e. negotiator – has of the starting point, the more likely they will choose the optimal route to the destination.

It is very important to know our departure point. The clearer the picture you have of this point, the more likely it is that you will be able to get where you want to go.

Let's say someone really wants to get rich. They are completely obsessed. Eventually they make some random steps towards this goal (going to a casino, for example). This is a huge mistake. The first thing they should have done is pinpoint their starting point: calculate their savings and debts – in short, figure out their starting balance. This would have helped them to calculate the level of risk they were willing to accept to achieve their goal.

In negotiations, this point also has huge strategic importance. It is important to know your initial position, the starting point of the negotiation process. And it is even more important to create an adequate forecast of the negotiation results (we already looked at forecasting in Chapters 1 and 3).

To answer the question *What do I have at the start of my journey?* you will need a fairly broad, in-depth picture of the current situation. In other words, you need to gather and analyse information.

Our modern world is a virtual torrent of information, and it is crucial to be able to navigate our way through this flow clearly. This includes being able to tell fact from opinion and gather significant data that could have an impact on the negotiation process. It is also important to scrutinise information and find the details that might at first glance seem insignificant, but that, if not given enough attention, could play a decisive role in the negotiation process in future.

Information that is easily assimilated and remains exactly where it can have the biggest impact rarely falls into the hands of those who are looking for it, as we know from the history of diplomacy. So it is essential to learn how to extract essential information directly in negotiations from the people who are close to the source of that information.

Some 2,500 years ago, the famous Chinese commander Sun Tzu said: 'Spies are a most important element in war, because on them depends an army's ability to move.'[49] It is hard to dispute that whoever governs the information governs the situation. In line with this, gathering information, drawing conclusions, creating an accurate picture of the present as a pre-requisite for further action – all of this work is, in itself, an integral part of the negotiation process. If this work is completed successfully, then the result can offer us the right landmarks so that we can pick out our next steps or even predict their success.

In 1940, Sergei Vinogradov was named envoy to the Soviet Embassy in Turkey, the second most senior position behind that of ambassador. Soon, after becoming the charge d'affairs in Ankara, he was entrusted with the role of ambassador. He was then thirty-three years of age.

The post of our representative in Turkey was – and still is – regarded as one of great responsibility. But its importance grew even more after Nazi Germany declared war on the Soviet Union. Turkey did not participate in the war, but it did, however, play host to embassies of the USSR and other Allied states, as well as the German embassy. A great deal depended on the side that Turkey, a country of great military and strategic importance, would take in the war. For the USSR, if Turkey were to enter the war alongside Germany, it would spell immense danger. Turkey's intentions, however, remained a mystery, so the USSR kept a major contingent of troops at its border with the country.

Now, our case in point took place in the autumn of 1942, when fighting along the Soviet–German border was at its peak. The eyes of the entire world were turned on Stalingrad. There, a battle was unfolding on which much rested, not only for the situation on the battlefields of the Great Patriotic War, but for the entire world. In the south, Hitler's tank armada was tearing towards Baku, in order to open up a route for Germany to Iran and the Middle East. Hitler's army had taken a pass along the Main Caucasian Ridge, and as a result only a narrow strip of Transcaucasia separated the Front from the USSR's border with Turkey.

At that moment, Vinogradov was urgently summoned to Moscow, with no explanation as to why. And at this period in time, simply getting to Moscow was no small task. Anyway, as soon as his flight arrived, Vinogradov rushed to the Ministry of Foreign Affairs, but he found no explanation there either. Everyone he spoke to simply shrugged and pointed at the sky indicating that the summons had come from the very top. Vinogradov was put up in a hotel and told to wait for a signal. That signal came in the middle of the night, in the form of a short message: 'A car's coming for you.' I will recount the following, trying to retain the flavour of Vinogradov's own narration.

The car took Vinogradov to Stalin's so-called 'nearer dacha' in Kuntsevo, on the outskirts of Moscow. When he entered, Vinogradov found himself face to face with Stalin himself. He was sitting at the dinner table with a few members of the Politburo. Vinogradov greeted them, to which Stalin replied: 'Give the ambassador some vodka.'

A glass of vodka was poured.

'Drink, ambassador.'

Vinogradov did as he was told, naturally drinking to Stalin's health.

'Tell me, ambassador, is Turkey going to wage war against us or not?'

'No, Comrade Stalin, they are not.'

'Give the ambassador some more vodka.'

Another glass was poured.

'Drink, ambassador.'

He drank, repeating his toast.

'So is Turkey going to wage war against us or not?'

'They are not, Comrade Stalin.'

'Good, ambassador. Go back to Ankara. But remember the commitment you have made here.'

Vinogradov returned to Ankara. Stalin gave the order to remove the Soviet troops positioned defensively along its Turkish border. These troops were relocated to Stalingrad as reinforcements, at a decisive moment in that battle of great historical importance.

And thus, from the recollections of Yuri Dubinin, professor at the Moscow State Institute of International Relations and author of the book *Masterstvo Peregovorov* ('A Mastery of Negotiation'):

'When I heard this story, it made a great impression on me. I asked: "Sergei Alexandrovich, what made you take such a position with Stalin? Had you heard any whispers from your Turkish counterparts? Or did you have some other information?"

'"No," he replied, "nothing of the sort. Turkey's representatives were very correct in their dealings with me: I played the odd game of chess with the Minister of Foreign Affairs, but they never shared any state secrets with me. I didn't have any top-secret information. But I was absolutely sure of the answer I gave Stalin." He then explained: "That was the conclusion I had drawn from all of my observations of the mood in Turkey and its leadership. At times that can hold more weight than familiarity with some *top-secret materials*."'[50]

We can make a distinction between two ways of obtaining information.

In the first, the information is precise, to the point, and clearly formulated when it reaches us.

In the second, we have to deduce it. The information has not been clearly formulated, so we must draw our own conclusions from a huge flow of information. This is the way demonstrated by Vinogradov's example. It builds on the following rule: in negotiations, there are no such things as trivial details or small points. It is very important to take everything into account.

At times it might seem that the less-than-top-quality items we supplied to a buyer last year are already ancient history. When in reality our opponent remembers them clearly; in fact, they are still at the top of their mind.

When analysing information, it is also important to bank on intuition.

Let's turn once more to our great negotiator, Andrei Gromyko. He was Minister of Foreign Affairs for a superpower for some twenty-eight years, so everything that he did has been put under great scrutiny. However, not one false move on his part has been found.

He wrote that intuition is extremely important in any diplomatic act. Nothing can be more important than keeping a picture of events in your mind. But nothing can be more important than the ability to forecast what is coming next, either.

Since ancient times, people have taken an interest in intuition, that indistinct feeling that comes up spontaneously based on our previous experience, suggesting what the right decision might be.

Logical decisions are the product of extrapolation, facts and intuition. John F. Kennedy was an outstanding president. He said: 'I've got thousands of advisers who can tell me how to build a pyramid, but not one who can tell me whether I need to build one or not.'

Life presented him with the opportunity to demonstrate this in practice. After the USSR had sent Gagarin into space, America, for all its achievements, was stunned – as was the rest of the world. While everyone chattered about Soviet superfuels and educational excellence, Kennedy created an expert commission to find out what should be done to prevent the USA from losing its standing in the world. To the question of whether an American lunar mission was necessary, the commission's response was no.

Kennedy, however, came to the opposite conclusion. That was his intellectual feat, his innovation. Do you remember the first words said by Neil Armstrong when he took his first step onto the surface of the moon? 'One small step for man, one giant leap for mankind.'[51]

So, the results of our information-gathering and analytical activity should be a clear and exact image of what is going on in the negotiation process at that specific moment.

**Information on the opponent**

What do they want?

What will their arguments be?

What is important to them?

What do they know about me?

What do they think of me?

What are their interests?

What is their key issue?

What problem do they want to fix?

This includes everything we know about the opponent and everything they know about us. Our strengths and – perhaps more importantly – our weaknesses. Our competitive edges and our non-business advantages (connections, contacts, patronage).

**What is important to know**

Where they work (company, department)

What they like

Who their friends are

Where they live (country, city)

I have already written that the best way to prevent blows is to know where your own weak spots are. You can have no doubt that if you have previously made a mistake in your dealings with your client, they will remind you of it at the most inopportune moment. But if you are prepared for this, the blow will miss you and you will be protected. Any minus, when acknowledged and not feared, can easily be turned into a plus.

'Rabinovich, yesterday after you left we realised that all of our silver spoons have gone!'

'Hey, I didn't take them, I'm a decent guy!'

'But they're gone! So don't come back!'

The next day, Rabinovich gets another call.

'Rabinovich, we found the spoons!'

'So does that mean I can come over again?'

'Oh no, we might have found the spoons, but that doesn't get you off the hook!'

I was once invited to talks with a major company. These negotiations were organised by the HR director, who had taken a liking to me. She immediately warned me that for many years they had been going to one and the same coach for their training needs, and that everyone felt very loyal to him. I was supposed to be negotiating directly with the CEO – let's call him Ivan Sergeyevich.

I asked myself the question: what am I starting these negotiations with? As is to be expected, my plus immediately came to mind: I had the HR director on my side. But there was also a minus: loyalty to the coach they were already working with.

Here's how the negotiations went:

**HR:** Ivan Sergeyevich, meet Igor – the trainer I've been telling you so much about.

**IS:** Yes, Igor, nice to meet you. But I should say we already run negotiation and sales training, and that our guys trust the coach we have. I doubt anyone would be able to offer anything new.

**Me:** Well, thank you both for inviting me to this meeting. Now, if I have understood you correctly, then no matter what I tell you – no matter how colourful the picture I draw of my methods, no matter what reviews I show – it won't mean anything?

**IS:** *Slightly dumbfounded, nods.*

**Me:** And that's because you're used to your current coach, which is great. But did I also catch a hint that you might be interested in trying something new and different?

**IS:** Yes.

**Me:** Then I'd propose you come to a session at our management (negotiation) duelling club and see for yourself. The sessions run every Thursday. Then you can decide for yourself whether my training style and techniques would suit your company or not.

> After attending the club, the company commissioned a series of workshops from me.

This example shows that when you know what your weak points are, you have a chance to turn the situation in your favour.

**List the moves that I used in these negotiations**

If six months ago you supplied defective goods, made a late payment or didn't send that letter you'd promised, then remember this. Prepare, acknowledge your shortcomings and move on. Don't be afraid to put your minuses on the negotiating table. Mistakes that are acknowledged and discussed stay in the past; the only thing that comes with you into the present is the fact that you know how to acknowledge and correct these mistakes. This fosters trust.

Before negotiating, it can be useful to fill out a table like the following:

| My pluses | My minuses |
|---|---|
|  |  |
|  |  |
|  |  |

*Question 2: Where do I want to get?*
In other words: what do you want to get out of these specific negotiations? What is your goal?

Picture yourself driving along the autobahn. It's a long, monotonous road, the radio is playing and your thoughts begin to drift. Soon, without noticing, you start coasting slightly to one side. But as you hit the hard shoulder, your car starts to shake as though it's on a washboard. Suddenly your mind comes back to your lane and you get back into it.

A goal works the same way. When it's there, it makes it very difficult for you to be drawn out of your lane. And even if that does happen, you will get back into the right lane when you remember your target destination.

During divorce proceedings:

'For over twenty years this woman has been throwing whatever she can at me!'

'You sure held out for a long time!'

'Well, it's only lately she's been getting her shots on target.'

Before we move on to look at how to set goals, let's discuss what the results of negotiations can be. Basically, all results can be divided into two groups:

1. Progress made: some sort of concrete step forward has been made, the next meeting has been scheduled, terms have been discussed, etc.

2. Your guess is as good as mine: no concrete step has been made. You had a nice chat, etc.

When you have a goal, you approach it step by step without deceiving yourself or justifying unsuccessful meetings that had a snowball's chance in hell of coming off.

**Some rules for setting goals**

Goals should be within the realm of your control. Closing a deal is not a goal.

It is important to have a clear understanding of what rests on you and what doesn't. Remember Bulgakov's words: 'to rule one must have a precise plan worked out for some reasonable period ahead. Allow me to enquire how man can control his own affairs when he is not only incapable of compiling a plan for some laughably short term, such as, say, a thousand years, but cannot even predict what will happen to him tomorrow?'[52]

A Roman dignitary decides he wants to learn how to ride a chariot and signs up for a course with a famous trainer. At the end of the course, he wants to test out his new-found skills, so he challenges his trainer to a race. He is desperate to win. They race three times, and the dignitary loses every time.

'You didn't teach me everything you know!' he complains to his teacher.

'What are you saying? Of course I did!' the trainer replies. 'I taught you everything. You just couldn't use the knowledge I gave you in the right way. In a race, what's most important is for your horse to feel at ease while running. That's why it needs to be harnessed properly, and during the race you have to control it so that it holds the right direction, at the right speed. But when I was overtaking you, you were doing everything in your power to outpace me. And when you were in front, you were thinking about keeping me behind you. By putting all of your energy into keeping ahead of me at all times, you forgot your main task – to control your own horse. That, and that alone, is why you lost.'[53]

Here, the dignitary does everything in his power to overtake everyone. In his obsession with results, he forgets that you can only control what lies within your power. In the same way, during the negotiation process we should focus on what we can control – manage our sense of 'need', ask questions, use all of our skills and knowledge, and gather and analyse as much information as possible. When we do this, the results will come organically.

I'm a keen table tennis player, and I practise with guys who are technically much better at the sport than me – losing to them, of course. But when playing against masters, what matters is how much you lose by. I've noticed that, while playing, if I'm only thinking about how to win that point, then I get tight and lose it. But if I focus on hitting the shot correctly, then the ball always goes where I intend it to, and then (if I'm lucky!) the master might just miss. When I play this way, I win more points.

We can't control the results. We can only guide the process by controlling our behaviour and the way we demonstrate our knowledge and skills.

**A false goal:**

Win a lucrative contract.

**The right way to formulate a goal:**

Find collaboration opportunities. Show our opponents the potential benefits of a partnership with us.

With these provisions in mind, try to formulate the goal that your company would like to reach in negotiations, based on the desired results as given on the next page.

**Formulate your goals based on what you can control**

Secure an order worth 1 million roubles

Get compensation for a defective delivery

Repay a debt

Increase the price by 16 per cent

Your goal should be formulated like a resolution. As renowned American entrepreneur, writer and teacher Robert Kiyosaki wrote: 'goals have to be clear, simple and in writing. If they are not in writing and reviewed daily, they are not really goals. They are wishes.'[54]

Goals shouldn't contain any hidden meaning. If you want to find out whether your proposal has been accepted or not then it is best to formulate your goal in the following way: 'Find out whether my opponents accepted my proposal or not.'

If the goal is formulated as: 'Get a response to my proposal', then chances are you will get a fuzzy, unclear response along the lines of 'your guess is as good as mine'. The former option gives you a chance of getting a concrete response and working with it.

By the way, creating a table to evaluate your negotiations can be a very good idea.

| Opponent (fill in prior to meeting) | Planned result (fill in prior to negotiations) | Actual result (fill in after negotiations) | Actions that led to the actual result |
|---|---|---|---|
|  |  |  |  |
|  |  |  |  |
|  |  |  |  |

In creating a table like this, you will be able to see the plays and steps that lead to positive results, and the ones that don't. You can then take this analysis and use it to adjust future plans accordingly.

### Question 3: Is it realistic?

This question has to be asked before you move forwards. If your answer is 'yes, it's completely achievable and realistic', then move on to question four. But if you feel that your goal may be difficult or even impossible to achieve then I would recommend going back to question two and finding a different answer.

Your goal should be formulated as clearly as possible. Before setting your goal, make a thorough, realistic assessment of your own capabilities. Unrealisable expectations are the product of over-ambitious goals, which will inevitably create difficulties during negotiations. It is also worth refraining from excessive detail, as this can inhibit flexibility.

In general, negotiators tend to set ambitious goals. For example: 'Get a contract with this holding company' or 'Get a pay rise'. Now, setting ambitious goals can be a very good thing. But to prevent yourself from straying from your intended path, you should follow Sun Tzu's rule: 'Doing a hundred *li* in order to wrest an advantage, the leaders of [your] divisions will fall into the hands of the enemy.'[55] In other words, don't over-exert yourself: break your large goal down into smaller ones.

Achieving one big goal is much easier and more manageable if you break it down. These smaller goals will become check-points in kind, from where you will be able to evaluate your negotiating position and decide what to do next.

**Goal:** Get the other side to agree to offer compensation. Agree on the sum and payment deadlines for this.

This is a rather bulky goal, which will be difficult for you to reach in one move. So let's put up some checkpoints that will bring you, step by step, closer to your goal:

**Step 1:** Get the other side to agree that the goods they delivered were faulty.

**Step 2:** Get the fact of the damage put down in writing.

**Step 3:** Discuss possible solutions.

**Step 4:** Finalise the agreement.

As you can see, each one of these steps gives scope for different approaches or moves. Where necessary, you can even take a step backwards.

> Setting achievable goals before – and not after – negotiations is crucial. Note where your checkpoints are, so that you will be able to take in and weigh up your next steps.

> Break down the following goal into steps: **Get the opponent to agree to do business with the entire holding.**
>
> Step 1
>
> Step 2
>
> Step 3

*Question 4: How will I progress towards this goal?*
This question is one of tactics. It is important to have a clear idea of the toolkit you have at your disposal for negotiations, and how you are going to use your negotiation 'weapon' (which methods, rules of influence, etc.). However, most important are the questions of when, how and with whom you plan to negotiate, as well as how to approach your opponent.

Let's take a look at these four components in more detail.

## Who to negotiate with

In negotiations, it is very important to know *who* you will be speaking to and *who* will be participating in the decision-making process. Why this distinction? Because the person doing the negotiating isn't always the person calling the shots.

Imagine holding long and drawn-out talks that demand a huge amount of time and effort, only to find out that you weren't talking to the person who makes (or even influences) the final decision. This is why it is important to think about and find out who might actually be calling the shots – or who is in a position to influence the outcome of negotiations – before getting into the process.

As regards the number of participants, we can categorise negotiations as either complex or simple. If the decision is being made by one person, then these will tend to be 'simple' negotiations. One and the same person negotiates, assesses the situation and makes the decision. They can do it right there on the spot.

However, when the negotiations involve a team or complex organisational structure, the decision-making process will be much more convoluted, potentially requiring multiple approvals.

In situations like these, the negotiator's job is to understand who affects the final decision, and how.

A family – a mother, father, daughter, son, grandmother and grandfather – have come to a holiday compound to view a few cottages they are interested in buying. While the grown-ups view the houses and study the terms of the deal, the kids play outside with their dog. The grown-ups get stuck on one of the terms, and go through its wording with a fine-tooth comb. Eventually, it looks as though they have decided to go for it. At that point, the enthusiastic adults step out to the kids and ask: 'Kids, do you like it?' The kids scowl and say no. And what do the parents do? They shrug and walk away without making the buy.

This is why when holding complex team negotiations it is very important to work with all of the participants involved; to find the key to that secret chamber, as it were, and figure out who inside there influences the decisions and how.

I'd like to pause for a moment on a very common misconception among negotiators: the higher the position their opponent holds, the more likely that this person is the decision-maker. This is often not the case. I mean, surely a manager can delegate their authority to their subordinate? Or the reverse: even if a CEO is negotiating personally, they might be doing so only nominally – the decision may in fact fall to a board of shareholders or owner, i.e. those not participating in the negotiations at all.

In such a way, to assume that you already know everything about the decision-making process in your opponent's company is one of the biggest blows you can deal yourself.

Straight after graduating, I went to work for a distribution network. I was hired as lead software engineer, but my boss soon realised software engineering wasn't really my forte, so instead he would assign me the administrative and housekeeping tasks, which I was happy to do.

We moved into a new building in the centre of town. It, apparently, had some mice. The boss called me into his office and told me to get a cat. So Mashka the cat also moved in, and her main task was mouse-catching. But, much to the boss's dismay, it was a job she did only sporadically – generally when the boss was already beside himself with rage at the mouse situation.

Soon, a clear pattern emerged: whenever Mashka caught a mouse and pushed it under the door to the boss's office, you could count on him very soon being in an excellent mood. So then everyone would run to him with their holiday requests, applications for a pay rise, hints at bonuses . . . and he would sign off every one.

As you can see here, the person making the decisions was our boss, but the one who was influencing these decisions was Mashka the cat – or, I suppose, the poor mouse that fell into her clutches.

Yes, this is a humorous story, but think about it: how many cats do we dismiss in the negotiation process?

To maintain an accurate worldview you must continue to analyse a situation as it develops, questioning who else might have an interest in the decisions being made. How do you go about this? Well, you need to investigate and analyse:

• The vertical hierarchy in the organisation: who reports to whom and how.

• The horizontal hierarchy: who stands beside whom, who is an influencer, who is the *éminence grise* wielding the power behind the throne.

| Position | Which decision-making processes do they participate in? What sway do they hold (max. or min.)? | Who can they influence in their organisation? | Who can influence them? |
|---|---|---|---|
| | | | |
| | | | |
| | | | |
| | | | |
| | | | |

Let's take a domestic example. Every evening, a father tries in vain to calm down his three unruly children. First he tries to explain why they need to stop running around the apartment, and when that doesn't work he tries to appeal to his oldest son, knowing how important the hierarchy of age is to kids. But it all comes to nothing. With every passing day, the kids are getting more and more out of control.

Then one day he gets home early from work only to find his wife and mother roaring with laughter as the kids chase each other around the apartment, literally smashing the place to pieces. Clearly the father hasn't been negotiating with the right people. He should have realised that two people who have a strong influence on the decision-making process in this situation are the kids' mother and grandmother. They are the ones he should have been negotiating with.

He explains his position to the two women. Once they lose the encouragement of their mother and grandmother, the kids start to listen to their father.

During the negotiation process, don't let the obvious vertical hierarchy be the only thing to guide you. You need to do some reconnaissance work; seek out the person standing in the wings, so to say. The search for the *éminence grise* is an important task for any negotiator, regardless of the level at which the negotiations are taking place.

In organisations, a role of no small importance in the decision-making process is played by the so-called 'blocker'. In this context, a 'blocker' is someone who doesn't let us into the decision-making process. Many authors recommend sidestepping this blocker. However, I would recommend learning to work with them, collaborating with rather than contending against them.

Remember: blockers are not the enemy. All being well, blockers can be potential sources of information, but you need to learn how to use them. To do this, it is important to understand why they aren't letting you access the decision-maker.

There can be a few reasons for this. When we figure out which one it is, the key we need to the secret chamber is suddenly much easier to find.

Here are some of the main reasons:

- A desire to feel important or respected.
- A desire to appear important, competent, or higher in rank than they really are.
- This is part of their job; they are simply following orders.
- Loyalty to a competitor.

The chief executive of a pharmacy chain travels to meet with a regional official (the deputy mayor of a small city) to discuss plans for the chain's expansion in that city. There are other pharmacy chains operating in the region, and these are popular among residents. Prior to this meeting, the chief executive has only met this official once; all previous discussions have been held directly with the mayor. The chief executive walks into the official's office and says: 'Nikolai Ivanovich, your boss has told me to get a couple of papers signed.' To which the official says: 'Well, if he told you, then sign them yourself.'

It's clear what the main reason for this block is. Feeling on top of the situation and all-too-aware of the nominal influence the deputy mayor has, the chief executive has strutted into his office and demanded the signature as though the decision has already been made. Of course this would grate on his opponent. Clearly, after this start, negotiations aren't going to be easy. People always like to feel more important than they really are.

If someone is lacking in status, give them a chance to feel more important. Never show your negative attitude to a blocker. The blocker can potentially be a good source of information. But in order to win this information, you need to first show them some attention, and second, ask questions like:

- Of course I'll show you our proposal, but could you please let me know who else might have an interest in seeing this decision made?
- Is there anyone who might be offended if they don't get to see the proposal?
- Could I ask you to take a look and let me know what you think, or if there is anyone else I should invite for a final discussion?

If you come to a blocker with a 'request for advice' when resolving an issue, then it is highly likely that they will help you and become an ally. But if you start to make demands and show a negative attitude, then the wall standing before you will only grow taller.

The following advice on overcoming a blocker comes from a woman who spent fifteen years as an executive assistant. Blocking was part of her job description.

There is a way to get information to the person it needs to reach, and it's pretty simple. Send your business proposal by email — as any sales clerk will have heard secretaries say hundreds of times. Some coaches recommend avoiding that at all costs, but that's missing a trick.

You see, it's all about how you position yourself. A business proposal has every chance of ending up on an executive's desk if it looks like an official letter rather than an advertising brochure: for example, if it has a reference number, a date, a company letterhead and comes with what looks like a real signature. These sorts of documents get registered by the secretary and will normally reach the director for perusal, and in turn they will pass it on with a decision or instruction, which in most cases the secretary will be able to update you on.

And you will then be able to work closely with whoever 'inherits' your letter, using all of your professional secrets.

**Remember:** blockers aren't the enemy. If you're lucky, they can become an ally. It's also worth remembering that people who like to feel important love any sign of attention. Here, the reciprocity principle works very well. In days gone by, officials' briefcases used to be littered with little chocolates and perfume samples. Why have we forgotten this nowadays? Why do we think that approaching the person – giving them a compliment or a small gift – is ineffective? In reality, the opposite is true – it's very effective. If we gain a blocker's favour, we can find out a lot, and they might just come to help us, too.

For example, we might unexpectedly learn that although formally and legally decisions are made by the CEO, whatever Ella Leopoldovna, the CEO's deputy for general affairs, writes in her resolution is what gets actioned. This sort of information is priceless!

If you want to get around the blocker, I can recommend a few different techniques, but the important thing to remember is that blockers are people, too. The following story, told by an active participant on my Facebook group (facebook.com/ryzov. igor) serves to confirm this fact.

For the longest time we couldn't get to the person we needed in the organisation. To all appearances, he was the key decision-maker in the process. And nothing we tried worked: there was always a stern secretary standing in our way, and neither compliments, nor flowers, nor persuasion helped us to get past her. So, almost out of despair, we decided on an unconventional approach. We made her a gift: a set of new business cards with her details and the words: IVAN IVANYCH SPECIALIST. The secretary was in fits of giggles about it all morning, and Ivan Ivanych himself asked for twenty of them, 'to show the boys at the bathhouse', as he put it. In the end not only did they hear us out, we closed a really good deal.

⚠️

In large organisations, decisions are never made by one person alone. They will always be influenced by someone. Which is why you need to approach decision-making as a process.

All of this might give the impression that the search for decision-makers is some sort of reconnaissance work. And in essence, it is. That is exactly how you should approach it. This work has to be done scrupulously and – not least – with a hint of imagination.

## When to negotiate

Timing is important. The time of day and day of the week that negotiations take place on are both significant. At times, when arriving for negotiations, a negotiator may be met with inexplicable aggression from their opponent that they can't understand.

Anger is an internal state caused by certain physical and physiological processes in the body.

Anger is mainly caused by:

1. Tiredness.

2. Unfulfilled expectations: a plan that doesn't work out.

So, if we are looking for productive negotiations where there's going to be no anger dumped at our feet, we need to choose our time wisely.

Picture this. A person gets up early on a Monday morning and on the way to work their car gets clipped. Or, as soon as they arrive at work, their boss gives them a lecture about something. And then you appear at 9.15 for negotiations as planned. What do you think – how are they going to behave? You guessed it: nothing good is going to come of it. These negotiations are going to turn into an emotional tussle. All of the negativity that person has faced that morning will be dumped on you, with not-very-constructive results.

Or else picture this. This person has been working all day and they're tired and have a lot of pent-up aggression. And then you show up. You can rest assured they will not be taking that aggression home with them: they will throw it onto you. At best you'll leave with nothing; at worst having lost your benefit.

So the conclusion is simple: the best time for negotiating is either in the morning between 10.00 and 12.00, or immediately after lunch. On a physiological level, it is hard for a person to be in an aggressive state after lunch (after eating, the blood flows to the stomach, whereas in the presence of aggression it flows to the face and hands).

For the record, the best lawyers in America try to schedule hearings for complicated court cases immediately after lunch. Statistically speaking, sentences are much softer after lunch.

This is why timing is so important. The same goes for the days of the week. Monday and Friday are the worst days on which to negotiate.

## How to negotiate

A participant in one of my online courses sent me the following conundrum: 'I arrived for negotiations alone and there were eight people there. What should I have done? I felt trapped.'

These problems come up when we neglect crucial components of the negotiation process, such as establishing negotiation guidelines and a negotiation agenda.

Negotiation guidelines are often viewed as a purely technical issue, a question of protocol at best. This comes with the assumption that agreeing on the substance of the matter trumps all other considerations. Formalities, after all, are just that: formalities. In other words, we once again see the Napoleonic principle of 'We'll engage in battle, and then we'll see' kick into action.

Drafting negotiation guidelines is, in fact, an important part of the negotiation process, no less so than the discussion of the matter at hand. It's worth noting that, without a mutual understanding of the guidelines for negotiation, it could be impossible to even discuss the fundamental problems, let alone agree on them.

Guidelines are often split into several parts.

*Participants*

This is an important consideration. It is very important to understand who will be participating on either side prior to the negotiations commencing.

*Scheduling*

The time the negotiations will take must be planned and agreed with all participants. If this isn't discussed from the very beginning, then unexpected demands or requests for postponements could arise, or the negotiation process could be interrupted at a particularly inopportune moment for one of the sides.

*Place and time*

Experience shows that negotiations on one aspect alone – location – can turn out to be fairly complicated in and of themselves. It is a widely held opinion that it is better to negotiate on your own territory. This is undoubtedly true. First, it means that it is always possible for you to quickly consult with the individuals on your side who will be affected by issues under discussion. Second, you can do other business in parallel. Third, you are surrounded by your own 'home comforts', while the opponent is psychologically aware that they are speaking to the 'host' and not vice versa. Not to mention the economics of finances and time.

There are, however, pluses to negotiating on an away ground. It gives you the opportunity to focus on the negotiations alone, whereas there will undoubtedly be more distractions on your home turf. You will always be able to withhold information, falling back on the pretext that you don't have it on you at the time. You also stand a higher chance of meeting directly with managers. Finally, the time spent on organisational issues and financial expenses always falls to the 'host'.

## How to approach opponents

Every negotiator must face one very pressing question: how to approach the opponent – as an enemy or an ally? I often hear sales managers talking about 'beating the buyer' or 'storming the fortress'. Thoughts like these translate into relationships. If we approach negotiations like war, then war is precisely what awaits. For this reason, I am categorically against calling my colleagues in sales and purchasing departments 'warriors' or 'soldiers'. In Russia we have an old saying: 'As you name a boat, so it will sail.'

A young couple buy an apartment. The wife takes their documents to the registration office to register herself and her husband at that address, but it can't be processed: she needs to provide another certificate. Back at home, she rants to her husband about what happened. He is outraged: 'How dare they not register us!' he exclaims. 'This is my apartment! I'll sort this out.' What is the outcome? It takes them three months to register at their address, which, in Russia, is quite a big deal. The young man comes to me and asks me: 'How do I beat this bitch?' Those are his exact words.

I'm sure between us we could come up with millions of similar stories. What has this woman actually done to him? Or what does the security guard who refuses us entry to a building without ID do to us? They are either just doing their job, or trying to feel important. In the former case they deserve our respect, and in the latter, our pity. As Confucius said: treat others with kindness. It's worth emphasising: not condescension, but kindness – an understanding that we're people, not robots. We all have our flaws. None of us are perfect.

Of course, there is an important difference between combat and collaboration. But targeted combat and all-out war are very different things.

**Always treat your opponent with respect**

In any situation, no matter what happens, the recipe for success is respect for the opponent. Respect is the only way.

If you negotiate in a negative mindset, you can be sure that your opponent will intuitively pick up on this negative. Which is why the only right decision is to take a respectful approach to the opponent. Maximum respect inspires mutual respect.

*Question 5: What will I be happy with?*
Knowing the answer to this question is crucial. If we don't, then we aren't fighting for a benefit, but for our ambitions. We have already seen what negotiations like these lead to.

Prior to negotiations, don't forget to construct a polygon of interests, which you will remember from Chapter 2. Draw your red line. Figure out your desired position, and from there find your stated one. When constructing this polygon, I recommend that you let your past experience guide you, but don't forget any future concerns. With a polygon of interests, you will always be able to determine whether what you are being offered (or what you are offering) is in your interest or not. Having this polygon does not, however, necessarily mean being the first to put forward a proposal, nor that you are under any obligation to offer much. It simply means being prepared to fight for a benefit, not for your ambitions. And to negotiate from a rational standpoint.

As a reminder, here's a summary of how to build a polygon of interests:

**Step 1.** Single out what your interests are. List every possible interest. Don't get stuck on your key interest; consider what else might be exciting.

**Step 2.** Monetise the faces of the polygon. Every face (or interest) is given a value in relation to the main interest. You need to know what is worth what; how much you are prepared to pay for a relationship or for favour.

**Step 3.** Construct a polygon that represents your desired position. Give values to all of the faces based on your key interest.

**Step 4.** Create a new polygon of interests based on your red line. Don't forget to ensure the overall perimeter of the polygon always remains the same. As your position gets closer to the red line, the total sum of your interests should not change.

**Step 5.** Now figure out your stated position. This is the position that you declare at the start of the negotiation process.

*Question 6: What will I do if I get a 'yes'?*
This question may sound completely redundant: a 'yes' means we've reached our goal! What else is there to do but crack out the champagne?

However, if you don't look for the right answer to this question when creating your negotiation roadmap, your success will be short-lived, or a one-time-only event. It may even leave question marks over the matter at hand, in spite of the positive response.

It's hard to predict how the results of these negotiations will be codified, or how this positive response might be formulated (for example, there may be different interpretations on certain points), etc. For this reason, the answer to this question needs to be quite meaty.

First, your answer should anticipate any possible versions of the proposed solution that either give rise to different interpretations or that don't completely resolve the problem. You will need to prepare a route for further work from each of these versions.

Second, a positive response to the issue under discussion is a good reason to take even the most cursory of glances into the near future: what else can you get from the opponent now that you appear to have established a relationship? Might there be a way of aligning your shared interests even further, in view of your mutual benefit?

Third, a positive response in these negotiations will inevitably have some sort of impact on your competitors' position, and they will naturally start to respond in some way. What might this response be? What will you need to do to prevent it from affecting your relationship with your new partner?

Once you have noted all of these possible consequences of this positive response on your roadmap, you need to anticipate what action you will need to take to avert any negative consequences and to reinforce the likelihood of a positive outcome. Then you will need to plan a 'start-up phase' for these actions that you can begin to implement directly from these negotiations.

*Question 7: What will I do if I get a 'no'?*
A participant in one of my online courses came to me for advice.

'Igor, I'm in a tricky situation. When I was let go from my previous job, they promised to pay me all of the bonuses I'd earned up to that point. This was quite a nice amount: 3 million roubles. But there weren't any documents to confirm what the firm owed me. For ten months, my former manager paid me 200,000 roubles per month. But he hasn't paid me anything for three months now, and he's giving me the runaround. I want to go to see him and ask him point-blank.'

It's a good thing this young man paused and asked for advice before unsheathing his sabre. You can only fire out questions point-blank, make threats or, indeed, hold complex negotiations on one condition: you truly know what you will do if you don't reach an agreement, if none of the options proposed and discussed fall within your polygon of interests, or if you're being pushed below your red line. People generally neglect to answer this question, leading them to either make concessions or get more aggressive at the negotiating table.

I asked the young man what he would do if his former manager told him to take a hike? He simply shrugged.

Amidst the turbulence of the mid-nineties in Russia, gas pistols and firearms started to gain in popularity. Getting a licence for these weapons was easy, and I, like many others, took a one-day course and got the licence. I was still choosing which pistol to buy when one evening I got into a very interesting conversation with my neighbour on the stairwell. My neighbour, Edward Viktorovich Dachevskiy, is an Air Force colonel who has gone through fire and water in his life. He asked me: 'Igor, would you be able to shoot someone?' This question daunted me. Stalling, I gave him a mumbled response. 'Remember: only get out a weapon if you're truly prepared to use it. Otherwise it'll get turned on you.'

Having answers to questions six and seven is crucial. These are what will help you to gain that 'strength in indifference' we saw in Chapters 2 and 3. Together, these questions help us to understand what to do going forward, turning singular negotiations into a negotiation process.

Remember: negotiations cannot be won or lost. But what you can – and must – do is know where you currently are in the negotiation process, and what steps you need to take next.

Now, back to our 'golden parachute' example. After speaking to me, the young man kept his pause going all day. Then he called me and said: 'I know what I'm going to do. I'm simply going to give him the right to decide whether to pay me or not. And I'll give him time to think; I won't call him. I've already got more than I initially wanted, anyway.' He was paid the full amount within a week.

Whenever people come to me saying things like: 'Our buyer's refusing to accept our price increase, we want to write them a letter threatening to break contract to scare them,' or 'My husband isn't paying me enough attention, so I'm going to tell him I'm moving out,' I ask them: are you really prepared to go through with those things? What would you do if your opponent accepted your threat?

THE KREMLIN SCHOOL OF NEGOTIATION

A husband and wife have had a fight. The wife has gone to stay with her mother and tells her: 'Mum, when I left I heard a bang. You don't think he's shot himself, do you?'

Her mother replies: 'He's probably cracked open the champagne!'

Knowing the answers to these questions isn't a substitute for ideas or a withdrawal from a fight for the benefit. Quite the opposite: it's a clear pursuit of your interests and the knowledge that, below the red line, you will proceed in a considered manner rather than rushing headlong into anything.

**General conclusion**

To create an up-to-date negotiation roadmap, you should ask yourself the following questions:

1. What do I have at the start of my journey?

2. Where do I want to get?

3. Is it realistic?

4. How will I progress towards this goal?

5. What will I be happy with?

6. What will I do if I get a 'yes'?

7. What will I do if I get a 'no'?

Everyone designs their negotiation roadmap in their own way. I recommend doing it in the form of a table like this:

**Roadmap**

| Question 1:<br>What do I have at the start of my journey? | Who will be taking part in the negotiations? | |
| | What strengthens my position? | |
| | What weakens my position? | |
| | Other important information | |
| Question 2:<br>Where do I want to get? | Goal | |
| Question 3:<br>Is it realistic? | | |
| Question 4:<br>How will I progress towards this goal? | Step 1 | |
| | Step 2 | |
| | Step 3 | |
| | Step 4 | |
| Question 5:<br>What will I be happy with?<br>Range of possible options | Desired position | |
| | Red line | |
| | Stated position | |
| What next? | Question 6:<br>What will I do if I get a 'yes'? | |
| | Question 7:<br>What will I do if I get a 'no'? | |

Read 'A not-so-funny story'. **Make a roadmap for Alexei** using the table overleaf as he faces a conversation with the foreman. I recommend reading the case a few times over, as this will help you to get to the heart of the matter and pick out important details.

### A not-so-funny story

Alexei is renovating his apartment. The works are nearing their completion. Alexei and his wife have bought new doors to install throughout the apartment, at a cost of 90,000 roubles.

When purchasing these doors, the salesperson offered Andrei and his wife a number of services, including having a specialist come out to take measurements to ensure accuracy. This service cost 2,000 roubles. Wanting to avoid any unpleasant surprises, Alexei paid for this service. However, he turned down the door installation service, as the foreman responsible for apartment renovations, Mikhail, had said he could do this for no extra cost. This was a bonus: the salon would have charged another 15,000 roubles for this service.

Alexei lets Mikhail know that the measurements are going to be taken two days in advance. Putting his trust in the two professionals, Alexei feels relaxed and looks forward to seeing the new doors.

One month later the doors arrive. Alexei is there to receive them and signs all of the necessary paperwork. For technical reasons, however, they only start installing the doors three weeks after they are delivered. When doing so, they realise that the doorways are all ten centimetres taller than the doors, leaving an unsightly gaping hole above each. Lowering the doorways would be problematic: literally days prior, the walls were decorated with an expensive Venetian stucco effect. Even if they were to attempt to recreate this on the lowered doorway sections, it would not be completely consistent with the rest of the walls, drawing extra attention to the patch job.

When Alexei complains, the specialist who took the measurements says that he had raised the issue of the doorways being taller than the maximum height of doors with a workman onsite (Mikhail hadn't been in the apartment at the time). He had written the information down on a piece of paper, which he had also given to the workman. Mikhail says that he was never given the paper, and that the doors aren't his responsibility. He was under the impression that the measurements were being taken because the doors would be made to measure.

Alexei is appalled. He was expecting his 'turnkey' apartment to be ready the following week.

Mikhail offers to fill the gaps with spruce branches in an 'artistic' way, giving the apartment a 'festive' feel all year round.

Alexei isn't blessed with Mikhail's subtle artistic flair, so he tells him he won't make the remaining payments until he does whatever needs to be done. The remaining figure due is 120,000 roubles. Mikhail responds that in that case he won't give Alexei his air-conditioning equipment (of a value of 200,000 roubles), which he took away to his dacha along with the documents and receipts to prevent – god forbid! – something from happening to them during the renovation.

You can send your versions of this roadmap to me at igor@ryzov.ru, and I'll make sure to get back to you to discuss where your routes would have got our heroes.


## SOME PERSONAL IMPRESSIONS ON NEGOTIATING WITH INTERNATIONAL OPPONENTS

While the below can be seen as a bit stereotypical, there's a reason the stereotypes developed, and these general observations may be useful.


### France

The French have a heightened sense of independence. Indeed, this could also be viewed as a heightened sense of superiority; a sense of self-sufficiency. After all, they have mountains, sea, good cheese, meat, wine . . . why would they travel?

The French react with great distaste to English or German being used as a working language in negotiations; this hurts their national pride. Practically all French people prefer to hold negotiations in their own language. Of course, if necessary they will find someone who knows English or even Russian, but a bitter aftertaste of having to do so will remain.

In their negotiation opponents, the French value a knowledge of their traditions, history, geography and culture. They are flattered by an interest in their country. Connections and relationships are very important. They don't like risk, instead preferring to weigh up and carefully consider any decisions.

It is quite natural for a French negotiator to interrupt their opponent, openly declare their position and defend it fiercely.

They speak courteously and politely, joke and smile, but this doesn't mean they avoid conflict – no: they are quite happy to confront issues head-on.

Agreements made in negotiations with a French party should be concrete, concise and very precise in their formulation. Sentences are short: between ten and fifteen words.

The French elect to make important decisions not only around the negotiation table, but also around the lunch table. In France, a business lunch is an opportunity for informal discussion. The French love food and are experts in it. For them, lunch is not only a means of satisfying physical needs, it's a sort of ritual. But when it comes to food and wine, their sense of superiority is even greater than in matters linguistic. If you are with a French person, you would be advised against praising Italian wines or Swiss cheeses, and Russian viticulture is definitely no topic worth broaching. It is also good to avoid political discussions; the French aren't fond of these.

The French are tremendously attached to their lunch breaks and their weekends. To them these are sacred, and they will react very negatively to being interrupted during these times, even if the matter is urgent.

I once called a French business partner on a Saturday to check whether they had been able to load and send me the products I had ordered on the Friday evening, as planned. I got a very rude reply along the lines of: 'It's my day off, I'm with my family, I'll reply to all of your questions on Monday.' I was left racking my brains as to what I could possibly have done wrong. And then on Monday my partner called me as though nothing had happened and we had a friendly, polite chat.

Bureaucracy flourishes in France, both anecdotally and in real life. Anyone who considers Russia a country of officials and unnecessary paperwork should visit France. You'll see what I mean.

## Germany

A distinguishing feature of Germans is their pedantic, dry nature. They avoid empty or meaningless phrases, and aren't fond of hearing these, either. Germans tend to enter into negotiations when they can already quite clearly see a possibility of reaching a decision that suits them. They only negotiate when they are sure an agreement is achievable. They don't like manoeuvres, and generally tend to fight for their benefit from the start, preferring clear guidelines and consistency when discussing issues. Any proposals should be strictly businesslike and clearly follow any guidelines. For them, proposals need to be quick as a shot.

When dealing with Germans, you should pay particular attention to hierarchy and titles. I would recommend clarifying this information in advance. Germans are not keen on jokes at the negotiation table.

Germans are precise and scrupulous when it comes to implementing any agreements reached, and they demand the same of their partners. No agreements will be signed without exhaustive guarantees that they will be fulfilled. If you have even the slightest doubt about being able to meet *all* of their agreement terms, then it is better to turn down those proposals.

For many years we worked with a German supplier. It took some time, but we eventually reached an agreement on deferred payments. We were given a payment period of twenty-one days from the point at which the products were unloaded. I had never seen such precision before: on the tenth day, they sent an email to everyone involved in the deal – from the accountant right up to the owner of the company – to remind us that payment would soon be due. This was re-sent five days before the deadline, and then again the day before. Of course, any hopes we had of following our 'normal' procedures were quickly shattered. Not to mention paying a few days late. Once, our truck happened to arrive at their factory to pick up a shipment on the day that payment was due for the previous delivery. For objective reasons, we had only made the transfer that day. They only allowed the products to be loaded onto our truck when they could see that the payment had come through. This was despite a friendly, long-standing collaboration.

## Italy

The Italian negotiation style is characterised by a very active development of partnerships and even friendships. In contrast to the French, little red tape is involved, with the Italians instead favouring friendly, informal dealings with their partners. They welcome a sense of trust and goodwill. In any contentious issues, they prefer to meet their opponent halfway.

Italians have a strong sense of national pride. Like the French,

Italians are delighted when business partners show an interest in their nation's history and culture.

Italians like to dine with their partners, meals that are always long and unhurried. Three important topics of conversation around the table are football, food and women. Business matters, however, should be kept away from the table. Similarly, you should not call Italians between the sacred lunch hours of 12.00 and 14.00.

I was in the middle of some very complex negotiations with the sales manager of a wine producer. My opponent was a loud and curt young woman between thirty and thirty-five, and she was forcefully demanding that I accept payment terms that would be unprofitable to me. From 10.00 to 12.00 we held very tough negotiations. My opposite number was jumping around and waving her arms, and more than once she said it would be easier for her to turn down the contract than to agree to my terms. But then, with the last chime of the clock at 12.00, it was as though she were substituted by a different person. The stern businesswoman's mask fell from her face, and she invited me to lunch in a friendly, even mildly flirty, way. We went to a very nice restaurant, where we were served delicious Italian food and wines. The conversation was free and easy, and I learned that Laura liked motorcycle racing, and that her husband was a Juventus fan. We talked about Rome, Florence and the ski slopes in Madonna di Campiglio, and when we arrived back at the office at 14.30 our negotiations continued in the gentle form of a heartfelt conversation between two bosom buddies. The best part was that we found where our interests intersected.

## China

The Chinese are some of the most difficult negotiators. They have an in-depth knowledge of the concept of a negotiation budget, and they will do whatever they can to inflate yours. It is not uncommon for them to invite large delegations to visit them for negotiations, and not just for a day. During their stay, they will show their guests the country and shower them in gifts. Negotiations will generally begin shortly before their opponents are scheduled to leave, and will be of a somewhat declaratory character. So, when preparing for negotiations with Chinese opponents, you should ensure that you have sufficient time, energy and money.

Now that I know about their negotiation tendencies, I prefer to act in the following way. We go to negotiations loaded with gifts, so that we can immediately reciprocate any that we receive. And when on the final day the Chinese party announce their terms, we are already prepared. A designated person will immediately extend our hotel stay and change our return flight. In doing so, we show that we have enough reserves in our negotiation budget to sustain us through further talks.

While negotiating, the Chinese side will seek to clearly delineate the individual stages of the process, from the initial clarification of positions to discussion and conclusions. During the initial stages, they will pay a great deal of attention to their opponents' appearance and behaviour. From this they will try to deduce the status of each of the participants, after which they will clearly direct their attention towards those who are, officially or unofficially, considered to be of a higher rank.

As a rule, Chinese people make the final decision at home and not at the negotiation table in the presence of their opponent.

Their delegations are often large, as they will contain experts on every possible subject on the negotiation agenda.

Practically all negotiations with Chinese opponents include technical and commercial stages. During the technical stage, the success of the negotiations will come down to the extent to which you are able to convince your partner of the advantages of collaboration. For this reason, when negotiating with Chinese opponents it is essential that your delegation contain highly qualified specialists who are capable of dealing with technical questions on the spot, and a good negotiator who is familiar with the specific terminology of the technical issues at stake. Then the commercial stage of negotiations can begin. Chinese companies are generally represented by experienced personnel who are well versed in questions of commerce. These represent-atives will be extremely well informed, and they will often make reference to previous advantageous contracts they have made. For this reason, if you are negotiating with Chinese opponents, you need to be prepared. You will need a good understanding of the current state of affairs on the world market, as well as in-depth technical and economic analyses and concrete materials at your disposal.

Usually the Chinese side will be the first to 'reveal their hand', express their point of view or make a proposal. In general, they will only make concessions at the very end of negotiations, once they have assessed the full extent of their business partner's options. It isn't unheard of for concessions to appear only once it feels like there is a deadlock. However, even in situations like these, they will skilfully exploit any errors or slips that their opponents have made.

Chinese negotiators never make any decisions without thoroughly studying every aspect or potential consequence of the agreements being proposed. If it is a subject of considerable importance, the decision will be made collectively and with multiple agreements at each level. Central approval for any agreements reached is practically essential.

In negotiations with Chinese opponents there is also a heightened risk of taking a blow below the belt. They are experts at incorporating sudden changes in terms into the negotiation process, and in some cases they will even start collaboration only to then change terms.

**A situation that comes up often when working with Chinese partners**

A company, Russian Field, decides to launch a new product line. They approach a Chinese factory, Chinese Forest, for their manufacturing needs. The purchasing manager of Russian Field negotiates with Chinese Forest, agrees all of the terms and signs the contract.

Russian Field pays the advance (30 per cent) and the factory starts production. Once the shipment is ready for delivery, Chinese Forest informs Russian Field that they incurred some unexpected expenses. They refuse to ship the goods without compensation for this.

Russian Field is faced with the decision: either lose their advance and that season's goods, or concede.

As a major manufacturer, Chinese Forest is risking virtually nothing: their production costs are already covered by the

> advance, and this order represents only a small proportion of their manufacturing portfolio. What's more, it would be fairly easy for them to shift the goods to a different buyer.

## USA

Americans are practically always competent negotiators. They are patriotic, which is important to remember: they won't accept any criticism. As business partners, they give the impression of being overly pushy, or even aggressive or plain rude. But rather than a reflection of their attitude towards their partner, this is simply their traditional style. On the contrary, on a personal level they are characterised by a pleasant demeanour, openness, energy and goodwill. They prefer a less official negotiation atmosphere.

However, generally speaking, little lies behind their outward display of friendliness. The results of the negotiations will depend entirely on how advantageous or not the proposal under discussion would be to them. The American negotiator's slogan is: 'The mouse's problems are of no concern to the cat.'

Americans often enjoy a strong position, which allows them to behave rather forcefully. They are normally quite determined to realise their negotiation goals, and they aren't afraid to haggle. They do absolutely nothing for free. When resolving virtually any problem, they try to predict how events will develop.

American negotiators like 'packaged' solutions. They take a negative view of unforeseen circumstances. They want to get a clear idea of the advantages of working with the party with whom they are currently communicating over any competitors.

When entering negotiations with Americans, you need to make these advantages clear. Otherwise they simply won't give you the time of day.

It is important to remember that in the USA recommendations hold a great deal of weight. When negotiating with Americans, it can be both important and useful to name the American firms and businesspeople with whom you have already had the opportunity to do business.

In the USA, lunch with business associates is a strictly business matter.

## Arab nations

Representatives of Arab nations are extremely sensitive to issues of national independence. Anything that could come across as interference in their internal affairs will be repudiated immediately.

They are characterised by respect and by their correct behaviour towards their negotiation partners. Before expressing their perspective on a specific issue, they prefer to demonstratively take counsel in order to convey a collective opinion from the start. It is not normal for one member of the delegation to play up their role in the decision-making process or in leading the negotiations.

When dealing with representatives of these nations, it is very important to observe local traditions and customs. In negotiations, Arabs will often make reference to the past, alluding to their roots. A key feature of their behaviour in negotiations is a continuation of their country's historic traditions. Islamic traditions in particular are significant in negotiations.

In Arab traditions, it is impolite to begin negotiations without bowing to one another.

Arabs tend to attach great importance to the level at which negotiations are taking place. They prefer to conduct a preliminary analysis of the details of the issues discussed in negotiations, and decisions are preceded by extremely long discussions.

One particular feature of concluding negotiations in the Middle East is that a verbal agreement and handshake are enough for an agreement finalised at that meeting to enter into force. This is a centuries-old tradition that sees the two sides, having achieved an approximate agreement, start to implement the conditions of that agreement immediately.

Another characteristic feature of negotiations here is the fact that practically any change in circumstance or new information can be considered sufficient cause to review a contract.


And with that, dear reader, you have reached the starting line. Yes, the starting line. Because ahead of you lies your chance to perfect these instruments and employ them in real-life negotiations. Bear in mind that negotiations are a sport; if you give it up for a period of time, then you will have to make up for lost time when you come back to it. I recommend regular practice, perfecting your skills, analysing previous negotiations and preparing for new ones. Always remember that negotiations are performed by people, not robots, and despite the logic we possess, we are also subject to emotions that can sometimes run the show. Good luck in your negotiations.

# SAMPLE ANSWERS FOR EXERCISES

## CHAPTER 1

**EXERCISE:** TRY TO FIND MIKHAIL AND IVAN'S REASONING.

There is no single correct answer to this question. Both are right in their own way. In Ivan's shoes, I would build on the fact that I did not agree to the changes, so in effect Mikhail assumed the right to manage my money. Whereas Mikhail did a good job, ensuring that nothing fell apart at the seams, as it were.

**EXERCISE:** HOW MIGHT THE CHIEF ENGINEER HAVE CONSTRUCTED A DIALOGUE, BASED ON THE PLAY 'SHOW YOUR ENEMY THERE IS A ROAD TO LIFE'?

**Answer:** He could praise or congratulate him, for example, giving him reason to hope that their relationship might be prioritised in later projects.

## CHAPTER 2

**EXERCISE:** BUILD A POLYGON OF INTERESTS BASED ON THE SITUATION GIVEN.

**Answer:** My polygon would have six faces representing the following interests: price, payment terms, dedicated technological specialist, access to holding company, supply volumes, and delivery and installation terms.

## CHAPTER 4

**EXERCISE:** WHAT EMOTIONAL STRINGS ARE THESE MANIPULATORS PLAYING?

**Answer:** 1. Curiosity. 2. Vanity. 3. Pity.

## CHAPTER 5

**EXERCISE:** RESPOND TO REMARKS 1–5 USING THE 'REVERSE' TECHNIQUE.

1. 'There's something about your proposal I don't like.'
**Question:** 'What would you recommend I add to my proposal to make it align better with your needs?'
**Appeal:** 'Please tell me which points you think I should change.'

2. 'For some reason your presentation style bothers me.'
**Question:** 'What style of presentation would you prefer?'
**Appeal:** 'Tell me how you think I should present.'

3. 'I don't find your proposal very constructive.'
**Question:** 'What would you like to see in my proposal?'
**Appeal:** 'Then how about you tell me what you had in mind and we can go through it together.'

4. 'You aren't looking very festive.'
**Question:** 'What would make me look more festive, in your opinion?'
**Appeal:** 'Tell me how I can make myself more festive.'

5. 'I'm not sure – do you think it's worth being so rash?'
**Question:** 'How would you recommend acting in this situation?'
**Appeal:** 'Please tell me what you feel the risks are.'

EXERCISE: RESPOND TO REMARKS 6–13 USING THE 'PARTIAL AGREEMENT' TECHNIQUE.

6. 'Don't you think you're being too cocky?'
**Answer:** 'You know, I *am* pretty sure of myself. Now let's take another look at the details of my proposal.'

7. 'What you're saying is arguable.'
**Answer:** 'I agree, some aspects will need discussing. Let's do that now.'

8. 'That's a very female assumption to make' [when addressing a woman].
**Answer:** 'Of course it is. I'm a woman.'

9. 'How can it take so long to explain?'
**Answer:** 'I agree that time is of the essence, but if we rush through this we're going to miss the details.'

10. 'You're too slow!'
**Answer:** 'I agree – I'm thorough, because I want to make sure everything I do, I do well.'

11. 'What you're saying gives me doubts.'
**Answer:** 'In that case, I agree that we ought to discuss this proposal again in detail.'

12. 'Petrov told everyone you're a slob.'
**Answer:** 'Everyone has a right to an opinion.'

13. 'I don't think your management trusts you all that much.'
**Answer:** 'I agree that it's impossible to 100 per cent trust anyone, but where these issues are concerned our points of view completely coincide. Now let's get back to what we were discussing.'

EXERCISE: RESPOND TO NEGATIVE MESSAGES 14–22 USING THE MARCUS AURELIUS TECHNIQUE.

14. 'I've heard you're always late on payment.'
**Answer:** 'On the contrary, we're always meticulous about our payment obligations.'

15. 'They say your employees are all jumping ship.'
**Answer:** 'Company X values its employees, and I'm living proof that its employees reciprocate.'

16. 'Your proposal is complete rubbish.'
**Answer:** 'I'm sorry you missed the key point of my proposal. I'll repeat: we supply high-quality equipment, and we would like to offer you significant productivity gains through . . .'

17. 'Come on, get to the point!'
**Answer:** 'To make our proposal as appealing as possible to you, I wondered if I might ask you a few questions.'

18. 'You aren't listening to me.'
**Answer:** 'I'd be happy to listen to what you have to say again.'

19. 'What nonsense!'
**Answer:** 'I think we should move away from mutual recriminations and try to hold a constructive discussion.'

20. 'Your market reputation is terrible.'

**Answer:** 'On the contrary, we have a solid reputation on the market, as our client's reviews confirm. I'd be happy to share them with you.'

21. 'Given your persistence, I'm taking it you're not particularly competent.'

**Answer:** 'We're letting ourselves get carried away with jabs and reproaches; I'd like to suggest we put that to one side and take our time to go through all of this again. Would that be all right with you?'

22. 'Ugh, enough of your so-called innovations!'

**Answer:** 'I'd be happy to run through our achievements with you; they truly are something to be proud of.'

**EXERCISE: IN THE SECOND AND THIRD COLUMNS BELOW, WRITE DOWN WHAT YOU INTERPRET THE TRUE MESSAGE HIDDEN IN THE ATTACKER'S WORDS TO BE, AND WHAT YOU FEEL WOULD BE THE APPROPRIATE RESPONSE.**

23.

| Phrase | True message | Reply |
|---|---|---|
| I'm tired of listening to your empty arguments. | I want to hear an argument that will convince me. | If I've understood you correctly, you want to hear some strong arguments? Yes. [Run through arguments one by one and after each check if that is strong enough for the opponent.] |

| Phrase | True message | Reply |
|---|---|---|
| I've had enough of this twaddle. | I want to hear something concrete. | If I catch your drift, you would like to cut to the chase?<br><br>Yes.<br><br>Then let's move on. |
| How many times must they send these simple clerks to negotiate! | I would like to speak to the decision-maker. | Would you like to speak to someone with full authority?<br><br>Yes.<br><br>Well, I have been given the full authority to make a decision here and now. |
| Your arguments are ridiculous. | I don't understand. | Am I right in understanding that my arguments aren't completely clear to you?<br><br>Yes.<br><br>Then let's take a look at what's causing the confusion. |
| Aren't you too young and inexperienced for this? | I'm not sure if this person has enough experience to resolve my issue. | You're confused by my age, and you think that means I don't have enough experience to resolve this issue?<br><br>Yes, exactly.<br><br>Well, I may be young, but the results my partners and I have achieved speak for themselves. I'd like to prove that to you in practice.<br><br>(This answer also uses the 'partial agreement' technique) |

| Phrase | True message | Reply |
|---|---|---|
| I know your 'Italy': I bet everything's made in China. | I, or someone I know, had a bad experience with a similar product, buying a 'designer' brand that turned out to be a cheap fake. | I take it that you have some doubts about the origin of our product? Yes, you just put your name on the tag. We'd be happy to show you documents confirming the origin of our products. We'd also be happy to show you samples. What evidence would you need to convince you of the origin of the items? (Combines an answer with the 'reverse' technique) |

EXERCISE: FORMULATE YOUR OWN QUESTIONS IN RESPONSE TO STATEMENTS 24–28, WHICH ATTEMPT TO DRAW YOU INTO AN EMOTIONAL MODE.

24. 'You'll never be able to finish this task, you're too dim!'
**Answers:**
*Questioning intent*: 'What do you mean by the word "dim"?'
*'Predator' question*: 'If I've understood you correctly, you're concerned whether I'll be able to keep to the schedule?'

25. 'I never realised you were so sharp.'
**Answers:**
*Questioning intent*: 'What is it that you actually want to discuss with me?'
*'Predator' question*: 'Am I right in guessing you didn't expect such a quick reaction from me?'

26. 'I'm sick of all this empty chat.'
**Answers:**
*Questioning intent*: 'What makes you say that?'
*'Predator' question*: 'I take it that you want to stop talking and start acting?'

27. 'Are you always this insistent?'
**Answers:**
*Questioning intent*: 'What is it that gives you concerns?'
*'Predator' question*: 'Am I right in sensing that you might want some time to think?'

28. 'You're being very provocative.'
**Answers:**
*Questioning intent*: 'Why are you making comments about my appearance?'
*'Predator' question*: 'Do I take it that you don't like parts of my wardrobe?' 'Yes.' 'Well, it's my way of expressing my personal style.'

**EXERCISE: RESPOND TO ATTACKS 29–37 USING A JOKE OR HUMOUR, BUT DON'T FORGET THE FORMULA: 'JOKE – RETURN TO ORIGINAL TOPIC'.**

29. 'You're hiding something – is this a deliberate stunt?'
**Answer:** 'Well, I do always save the best for last. And, as it happens, it's time for dessert.'

30. 'Are you having a laugh?'
**Answer:** 'Laughter is the best medicine, but right now I'm completely serious. I'd be happy to run through the main points again, if you want?'

31. 'You're too sharp for this job.'
**Answer:** 'Easier to slow a hare than to speed up a tortoise. But what is it that you take issue with?'

32. 'Do you even realise how risky your proposal is? What are you thinking?'
**Answer:** 'If you don't take a risk or two you'll never pop the champagne. I'd like to propose we think this through carefully but take the risk. I'm sure we'll be popping corks soon enough.'

33. 'What you're saying is arguable.'
**Answer:** 'Well, we aren't parliament – we haven't come here to argue. Let's take a look at the specifics.'

34. 'You are wrong and should agree with me.'
**Answer:** 'But if I agree with you then both of us will be wrong.'

35. 'Where's your head?'
**Answer:** 'It's right here, but I guess two heads are better than one anyway. Let's brainstorm this together.'

36. 'I shouldn't be having to chase you – you should be the one chasing me.'
**Answer:** 'Well, it's a good thing we seem to have plenty to chase. I'd like to propose we discuss these issues in a constructive way.'

37. 'Why are you looking at me like that?'
**Answer:** 'God gave me eyes, so I'm using them. But do let me know your thoughts.'

## CHAPTER 6

**EXERCISE:** YOU REPRESENT A GYM. YOU ARE EAGER TO SELL SUBSCRIPTIONS FOR 50,000 ROUBLES PER YEAR. HOW CAN YOU PRESENT YOUR PROPOSAL TO THE BUYER IN THE MOST FAVOURABLE LIGHT? TRY TO COME UP WITH A PITCH THAT USES THE CONTRAST PRINCIPLE.

**Answer:** The best approach would be to introduce an expensive offer and then something to compare it to. For example: a VIP subscription at 100,000 roubles, and the reasonable offer at 50,000 roubles.

**EXERCISE:** USING THE CONTRAST PRINCIPLE, TRY TO REWRITE THIS COPY: 'THREE PATIENTS OUT OF TEN WHO ARE TREATED IN OUR CLINIC FEEL RESULTS ALMOST IMMEDIATELY.'

**Answer:** There's no point using the figure as it isn't in your favour. It would be better to use the total patient numbers for a month or year. For example: more than 140 patients in the past year immediately felt the results of their treatment.

**EXERCISE:** THINK ABOUT HOW, USING THE CONTRAST PRINCIPLE AND COMPROMISE PLAYS, YOU MIGHT BE ABLE TO ENCOURAGE TALKS TO PROGRESS WITH THE BIOLOG- ICAL FATHER. PREPARE THREE PACKAGES.

**Answer:**
Option 1: You participate in her upbringing, pay for her school and hobbies, and take her on holiday once a year. Oh and of course, pay monthly child support.
Option 2: Court, alimony, etc.

Option 3: I'll relinquish any claim on money and support from you, and you relinquish your surname.

## CHAPTER 7

**EXERCISE:** FORMULATE GOALS BASED ON WHAT YOU CAN CONTROL.

a) secure an order worth 1 million roubles.
**Answer:** Get the client to agree to do business with us.

b) Get compensation for a defective delivery.
**Answer:** Get the other side to agree to offer compensation. Agree on the sum and suitable payment deadlines.

c) Get a debt repaid.
**Answer:** Get the opponent to repay their debt, or a timetable and additional guarantees for this repayment.

d) Increase the price by 16 per cent.


**EXERCISE:** BREAK DOWN THE FOLLOWING GOAL INTO STEPS: 'GET THE OPPONENT TO AGREE TO DO BUSINESS WITH THE ENTIRE HOLDING.'

**Answer:**
Step 1: Outline the terms of collaboration and whether this is possible or not.
Step 2: Finalise an agreement with one enterprise.
Step 3: Discuss the possibility of doing business with the wider holding company.

# NOTES

1  Niccolò Machiavelli, *The Prince*, translated by Tim Parks (London: Penguin, 2009).
2  Eliyahu M. Goldratt, Jeff Cox, *The Goal: A Process of Ongoing Improvement* (Great Barrington: North River Press; 2nd Rev edition, 1992).
3  Jim Camp, *Start with NO* (New York: Crown Business, 2002).
4  General Carl von Clausewitz, *On War*, translated by J.J. Graham (New York: Start Publishing, 2012).
5  Napoleon's motto was reputedly *'On s'engage et puis on voit'*. This phrase was popularised in Russia through Lenin's adoption of the motto.
6  Sun Tzu, *The Art of War*, translated by Lionel Giles (London: Luzac & Co., 1910).
7  General Carl von Clausewitz, *On War*.
8  Barry Bernandi and Jack Giarraputo (Producers), Peter Segal (Director), *Anger Management* (United States: Colombia Pictures, 2003).
9  Larry Wilson, 'Grow Or Die: Four Stages Of Transformation', published on Above + Beyond. Retrieved from: http://abovebeyond.ca/blog/grow-or-die-four-stages-of-transformation-pt-2/.
10  Sun Tzu, *The Art of War*.

11  Stephen Covey, *The Seven Habits of Highly Effective People* (New York: Free Press, 2004).

12  General Carl von Clausewitz, *On War*.

13  Sun Tzu, *The Art of War*.

14  General Carl von Clausewitz, *On War*.

15  Everett Shostrom, *Man, the Manipulator* (Nashville: Abingdon Press, 1967).

16  Jim Camp, *Start with NO*.

17  Sun Tzu, *The Art of War*.

18  Vladimir Tarasov, *Isskustvo Upravlencheskoy Borby (The Art of the Management Battle)*, (Moscow: Dobraya Kniga, 2016). Excerpt translated by Alex Fleming.

19  Andrei Gromyko, *Memories*, translated by Harold Shukman (London: Hutchinson, 1989).

20  Mikhail Bulgakov, *The Heart of a Dog*, translated by Michael Glenny (London: Vintage Books, 2009).

21  Popular proverb often attributed to Lucian of Samosata.

22  Robert Cialdini, *Influence: Science and Practice* (New York: Harper Collins, 2009).

23  Yuri Dubinin, *Masterstvo Peregovorov (A Mastery of Negotiation)*, (Moscow: Mezhdunarodnye Otnosheniya, 2006). Excerpt translated by Alex Fleming.

24  Vladimir Tarasov, *Isskustro Upravlencheskoy Borby*.

25  Sun Tzu, *The Art of War*.

26  Andrei Gromyko, *Memories*.

27  Kozma Prutkov, *Izbrannoye* ('Selected Works'), (St Petersburg: OLMA Media Group, 2013). Excerpt translated by Alex Fleming.

28  Dale Carnegie, *How to Win Friends and Influence People* (New York: Pocket Books, 2010).

29  Rudyard Kipling, *The Jungle Book* (London: Penguin, 2013).

30  Benjamin Franklin, *The Autobiography of Benjamin Franklin* (New York: P. F. Collier & Son, 1909).

31  Translator's note: this proverb also commonly appears as the French *'Fais ce que dois, advienne, que pourra.'*

32  Niccolò Machiavelli, *The Prince*.

33  Général de Division Armand Augustin Louis de Caulaincourt, Duc de Vincence, *Memoirs of Général de Caulaincourt – The Russian Campaign*, translated by Hamish Miles (Halstad: Pickle Partners Publishing, 2011).

34 Sergei Kharitonov, '*Model dinamiki aktivnosti zhivykh sistem*' ('A MODEL OF THE DYNAMICS OF ACTIVITY IN LIVING SYSTEMS'), retrieved from: http://www.rusnauka.com/26_WP_2013/ Matemathics/4_144087.doc.htm. Excerpt translated by Alex Fleming.

35 Astrid Lindgren, *The World's Best Karlson*, translated by Sarah Death (Oxford: OUP, 2009).

36 Leonid Kroll, *Peregovori s Drakonami* ('Negotiating with Dragons'), (Moscow: Klass, 2013). Excerpt translated by Alex Fleming.

37 Niccolò Machiavelli, *The Prince*.

38 Rudyard Kipling, *The Jungle Book*.

39 Robert Cialdini, *Influence*.

40 Eliyahu M. Goldratt and Jeff Cox, *The Goal*.

41 Robert Cialdini, *Influence*.

42 Andrei Gromyko, *Memories*.

43 Yuri Dubinin, '*Iskusstvo Diplomatiy*' ('The Art of Diplomacy'), retrieved from: http://russiancouncil.ru/analytics-and-comments/analytics/iskusstvo-diplomatii/?sphrase_id=22937921. Excerpt translated by Alex Fleming. A report on this lecture is also available in English at: http://russiancouncil. ru/en/analytics-and-comments/analytics/on-the-art-of-diplomacy/.

44 Count Sergei Witte, *The Memoirs of Count Witte*, translated and edited by Sidney Harcave (Abingdon: Routledge, 2016).

45 Count Sergei Witte, as above.

46 Count Sergei Witte, as above.

47 Sun Tzu, *The Art of War*.

48 Lewis Carroll, *Alice's Adventures in Wonderland and Through the Looking Glass* (London: Penguin, 2012).

49 Sun Tzu, *The Art of War*.

50 Yuri Dubinin, '*Iskusstvo Diplomatiy*' ('The Art of Diplomacy'), retrieved from: http://russiancouncil.ru/analytics-and-comments/analytics/iskusstvo-diplomatii/?sphrase_id=22937921. Excerpt translated by Alex Fleming. A report on this lecture is also available in English at: http://russiancouncil. ru/en/analytics-and-comments/analytics/on-the-art-of-diplomacy/.

51 This section is also based on information from Yuri Dubinin's lecture, '*Iskusstvo Diplomatiy*' ('The Art of Diplomacy'), retrieved from: http:// russiancouncil.ru/analytics-and-comments/analytics/iskusstvo-diplomatii/ ?sphrase_id=22937921. Excerpt translated by Alex Fleming. A report on this lecture is also available in English at: http://russiancouncil.ru/en/ analytics-and-comments/analytics/on-the-art-of-diplomacy/.

52  Mikhail Bulgakov, *The Master and Margarita*, translated by Michael Glenny (London: Vintage Books, 2003).
53  Vladimir Tarasov, *Isskustvo Upravlencheskoy Borby*.
54  Robert T. Kiyosaki with Sharon L. Lechter, *Rich Dad's Guide to Investing* (New York: Warner Business Books, 2000).
55  Sun Tzu, *The Art of War*.